**Mary Whitehouse,
Ann Gregory, Jane Vellacott**

Published by BBC Educational Publishing,
BBC White City, 201 Wood Lane, London W12 7TS
First published 1998

ISBN: 0 563 46120 9

Designed by Cathy May (Endangered Species)
Illustrated by Kathy Baxendale, Caroline Logan,
Pete Neame and Howie Twiner
Printed in Great Britain by Bell & Bain, Glasgow

500 BBC

Contents

Introduction

About BITESIZEscience

This book is a revision guide to help you to do your best in your GCSE science exams. You can help yourself in three ways: work through the activities and questions in the book; watch the TV programmes; and even log-on to the Internet to get more practice at the ideas you find difficult.

This book is a good basis for your revision. For people aiming to get A*A* in science, do not forget to use your notes from school and any textbooks you have too.

Read through this introduction carefully as it tells you how the book is laid out and how to make best use of it for your revision. It tells you about the television programmes, which explain the science, and how to make the best use of them alongside this book; a little bit about topics covered by the programmes and some general help with exams and syllabuses; a check list of the key things you should be able to do; and finally some tips to pick up those crucial extra marks in the exams.

About this book

This book is in three parts: Biology, Chemistry and Physics. Each part is divided into sections which cover important science topics.

Each topic begins with an introductory page to tell you what the topic is about. This summarises the main ideas in the topic. The next page is the FactZone which has key facts and definitions of important ideas in the topic, and sometimes there are equations you need to learn. The following pages give you more information, with activities to help you revise ◎; questions to do ?; and tips from the examiner.

There are Practice Questions, similar to the questions you might get in an exam, with answers at the back of the book. There are also longer Exam Questions to give you practice at doing a full exam question.

The book has been put together to go alongside the BITESIZE television programmes and the BITESIZE website. You will see the TV symbol in the text. This shows you where there is a link to the TV programme. When you are watching the video of the TV programme you could make a note in your book of the counter number in case you want to come back to that item.

KEY TO SYMBOLS

- TV A link to the video
- ? A suggestion to do
- ◎ An activity to do
- h A higher activity – ask your teacher if you need to do these

Using this book to revise

Planning your revision

Do you know when your exam is? How long have you got to revise? It is no good leaving revision until the night before the exam. The best way to revise is to break the subject up into BITESIZE chunks. That is why we have broken the GCSE science course into topics. There are 17 topics and 144 pages of science to revise in this book. You need to work out how many pages you need to do each day to get it all done before the exam. Use the Contents page to plan your revision. You could write the date by each topic, to show when you will revise it.

Of course, you have other subjects to revise too. It is often better to cover more than one subject in an evening - a change is as good as a rest, so they say. So how about planning all your revision by working out how much time you have before the exams start and then sharing the days out amongst your subjects. Do not forget to leave some time to relax too!

Revision tips

It is no good just sitting reading this book, to learn the material and understand it you need to be active. Here are some ideas to try:

- Do each of the activities shown by the ◎ or ⓘ symbols.
- At the end of each double page; close the book and write down the key facts from those pages.
- When there is a labelled diagram to learn, draw a copy of the diagram without the labels. Look at the labels in the book; close the book; label the diagram and then check how many were correct.
- 'Look, cover, write, check' is a good way of learning all sorts of things - including spellings, equations and formulae.
- Use information from the FactZone pages to make some flash cards: write a definition on one side of the card and the word on the other. Look at the word - can you write a definition? Look at the definition - which word is it and how do you spell it?
- Use flashcards to learn the Physics equations. Include the units for all the quantities in the equations.
- Use flashcards to learn the word equations for chemical processes. Write the name of the process on one side and the equation on the other side. Or write the word equation on one side and the balanced equation with symbols on the other.
- Revise with a friend - flash cards are more fun with a partner.
- Make a set of flash cards to fit in your pocket - great for the day when the bus gets stuck in a traffic jam or you have to wait for a dentist's appointment!

THE ON-LINE SERVICE

You can find extra support, tips and answers to your exam queries on the BITESIZE internet site. The address is http://www.bbc.co.uk/education/revision

Using the TV programme

You will have to record the BITESIZE science programmes - unless you want to do all your revision in the middle of the night. The great thing about watching the recorded tape is that you can go back over the bits you did not understand as many times as you like!

There are three BiteSize programmes to help you revise for your GCSE Science exams. There is one programme for each of Biology, Chemistry and Physics.

It would be helpful if you have this BITESIZE science book with you as you watch the tape. Do not try to watch the whole tape at one time - watch one Bite and then work through that topic in the book.

The TV will have references to show where the book has more information. The book has TV icons to show you where there is a piece of TV to watch to help you understand the science in the book.

GCSE Science

The National Curriculum for England and Wales sets four Programmes of Study and Attainment Targets for Science.

Sc1 Experimental and Investigative Science is assessed by coursework which you will have to hand in to your teacher for marking. This is a chance to gain as many marks as possible even before you go into the exam. This book concentrates on ways in which you can improve your marks in the exams.

Sc2 Life processes and living things You might also know this attainment target as Biology.

Sc3 Materials and their properties You might know this as Chemistry.

Sc4 Physical processes This is also called Physics.

Each of these attainment targets is worth 25% of the marks towards your GCSE in Science.

GCSE exams

The examining groups all provide GCSE Science syllabuses which cover these four attainment targets. There is some variety in the precise details of the syllabuses. You should find out from your teacher which syllabus you are taking and obtain a copy of the syllabus.

Linear or modular?

Most GCSE science syllabuses are linear. This means that the exams at the end of the course, in June, will test all your knowledge and understanding of the science you have learned in your GCSE course. You will have already completed your coursework when you take the exams. There may be three papers one for each of Biology, Chemistry and Physics; or the papers may be integrated, asking questions about all three subjects on each paper. You need to make sure you know what your papers will be like.

Other syllabuses are modular. If you are taking a modular syllabus you will have been doing short module tests during the course. The marks from these tests will contribute to the final mark for your GCSE. You will take one or two final exams at the end of the course. This book should help you revise for the final exams. You need to check which topics will be in the final exam.

Single or double award?

Most students take Double Award Science - this means when the results come out you will get a 'double grade' for science - DD or CC for instance. You need to know all the work in this book for Double Award Science. Some students spend less time on science and take the single award exam. If you are taking single award, you should check with your teacher which topics you need to know.

Foundation Tier or Higher Tier?

There are two tiers of examination in Science. Students taking the Double Award Foundation Tier exam can achieve grades between GG and CC. Students taking the Higher Tier papers can gain grades between DD and A*A*. Even if you do really well on the Foundation Tier papers you cannot get a better grade than CC. If you do really badly on the Higher Tier papers and do not get enough marks for a DD you will be ungraded. This means you must make sure you are entered for the right tier. You should discuss with your teachers and parents which is the best tier to enter. And when you get into the exam make sure you are given the right paper!

In this book the work that will only appear on Higher Tier papers is marked with **h**.

The exam papers

In the final exams you will write your answers on the question paper. The questions are usually in several parts. They often start with some information or a diagram. It is important that you read the information and look at the diagram to make sure you know what the question is about. Underline any important words in the information - they will help you in your answers.

The questions leave a space for you to write your answer or do a calculation. The marks for each part of the question are given. The size of the space and the number of marks give you a clue about how long your answer might be.

Some questions ask you to write at more length about some science. There are often several marks for this work and you will be asked to write several sentences to explain your ideas. Make sure that you write good legible English with correct spelling. There are more questions like this on the higher tier papers.

Maths skills

All the examining groups expect you to be able to do some maths. You will have to look at your syllabus for the specific details for your syllabus. However you should be able to do the following things.

For both Foundation and Higher Tier papers you should be able to:

- Add, subtract, multiply and divide whole numbers and decimal fractions
- Use tables and charts
- Understand and use averages
- Interpret and use graphs
- Plot graphs from given data and draw the best smooth curve through the points
- Solve simple equations
- Substitute numbers in to simple equations

For Higher Tier you should also be able to:

- Manipulate equations
- Choose appropriate axes when plotting graphs
- Understand and use inverse proportions

Picking up marks in exams!

Follow these tips to make sure you get all the marks you deserve. The examiners cannot read your mind - they can only give you marks for what you actually put down on paper.

- Read all the questions carefully, because they contain the clues to the answers
- Make sure you answer the question
- Sometimes you have to choose the correct words from a list. Use the words provided - do not make up your own answers!
- Check your spelling, punctuation and grammar - there may be marks for this
- Diagrams - use a pencil to add to a diagram, following the instructions in the question
- Graphs:

  label the axes and show the scale and units you are using

  plot each point neatly with a cross

  draw a line or curve smoothly with a single line

- Chemical equations
  - write out the word equation first
  - write down the formula for each substance in the word equation
  - balance the equation
- Calculations - you must show your working to get full marks.
  - write down a word equation to show the ideas you are using
  - substitute in the numbers you know into the equation
  - work out the answer and show the units

Even if you cannot do the arithmetic, you may get some marks for writing down the equation and writing down the units of the answer.

Good luck!

Life processes and cell activities

This section is about

- naming the main life processes
- describing the differences between plant and animal cells
- describing the functions of the main parts of a cell
- picking out features of some cells that are appropriate to their function

Living things are alive because of the activities that go on inside them. These are called **life processes** and they happen so that the organism works properly. By continually adjusting to changes, the various systems keep conditions inside the organism remarkably constant, despite the changing conditions outside the organism.

Living things are made of **cells**, which are the smallest units of living matter. Although all cells have some features in common, there are many different types of cells. This is because different cells carry out different jobs.

A group of cells of the same sort makes up a **tissue**. Tissues make up the **organs**, which have a special structure and perform a particular function. For example, the heart is an organ that pumps blood. It is mostly made from three tissues: **muscle**, which moves to make the heart beat; **blood**, which carries many substances, including oxygen; and **nerve tissue**, which coordinates the stages of each heartbeat and the rate at which it beats. Larger plants and animals are made up of a greater variety of tissues and organs than simpler living things and can carry out a greater variety of activities.

A major difference between the way that plants and animals live is the way that they feed. Plants are **food producers**. They transfer light energy to chemical energy in food during a process called **photosynthesis**. Because of this plants are at the start of all food chains and are food sources for other living things.

The **nucleus** of a cell is mostly **DNA**. This is probably the most remarkable chemical compound on Earth, responsible for both the moment to moment running of cells and for the inheritance of characteristics from one generation to the next during cell division.

FactZONE

Introducing living things

Cells

All living things are made of cells. The main features of a cell are:

- the **nucleus**, which contains genetic material
- the living contents or **cytoplasm** where chemical reactions happen
- the **surface membrane**, which controls what enters and leaves the cell

Plant cells have extra features, such as a **cell wall**, a fluid-filled **vacuole** and **chloroplasts**, where photosynthesis happens. Cells make up the tissues and organs of living things.

Life processes

You should know about these basic life processes common to all plants and animals:

- **respiration:** the transfer of energy from food to the organism
- **feeding:** this provides nutrition for living things, including a source of energy, raw materials for making new cells and substances needed to stay healthy. Nutrition in plants happens mainly through photosynthesis
- **sensitivity:** living things can detect changes that happen inside and outside themselves. They can use the information to survive
- **movement:** animals move from place to place to find the best conditions for life. Plants move slowly, by growing in particular directions
- **reproduction:** when living things mature they reproduce and have offspring, to replace individuals who have died
- **growth:** a permanent increase in size, which may take place throughout life or at a particular stage, e.g. when young
- **excretion:** chemical reactions in cells make products, some of which are wastes. Excretion is getting rid of wastes, such as urea (in urine), oxygen (a waste product from photosynthesis) or carbon dioxide (a waste product from respiration)

Cells, the building blocks of life

The picture below compares the main features of plant and animal cells.

■ **surface cell membrane** (animal and plant cells) controls what moves in and out of the cell

■ **cytoplasm** (the contents of the cell; animal and plant cells), which contains smaller parts called **organelles**. All the chemical processes happen in the cytoplasm and each organelle has its own job

■ **nucleus** (animal and plant cells) made of **genetic material** such as DNA. The nucleus acts as a set of instructions for the cell. It's also important when cells divide because new cells inherit their characteristics from the genetic material of the nucleus

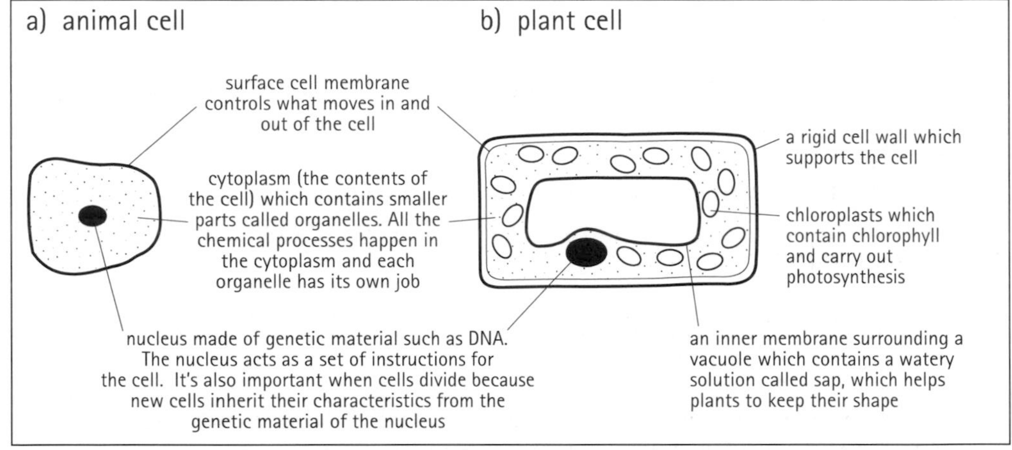

REMEMBER You need to know what the surface membrane, the cytoplasm and the nucleus do in a cell.

■ a rigid **cell wall** (plant cells), which supports the cell

■ **chloroplasts** (plant cells), which contain **chlorophyll** and carry out **photosynthesis**

■ an **inner membrane** (plant cells) surrounding a **vacuole**, which contains a watery solution called **cell sap**, which helps plants to keep their shape

◎ *Try sketching and labelling examples of an animal and a plant cell.*

◎ *Check the meaning of the words chloroplast, chlorophyll and photosynthesis.*

REMEMBER You need to know that the process of photosynthesis happens in a chloroplast.

Although the cells in the pictures below share some common features, they look very different. This is because they have different functions. The structure of each cell suits the job it carries out.

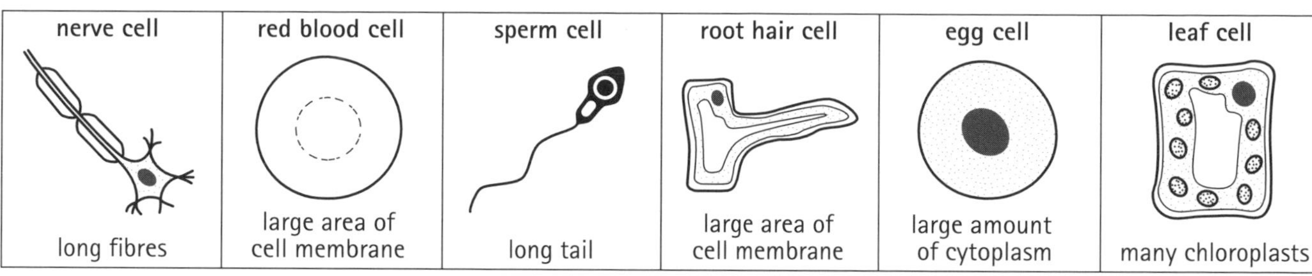

Which of the cells in these pictures are plant cells? How can you tell?

Cell division that happens when living things are growing or replacing worn out cells is called **mitosis**. Cell division that happens when sex cells are produced is called **meiosis**. There is more about this on page 48.

Why is it difficult to measure growth accurately in living things? Try to think of three ways this could be done.

Name three differences between plant and animal cells.

Sketch a plant cell and an animal cell.

The video section shows a variety of cells.

Practice Questions - Life proccsses 1

1 a) Name the life process that a plant cell can carry out but an animal cell cannot.

b) Suggest how the structure of each cell in the picture above is suited to its function.

2 Complete these sentences about some of the main life processes:

a) *Growth is an ________________ in size, which happens because the number of ________ increases.*

b) *Mature organisms can create new lives by a process called ________________.*

c) *During ________________, energy is transferred from food. Humans need __________ to carry out this process.*

d) *Getting rid of waste is called ________________. Two examples of human wastes are ________ and ____________.*

Humans as organisms

This section is about

- matching the main body systems with the jobs they perform
- nutrition, diet and lifestyle, and the basic processes of digestion
- the blood, the structure of the heart and circulation
- reasons for disease and ways we can maintain and improve health
- understanding how we breathe and the role of diffusion in gaseous exchange
- understanding the role of the nervous and endocrine systems in being sensitive to and responding to changes in the environment
- sexual development and the human reproductive system
- how the body regulates blood sugar level and temperature
- how the kidney balances the input and output of water and salts

Humans are active creatures, and life processes such as breathing continue at all times. Body systems are the parts of the body that carry out the life processes. Each body system is designed to carry out particular functions, and is made up of complex structures called organs.

All life processes need an energy source. They get it through respiration, which happens in all cells. The chemistry of cells is complex and requires coordination and control systems to continually adjust to the changes happening in the body. Keeping the body in balance in this way is called homeostasis.

We influence our health by the way we live. For example, a healthy, balanced diet and enough exercise are both very important for good health. Many people today are inactive a lot of the time, but it is important to build exercise into your daily routine.

Drugs such as caffeine, alcohol or illegal substances like heroin change the way our bodies work and can have harmful effects on our health.

There is no doubt that smoking and passive smoking (breathing in other people's smoke) are also dangerous to health. Scientists investigating the effect of smoking on health use information they have collected to provide facts about the harmful effects. Even so, many people continue to smoke.

FactZONE

Human body systems

The picture below shows the major body systems in simple detail. These body systems interact so that the body functions properly.

The **breathing system** involves the lungs, diaphragm, ribs and rib muscles. When we breathe, air moves in and out of the lungs because of air pressure changes inside the chest cavity.

The **blood system** is the body's major transport system. It is made up of the heart (the pump), tubes (the blood vessels such as arteries and veins) and blood. Blood is also important in fighting disease and in healing wounds.

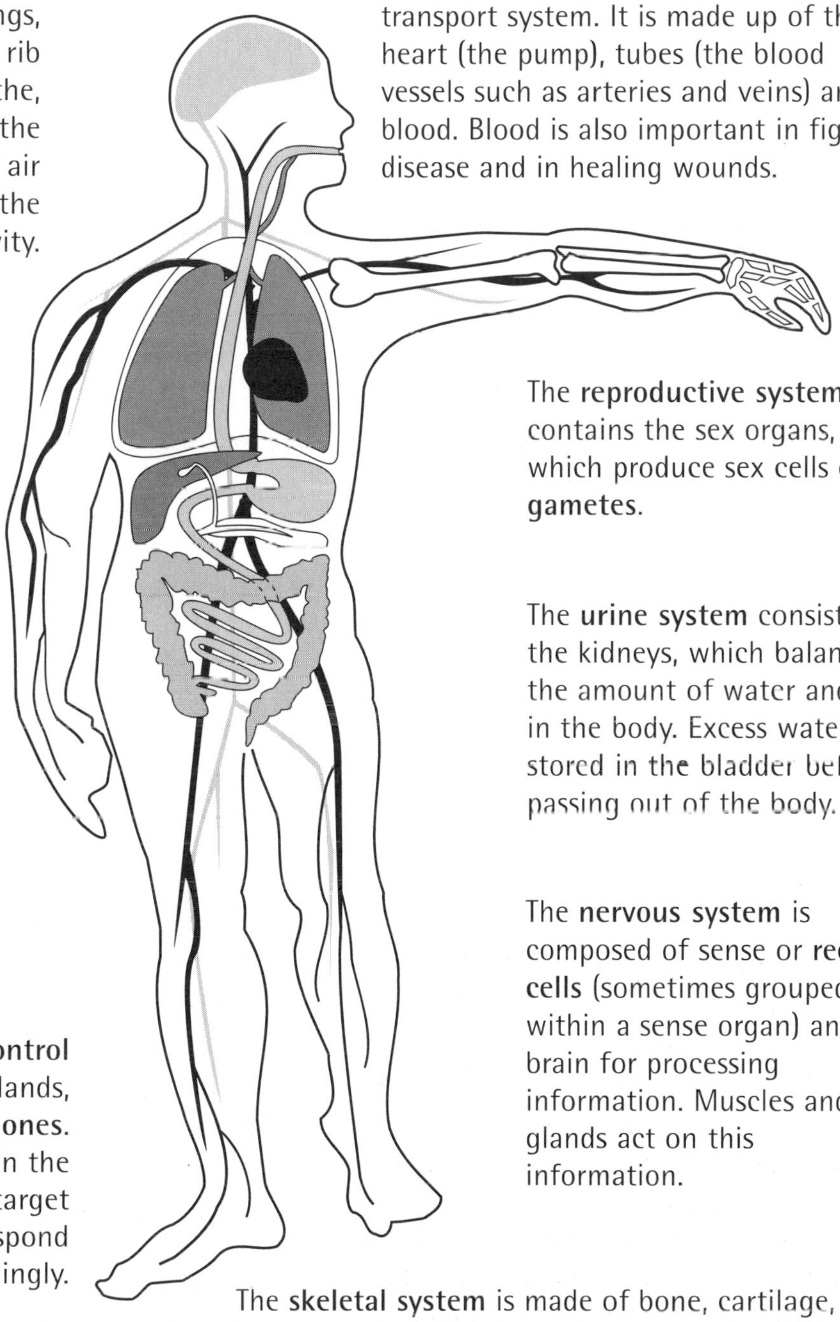

The **digestive system** is basically a tube from mouth to anus, with different features along its length. Food is broken down in the digestive system and absorbed into the blood. The liver makes **bile**, which passes into the digestive system and controls the level of digested food in the blood. Food that is not digested passes out of the body as faeces.

The **reproductive system** contains the sex organs, which produce sex cells called **gametes**.

The **urine system** consists of the kidneys, which balance the amount of water and salts in the body. Excess water is stored in the bladder before passing out of the body.

The **nervous system** is composed of sense or **receptor cells** (sometimes grouped within a sense organ) and the brain for processing information. Muscles and glands act on this information.

The **chemical control system** involves glands, which make **hormones**. Hormones are carried in the blood to particular target organs, which respond accordingly.

The **skeletal system** is made of bone, cartilage, tendon and muscle. It provides protection for delicate organs, supports soft tissues and helps us to move.

Human nutrition

We get nutrition, or *nutrients*, from our diet. The food we eat provides us with a source of energy, which we need for all the activities of life. It is also the source of the raw materials our cells need to make other substances. The table below lists some facts about the main types of food and how it is used.

food type	chemical elements in food type	how it is used in living things	items that contain food type
carbohydrates	carbon, hydrogen and oxygen	■ sugar as an energy source ■ glycogen as an energy store	■ sweets, cakes and fruit contain sugars ■ potatoes, rice, pasta and bread contain starch ■ vegetables, cereals and fruit contain fibre 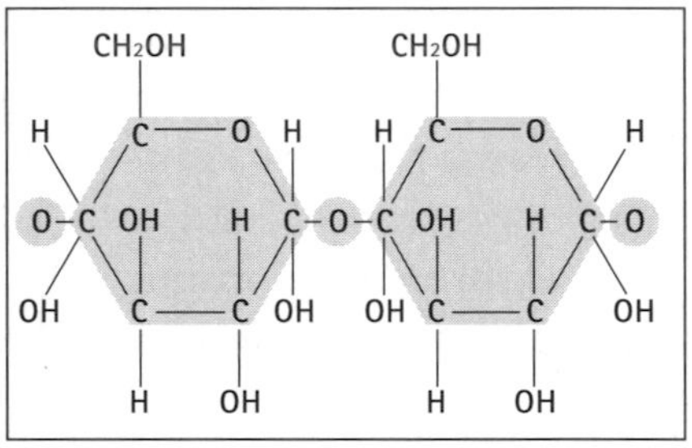 a polysaccharide
proteins	carbon, hydrogen and nitrogen	■ enzymes are molecules made of protein, which act as catalysts speeding up chemical reactions ■ cell membranes and organelles are mostly built of protein	eggs, beans and pulses (e.g. lentils), fish, meat, milk and cheese 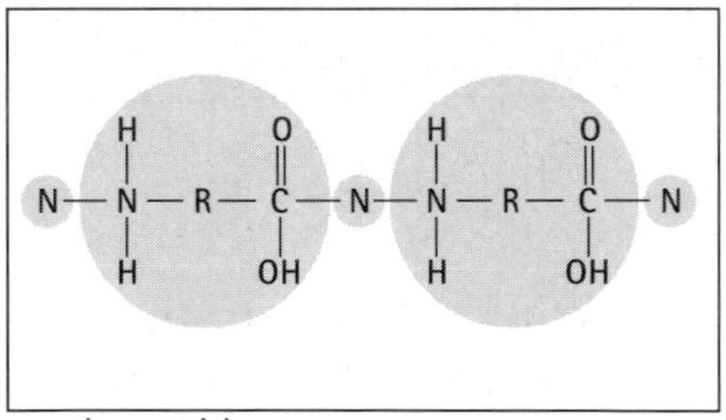 a polypeptide
fats (lipids)	carbon, hydrogen and a little oxygen	■ cell membranes contain lipid ■ fat deposits act as a layer of insulation ■ fat deposits cushion the body and prevent damage ■ a source of energy	fried foods, fatty meats, oily fish, butter, cheese 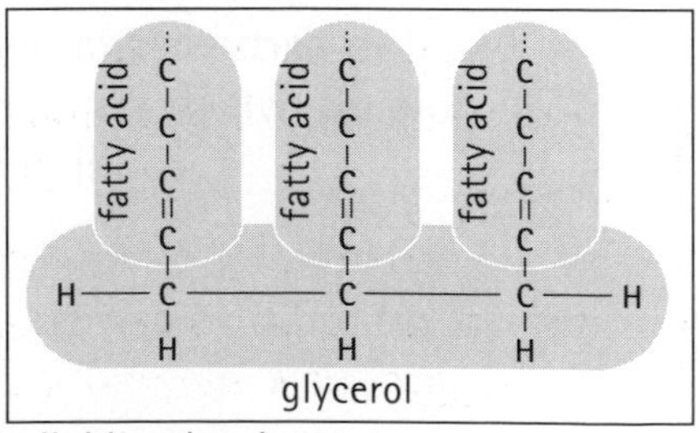 a lipid molecule

To stay healthy we need a balanced diet, which means eating a variety of different foods and the right amount of each food type. People need a diet that suits their lifestyle, which can change.

Keep a diary of your diet for a few days. Write the foods in groups according to food type. Which food type do you eat most of? Is yours a balanced diet?

Meat contains iron, which is needed to make new red blood cells. Calcium, needed for strong teeth and bones, is found in milk. Fruit and vegetables are particularly important in a diet because they provide minerals, vitamins and fibre. Vitamin C, needed to keep skin in good condition, is found in citrus fruits, such as oranges and lemons, and tomatoes. These substances keep us healthy, but some can be destroyed or lost during cooking.

What methods of preparing foods help to keep the vitamin content high?

Some people with certain medical conditions have to avoid some types of foods.

medical condition	things to consider about diet
high level of cholesterol in blood	eat low fat foods, like fruit and vegetables
diabetic	control sugar intake carefully
high blood pressure	avoid salty foods
kidneys not working properly	eat low protein diet

REMEMBER You need to know how to explain what a balanced diet is. You also need to know about the main food types and some examples of foods containing them.

REMEMBER In the exam you may be asked to link a suitable diet to a particular lifestyle.

Practice Questions – Humans as organisms 1

1 Why are salads and lightly cooked vegetables good for you?

2 What are three of the most likely reasons for someone being overweight?

3 Suggest three foods and one food type that might be avoided by someone with kidney problems.

4 a) Suggest two reasons why children need to eat more high energy foods than elderly people.

b) Aidee used to do a lot of sports when she was a student, but is about to start an office job. Suggest how she might change her diet because her lifestyle is changing.

5 Look at the picture and table below.

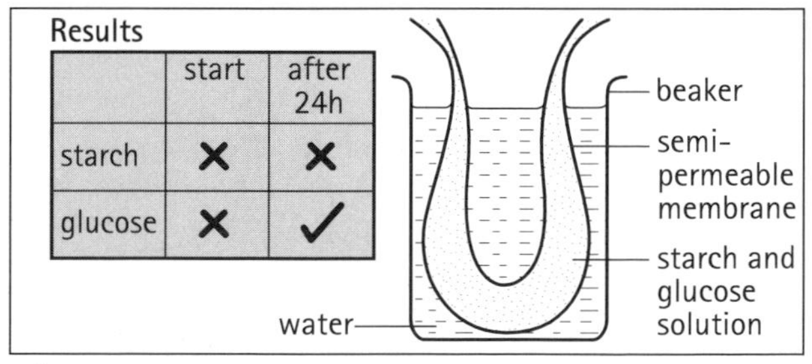

	start	after 24h
starch	✗	✗
glucose	✗	✓

a) What sort of substances are sugar and starch?

b) Explain why there is glucose in the water after 24 hours, but not starch.

c) Why is it important to test the water for both starch and glucose at the start of the experiment as well as the end?

Human digestion

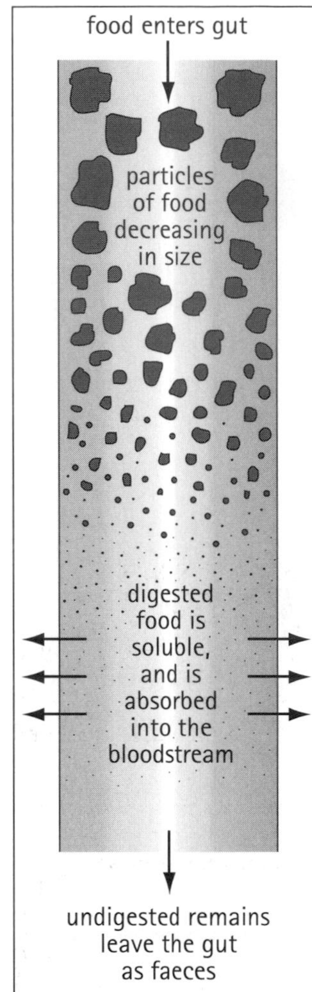

Food is processed as it passes through the gut, or **alimentary canal**. The size of the food particles gets smaller and smaller as the food travels along from the mouth towards the anus. Finally food particles are small enough to pass out of the gut and into the blood. Any food that is not digested passes out of the body at the anus, as a solid waste called **faeces**.

How is food broken down?

- teeth chop and grind food (this is called physical digestion)
- **enzymes** (biological **catalysts**) speed up the breakdown of large food molecules into smaller molecules. Enzymes are made in the lining of the gut and by the **pancreas**
- carbohydrates are broken down into **glucose** (sugar)
- acid in the stomach helps to break down proteins into **amino acids**
- bile made by the liver helps to break down fats into **fatty acids** and **glycerol**

The picture below shows the gut, the conditions within it and what happens at each part. In the insert picture, part of the lining of the small intestine called the **villus** is shown in more detail.

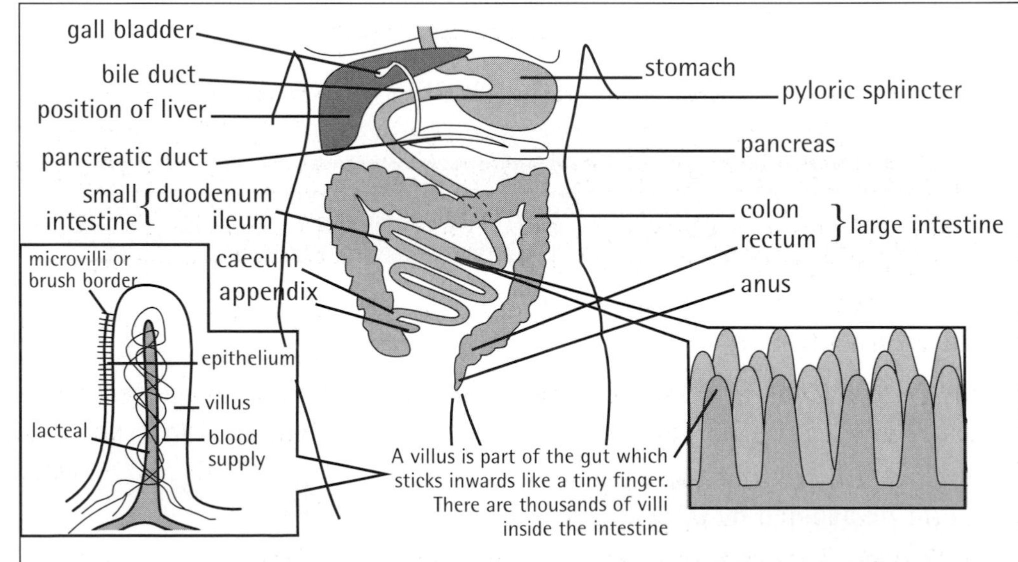

REMEMBER You need to know the order of the different parts of the gut, starting with the mouth, and what happens in each part.

◎ *Carbohydrates are digested into __________. Amino acids come from __________ and fat is broken down into __________ and glycerol.*

During **peristalsis**, food moves through the gut because muscles in the wall contract to squeeze it along. Fibre is important because it provides bulk, allowing the muscles to move food along the gut more effectively.

Enzymes and digestion

Enzymes are made of protein molecules. Each enzyme is made of a different protein and has a specific shape. The shape is particularly important and is called the **active site**. This is where molecules temporarily join to the enzyme and change, either by breaking into smaller molecules or by joining to form larger ones.

If an enzyme changes shape, it does not join with other particles and cannot speed up reactions. What conditions affect the shape of enzymes?

- high temperature (over 50°C), because the protein structure breaks down
- change in pH, because pH affects bonds between atoms in the protein molecule

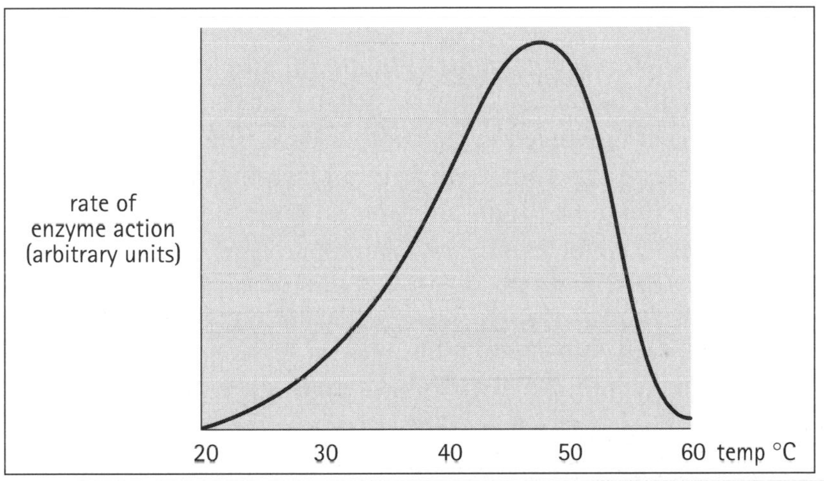

REMEMBER Make sure you can understand and explain graphs showing the rate of an enzyme-catalysed reaction.

Practice Questions - Humans as organisms 2

1 a) Use a mirror to observe the shape and number of human teeth. Find out the names of each type. How is the shape suited for the job each tooth does?

b) Which body system makes us aware of pain when a tooth is decayed?

2 Draw a flowchart using the phrases below to summarise the main events that happen in each part of the gut. Draw it on a large piece of paper and use lots of space.

events in the mouth

events in the stomach

events in the first part of small intestine

events in the last part of small intestine

events in the large intestine

3 a) Describe the effect of temperature on the action of an enzyme.

b) Amylase is an enzyme that speeds up the breakdown of starch in the mouth. When food is swallowed, amalyse enters the stomach. What would you expect to happen to the action of amylase in the stomach, and why?

4 Find out what a 'barium meal' is and why someone might be given one.

5 a) What is a sphincter muscle?

b) Suggest a reason why there are sphincters at both ends of the stomach.

6 The acid in the stomach kills most of the bacteria that enter with food. Why is this a good idea?

The blood system

Blood and circulation

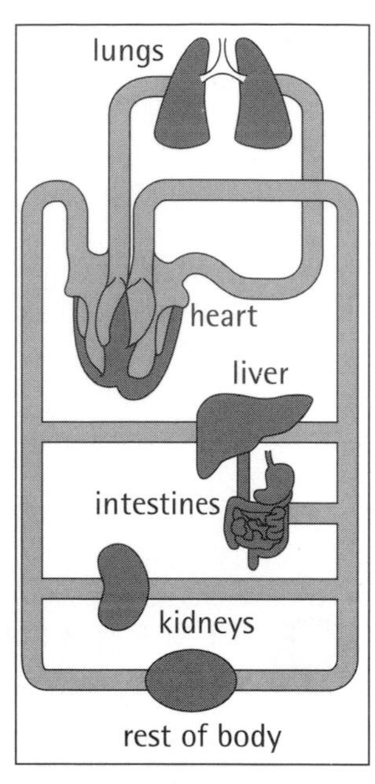

The heart is one of the most important organs in the body. It is responsible for the circulation of the blood. If the heart is diseased, in many cases it can be repaired by surgery. For example, valves can be repaired or replaced, blocked arteries can be by-passed, or a heart can be replaced entirely. Replacing a heart with another human heart is called a **transplant**. Rejection is a major problem with transplanted organs, and the patient may need to take **immunosuppressant** drugs for the rest of their life.

Overall, the structure of blood does not change much, apart from slight changes in the levels of glucose or salt soon after a meal, or perhaps the presence of medicines. When someone is fighting an infection, such as a sore throat, the number of white blood cells may be greater than normal. This is because white blood cells are involved in fighting disease. The number of red cells may increase if someone stays for a while in a place that is very high above sea level. The air is thinner at high altitudes so their blood needs more **haemoglobin** (see below) to collect and carry as much oxygen as possible.

REMEMBER You need to know that there are four blood groups: O, A, B and AB.

The blood is made up of a number of components:

- **red blood cells**, which contain haemoglobin transport oxygen to the cells and most of the carbon dioxide back to the lungs. The cells have a dent in the middle which makes them more flexible. The large surface area helps their uptake of oxygen
- **white blood cells** fight infection. They make **antibodies** and surround and overcome bacteria. Some white blood cells can change shape so their **cytoplasm** flows around particles
- **platelets** are cell fragments and are very important in clotting
- **plasma** is the yellow liquid part of blood. It contains many dissolved substances, such as glucose, salts and amino acids. It also contains plasma proteins, such as blood clotting factors

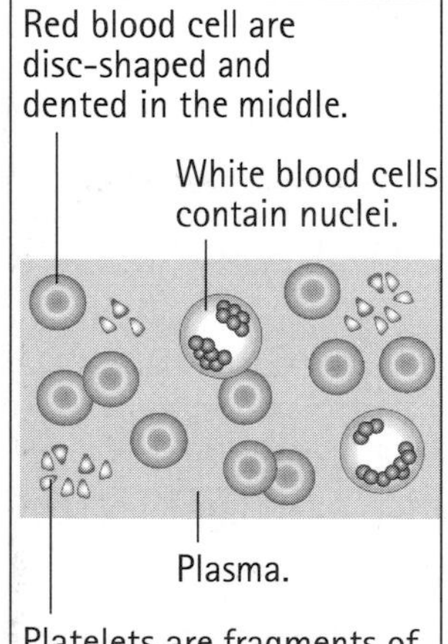

Haemoglobin is the substance in red blood cells that combines with and carries oxygen:

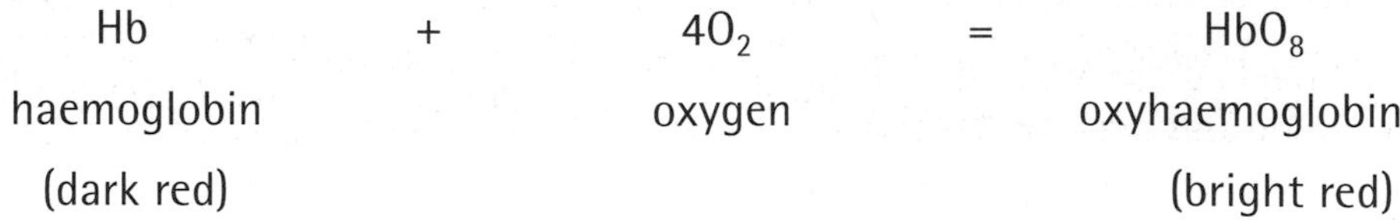

Hb	+	$4O_2$	=	HbO_8
haemoglobin		oxygen		oxyhaemoglobin
(dark red)				(bright red)

There is a higher concentration of oxygen in the lungs than there is in the blood passing through the lungs. The oxygen diffuses through the **alveoli** (air sacs) of the lungs and into blood. Haemoglobin in the blood joins with oxygen and circulates around the body as **oxyhaemoglobin**. In the tissues where oxygen is being used up, red blood cells give up their oxygen and pick up carbon dioxide.

The heart is the pump which drives the circulation of blood. It is made of muscle and beats continuously during life. Each heartbeat consists of the following sequence of events:

- the two **atria** fill with blood, which enters through the large veins
- the two atria contract or close, and blood passes into the two **ventricles**
- as the ventricles fill, blood presses against the **valves** between the atria and ventricles, closing them
- the ventricles contract strongly, pumping blood into the **arteries**
- the atria begin to refill, and the valves at the base of the large arteries close

REMEMBER You should be able to label a diagram of the heart and relate the structure of blood vessels to their function.

A summary of the features of blood vessels

feature	structure	oxygen levels of blood flow	pressure	speed and direction
artery	thick muscular and elastic wall with small space inside; resists high pressure and pulls back into shape	high	highest nearer the heart	high, since the blood is close to the pump; blood flows towards the organs and away from the heart
capillary	thin wall only one cell thick, small in size passing close to cells; the thin walls 'leak'	higher near an artery and lower near a vein		very slow, moving between an artery and vein within tissues, so more time for materials to exchange between blood and tissue fluid
vein	thinner wall than an artery, and the pressure is lower, but larger space inside; valves present to stop blood flowing the wrong way	lower than an artery	lowest nearer the heart and lower than an artery	slower than an artery since the blood is furthest away from the pump and has slowed in the tissues; blood moves away from organs towards heart

Practice Questions - Humans as organisms 3

1 a) Draw a picture of the heart. Label the diagram, including the names of the main blood vessels.

b) Where are the valves in the heart? Why are they necessary and when are they closed?

2 a) Name the blood vessels that carry blood:

(i) to the lungs

(ii) to the body from the heart

b) How does the blood pressure and the amount of oxygen carried in these two vessels vary?

Health, disease and immunity

REMEMBER Make sure you know the difference between an antigen and an antibody.

If you are healthy, your body works well, you feel happy (most of the time!) and you are able to cope with life. You aren't ill or unwell.

Poor health can have several causes, including:

- **infection**, e.g. a cold is caused by a virus, a sore throat is caused by a virus or a bacterium
- **injury**, e.g. the liver might be damaged in an accident
- an **inherited condition** like cystic fibrosis
- a **lifestyle habit**, such as drug abuse
- **mental illness**

Doctors sometimes use medicine to kill a bacterial infection. Find out what sort of medicine is used to cure a sore throat or ear infection.

How does your body defend itself against disease?

- the main defence against disease is the **skin**, which is the body's barrier
- if the skin is cut, it heals as new skin cells grow
- a cut blood vessel gets plugged by a clot, which then turns to a scab
- a 'non-self' cell, such as a bacterium which gets into the body, is called an **antigen**. Some white blood cells produce **antibodies**. These are are substances that lock on to antigens, damaging them or allowing other white cells to engulf them. Antibodies give us immunity against infection

Why does smoking damage health?

Smoking can seriously damage your health

Smoke damages the little hairs or **cilia** on the surface of cells in the air passages, so they do not sweep out the dirt particles so well. Dirt collects and damages cells lining the alveoli. Finally, the lungs lose their elasticity and fluid collects in the alveoli, making it much harder to breathe. This is called **emphysema**.

Tar contains chemicals (called **carcinogens**) which cause lung cancer. **Nicotine** causes the muscle in the walls of blood vessels to contract. This raises blood pressure, which can damage arteries by making them less elastic and allowing blood clots to form. Nicotine is addictive, so smoking is difficult to give up. Smoke also contains **carbon monoxide gas**, which combines with haemoglobin faster than oxygen, so the blood carries less oxygen around the body.

Women who smoke during pregnancy have smaller babies than those who do not smoke.

REMEMBER Any chemical we know causes cancer is called a carcinogen.

Why do people find it difficult to stop smoking?

Immunisation

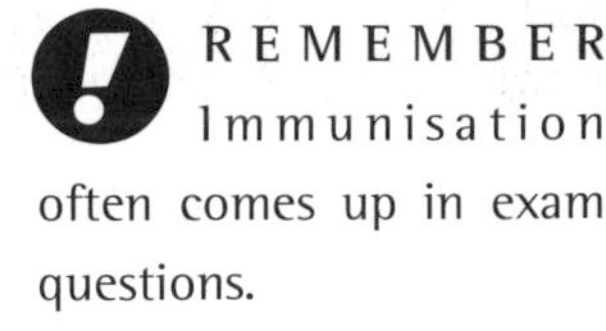

Immunisation is a way of protecting ourselves from infection. The picture below shows how immunisation uses the body's own immune system for future protection.

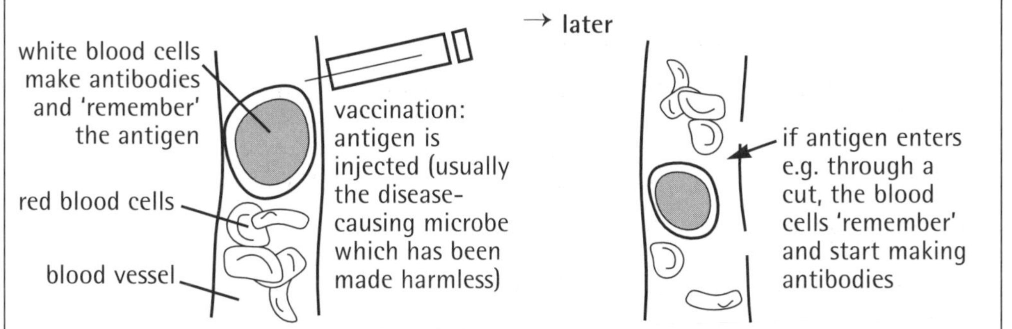

HIV is a virus that enters human cells, including white blood cells which normally protect us against infection. The virus particles take over the white blood cells, using them to make many more virus particles and destroying them as they burst out into the bloodstream. It is difficult to treat this infection because the virus particles are inside white blood cells, where they are protected from our defence system.

Make a list of the diseases that can now be prevented by immunisation. You can find the information at your local doctor's surgery or at the library.

Practice Questions - Humans as organisms 4

1 What type of health condition is:

a) an earache?

b) a broken leg?

c) an addiction to tranquillisers?

d) feeling depressed?

e) sickle cell anaemia?

2 Haemophilia is an inherited disease in which the blood doesn't clot normally. Suggest reasons why blood clotting is important to health.

3 a) What are antibodies?

b) Why are antibodies important for immunity?

Breathing

Living things need to exchange gases with their surroundings. Plants do this by **diffusion**, mainly through pores in the leaf surfaces. However, humans and most other animals are so active that they need a greater oxygen supply than could be provided by diffusion alone. The breathing system involves special organs adapted for getting air in and out of the body fast.

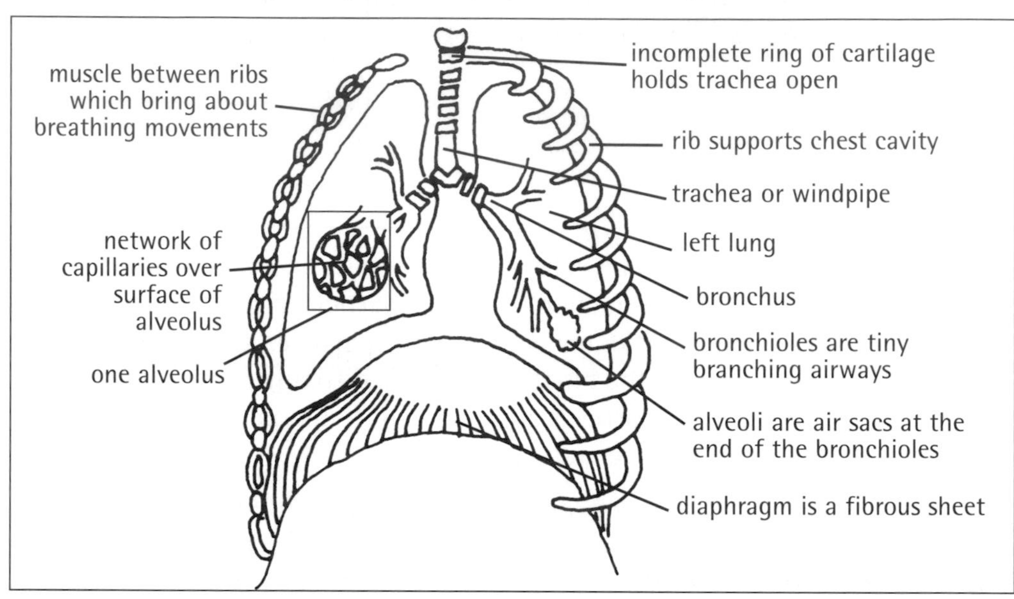

Breathing in: inhalation

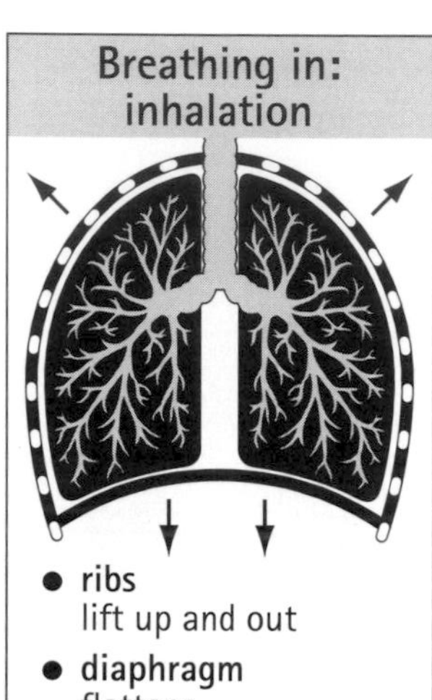

- **ribs** lift up and out
- **diaphragm** flattens
- **volume inside chest and lungs** increases
- **air pressure** drops
- **air flow** inwards

Breathing out: exhalation

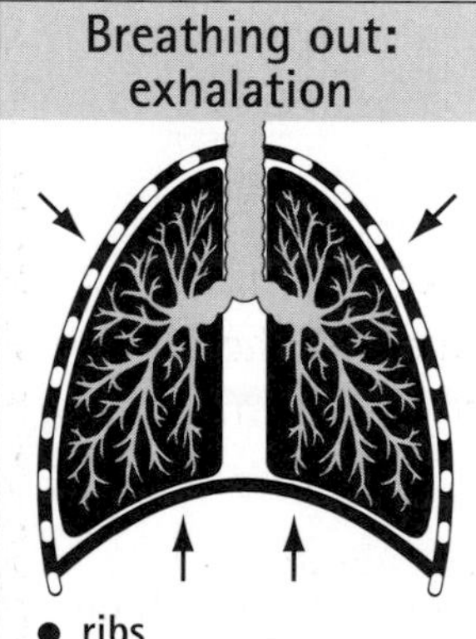

- **ribs** sink down and in
- **diaphragm** domes upwards
- **volume inside chest and lungs** decreases
- **air pressure** rises
- **air flow** outwards

The **lungs** are delicate organs which are pushed against the inside of the chest cavity by air pressure. Pleural fluid lets the lungs slip against this surface as they move during breathing. Inside the alveoli, oxygen dissolves in the surface moisture and diffuses through the wall of the air sac into a nearby blood capillary. Similarly, carbon dioxide gas can diffuse from the blood capillaries into the alveoli and is breathed out.

◎ *Sketch the outline of the chest cavity and lungs and try labelling them. Use the book to check if you've got the details right.*

Breathing is an active process which uses energy, because we need to move the muscles to make it happen, but it is controlled automatically so we do not have to think about it. The direction in which air flows when we breathe depends on the difference between the pressure inside the lungs and outside the body. If there is no difference there is no overall air flow.

Breathing movements make air move in and out of the lungs. These movements use:

- sets of muscles around the ribs
- the diaphragm

When we breathe in, or **inhale**, air pressure inside the lungs is lower than outside them so air is drawn or sucked in. When we breathe out, or **exhale**, air pressure outside the body is lower than in the lungs so air is squeezed out.

Compostion of inhaled and exhaled air (%)

	air we breathe in (inhale)	air we breathe out (exhale)
nitrogen	78	78
oxygen	21	18
carbon dioxide	0.04	3
noble gases	1	1

What do you notice when you breathe on a mirror or cold window? How does the composition of air change between inhaling and exhaling?

REMEMBER You should be able to relate the structure of the breathing system to the way it works and label its main features.

Practice Questions - Humans as organisms 5

1 a) How are the alveoli well adapted for gas exchange?

b) Name two materials which exchange between the blood and alveoli in the lungs.

2 Design a flowchart to describe the events that happen during inhalation (breathing in), and fill in the details.

3 A spirometer is a piece of apparatus that can be used to investigate the depth and rate of breathing. The diagram opposite shows spirometer traces for an individual before and after exercise. Raising lines on the traces show where the individual breathed in. Falling lines on the trace show where the individual breathed out.

a) What was the rate of breathing at rest?

b) What was the depth of breathing at rest?

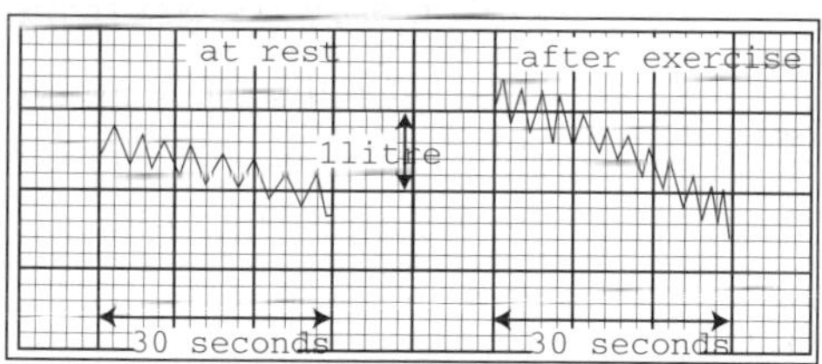

c) Ventilation rate can be worked out by multiplying the rate of breathing by the depth of breathing. The answer is given in litres per minute.

(i) What was the ventilation rate at rest?

(ii) What was the ventilation rate after exercise?

(iii) Suggest reasons for the difference in ventilation rate.

(iv) Explain why the variation in composition of the blood may affect the ventilation rate.

Respiration

REMEMBER You should know the difference between aerobic and anaerobic respiration.

There is life on Earth because of the unique conditions here. We have the Sun as an energy source and an oxygen-rich atmosphere. How is the Sun's energy transferred to the cells of living things? Mostly the energy is transferred by the process of **respiration**.

During **aerobic respiration** oxygen is used to allow the transfer of energy from glucose in every cell of the body:

glucose + oxygen → carbon dioxide + water + energy transferred to cells

Some living things, like yeast, can carry out **anaerobic respiration**. This type of respiration happens without oxygen. It is called **fermentation**:

glucose → carbon dioxide + ethanol + some energy transferred to cells

During vigorous exercise, muscle tissue may use up oxygen very quickly. When this happens anaerobic respiration takes place in the muscle tissue:

glucose → lactate + energy transferred to cells

Later, when vigorous exercise has stopped and more oxygen is available to the muscle tissue, the oxygen is used to respire the lactate. In order to respire lactate, oxygen is needed. So while lactate is building up in the muscle, we say the muscle has an **oxygen debt**.

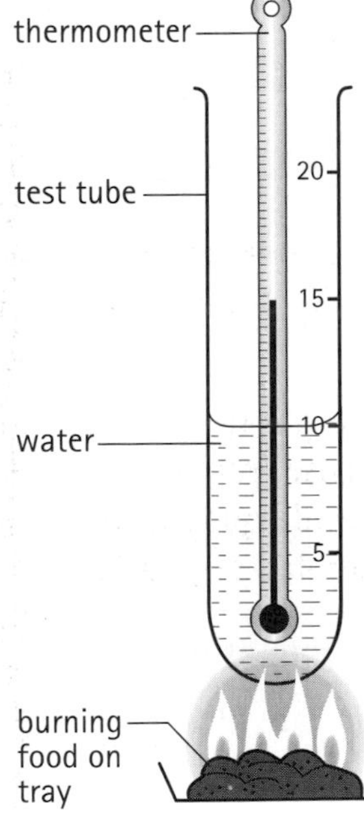

You can carry out a simple experiment to estimate the energy transfer when foods are respired. Burning food combines with oxygen, making carbon dioxide and water, and transferring energy to the surroundings. This is similar to the way food is respired.

A water sample is placed directly above the burning food, as shown in the picture on the left, so that most of the energy transfers to the water, raising its temperature. You can calculate how much energy is transferred like this. We know that 4.2 J of energy will raise the temperature of 1 ml of water by 1°C. So if you substitute the amount of water you used for your experiment and the rise in temperature you observed in the equation below, you will be able to work out how much energy was transferred:

energy transferred (J) = 4.2 J/ml °C x volume of water (ml) x rise in temperature (°C)

Practice Questions – Humans as organisms 6

1 a) Why do cells carry out respiration?

b) What is the difference between aerobic and anaerobic respiration?

c) Why does an oxygen debt sometimes occur in muscles?

2 The table below shows how much energy, in kilojoules, is needed to do various activities for one hour.

ACTIVITY	ENERGY USED FOR ACTIVITY (KJ / MIN)
SITTING	6
SLOW WALKING	13
STANDING	7
RUNNING	42

a) Use this information to finish the bar chart below. The first one has been done for you.

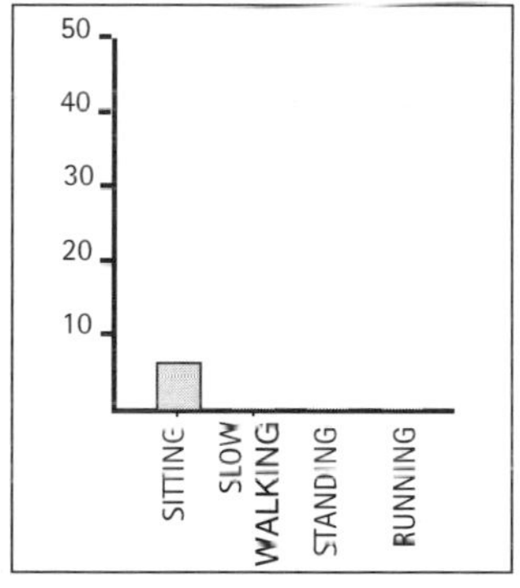

b) (i) Which activity uses most energy?

(ii) Why is energy needed while you are sleeping.

(iii) How much energy does the boy need to run for 30 minutes? Show your working.

3 The shrew is a small mammal that looks like a mouse. The picture above right shows the relationship between body mass and rate of oxygen consumption for various species.

a) Which species uses 7 cm^3 per gram per hour of oxygen?

b) (i) How much more oxygen in cm^3 per gram per hour does a sonoma shrew use compared to a short tailed shrew?

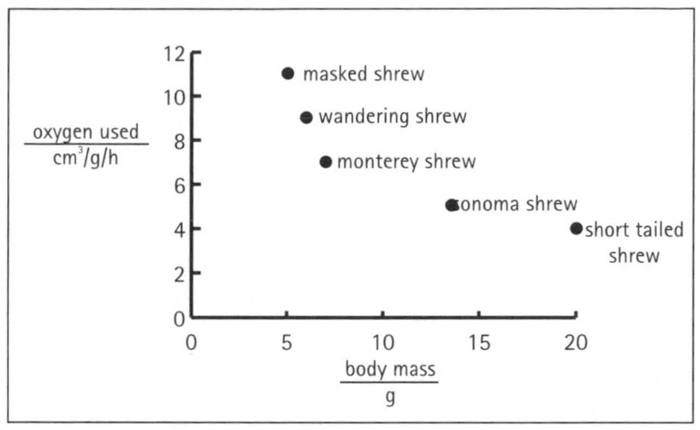

(ii) Suggest one reason for this difference.

c) Shrews eat food equivalent to 95% of their body mass each day. Which shrew would eat most food per day?

d) Describe the relationship between body mass of shrews and rate of oxygen consumption.

4 Long-distance swimmers are sometimes advised to eat a chocolate bar before swimming. One popular chocolate bar has the following nutritional information:

Each 100g gives you	carbohydrate	69.6 g
	protein	4.0 g
	fat	17.5 g
	energy	1892 kJ

a) Use this information to state one reason why the chocolate bar is suitable food for a long-distance swimmer.

b) Aerobic respiration in the swimmer's muscles uses oxygen and glucose from the bloodstream. Complete the word equation to the chemical change when aerobic respiration takes place:

oxygen + glucose → __________ + __________.

Sensitivity

Our survival depends on us being sensitive to, and responding to, changes that take place inside and outside our bodies. The nervous system gives us sensitivity. The main components of the nervous system are shown below:

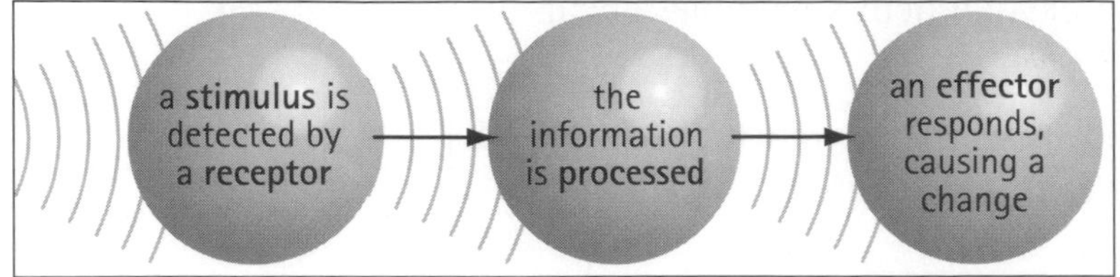

- a **stimulus** is a condition that is detected by the body, e.g. temperature
- a **receptor** is the part of the body that detects the stimulus. This could be a single nerve cell (a **neurone**), such as a pain receptor in the skin, or a sense organ (like the nose) with many receptor cells
- an **effector** is the part of the body that responds (e.g. a muscle, which moves, or a gland, which produces a hormone)
- the brain acts as a **processing centre** for all the information detected by receptors. It then tells the effector organ what to do. The nervous system coordinates all the life processes

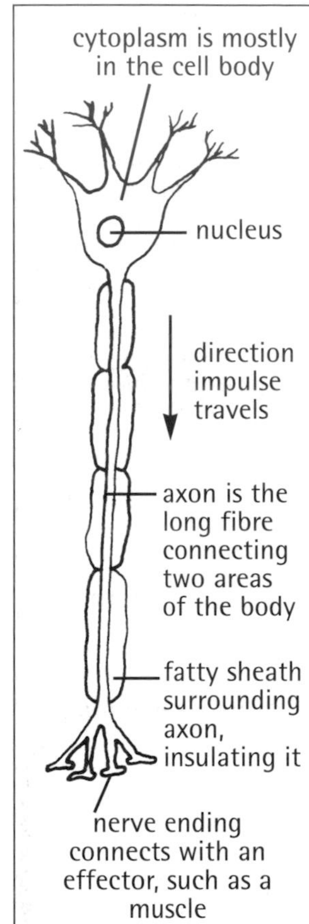

A single nerve cell

Reacting without thinking

There are lots of actions you make that you don't need to think about, like breathing and making your heart beat. Other actions, called **reflexes**, are automatic and do not have to be learned. The simplest pathway a reflex action takes can involve just three nerve cells.

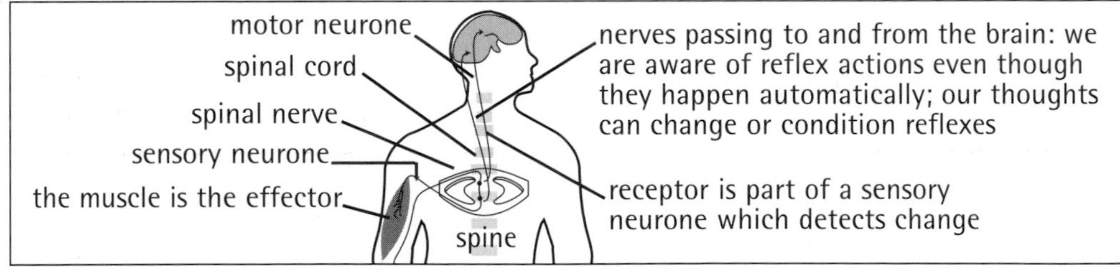

Why are reflexes important for survival?

The eye

The eye is a sense organ containing many receptor cells, which are sensitive to light. To see things clearly, light must come to focus on the retina. The eye achieves this by changing the shape of the lens. The pictures on the page opposite show how the amount of light entering the eye is adjusted by contraction and relaxation of the muscles in the iris.

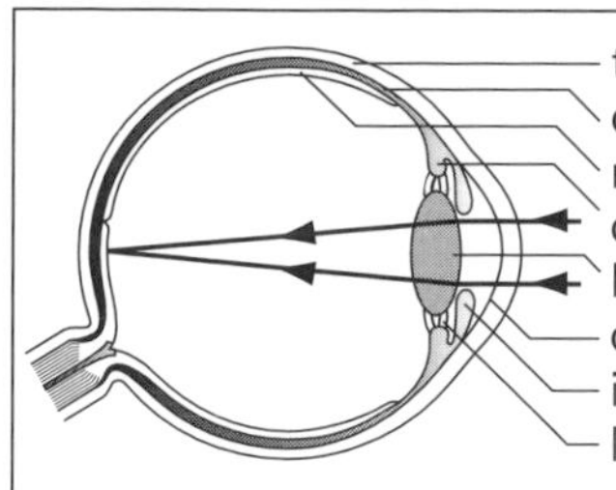

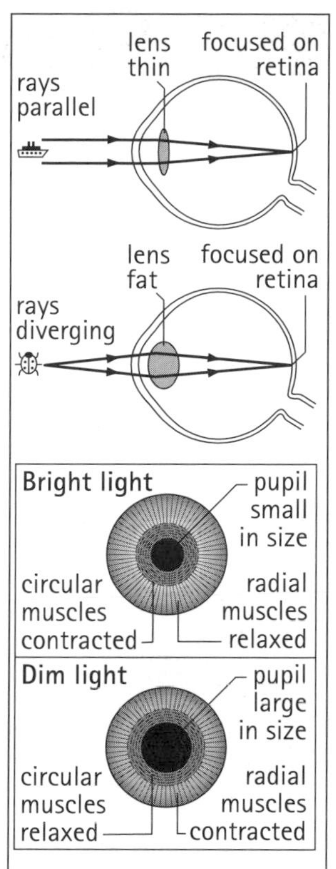

Seeing near and far

	looking near	looking far
reflected rays	spread apart as they enter eye	enter the eye almost parallel
ciliary muscle	contracted	relaxed
ligaments	slack	pulling on lens
lens shape	fat	thin
light rays brought to focus	to a greater extent	slightly
image	focused on the retina	focused on the retina

Correcting eye problems

  *Watch the video section on correcting sight problems.*

Exam questions often ask you to draw in the position of the lens, light rays coming to focus, or the type of lens for correction.

Practice Questions - Humans as organisms 7

Reaction time/milliseconds

Student	Before drinking the beer	1 hour after the drink	2 hours after the drink	3 hours after the drink	4 hours after the drink
Manjit	80	125	95	79	80
Lisa	90	160	100	95	90
Darren	70	150	120	100	90
Jo	85	110	84	85	85

1 In an experiment to test reaction times some university students were told to press a buzzer when they heard a bell ring. Their reaction times were measured. They then drank some beer and were tested again.

a) What effect did drinking the beer have on their reaction times?

b) Explain how you can tell that Jo recovered most quickly from the effects of the alcohol.

2 a) Why are long or short-sighted people not able to see clearly without glasses?

b) Why are different types of lenses used to correct long and short sight?

Chemical coordination

Hormones are chemicals that help to coordinate life processes. They work in different ways:

- immediately, e.g. insulin is produced because of a change in the level of glucose in the blood, and helps to keep it to the correct level
- over a period of time, e.g. growth hormones adjust the rate of growth in children

Glands produce hormones, delivering them directly into the blood which passes through them. The circulating blood carries the hormones. They affect particular organs, called **target organs**. For example, ADH affects the kidneys (see page 38). The **pituitary gland** has a special role because it produces some hormones which activate other glands. Hormones are broken down in the liver and excreted by the kidney.

REMEMBER Make sure you can label the glands shown on a diagram like the one on this page.

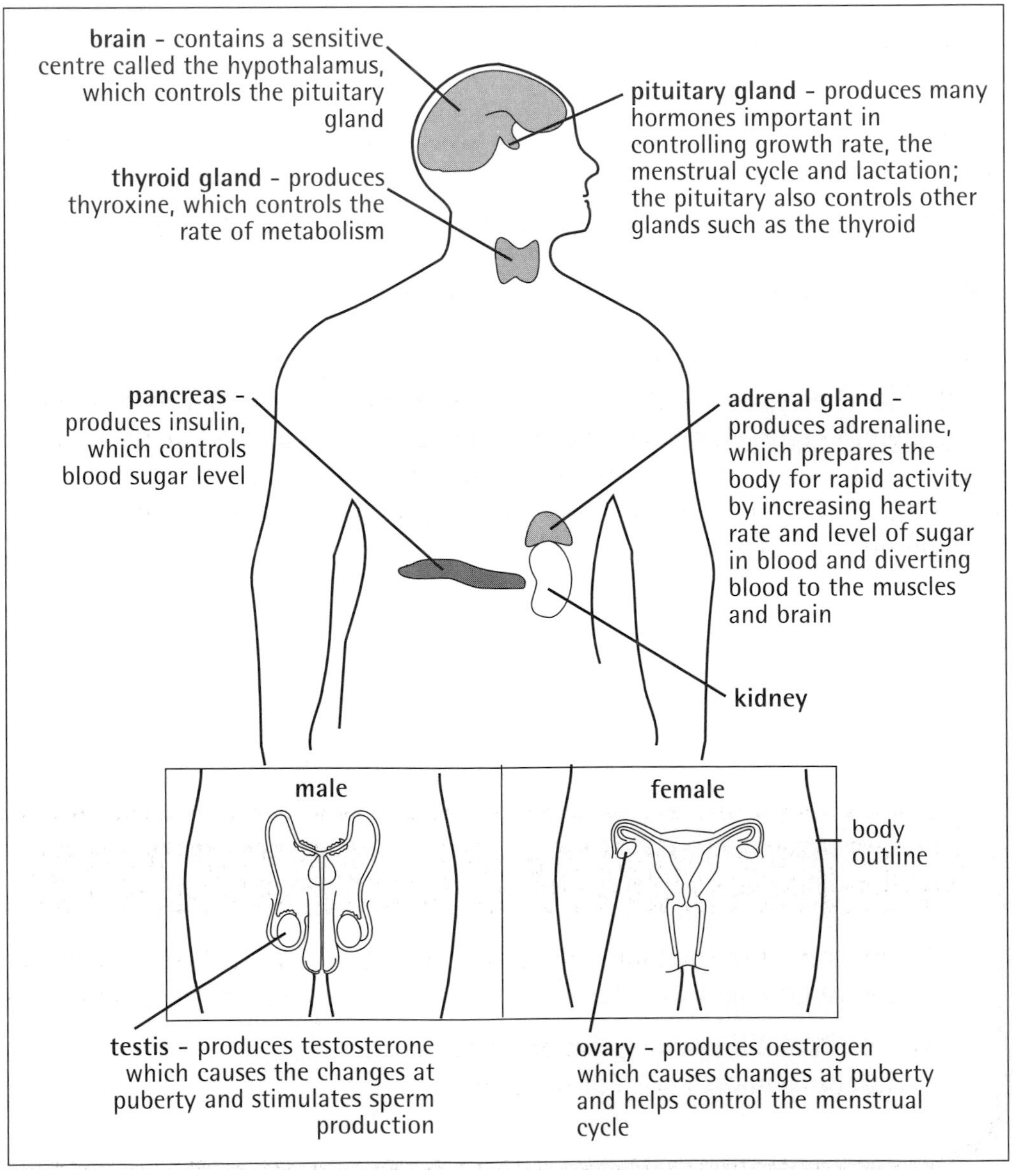

Controlling sugar level in blood

The amount of sugar in the blood is critical, because it has an effect on the nearby cells. If the blood contains too much sugar, it draws too much water out of cells and damages them. Low blood sugar is dangerous too, because sugar is needed as an energy supply for all cells. The blood sugar level needs to be adjusted constantly, because the amount and type of food we eat varies daily and the activities we're involved in affect how quickly food is used by the body.

Insulin and **glucagon** are the two hormones involved in controlling sugar level in blood. They are both produced by special cells in the pancreas. Together they keep the level of sugar within a safe range for cells.

Insulin and glucagon are sugar controllers.

sugar level rises, e.g. after a meal	sugar level drops, e.g. between meals
more of the hormone insulin produced	more of the hormone glucagon produced
more sugar taken into cells for respiration	cells take up less sugar (so it stays in blood)
sugar is converted to glycogen and stored	glycogen may be converted to sugar

? *Which hormone would be produced after eating a big bar of chocolate?*

? *What happens if there is a lack of insulin?*

Some people don't make enough insulin because they have an inherited condition called **diabetes.** A person with diabetes lacks a gene which codes for insulin production, so the special cells in the pancreas don't make that hormone. Nowadays, human insulin is made by bacteria which have been given the gene that codes for insulin production. The insulin is injected into the bloodstream in controlled doses.

Practice Questions - Humans as organisms 8

1 Describe how the pituitary gland is different to other glands.

2 Which glands are involved in bringing about the changes which happen at puberty?

3 How does a hormone pass from the gland cells into the bloodstream?

Sexual maturity

The human body changes during adolescence as children grow into adults. These changes are called the **secondary sexual characteristics** and they appear at puberty. This means sex organs develop and become mature and the person is capable of reproducing (see page 34 for details of the reproductive systems). Sex hormones cause puberty: **testosterone** in males, **oestrogen** and **progesterone** in females.

secondary sexual characteristics for boys	secondary sexual characteristics for girls
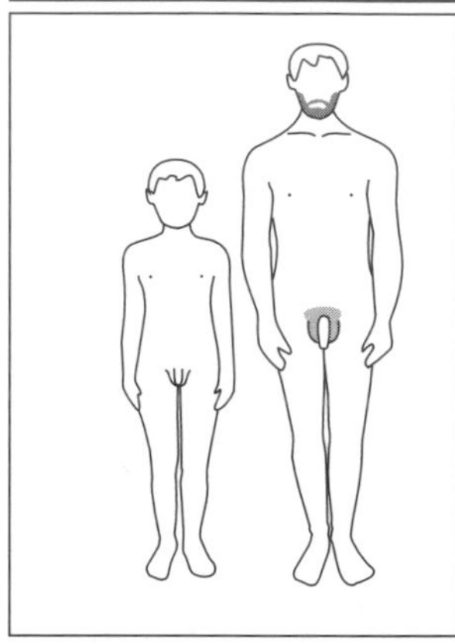	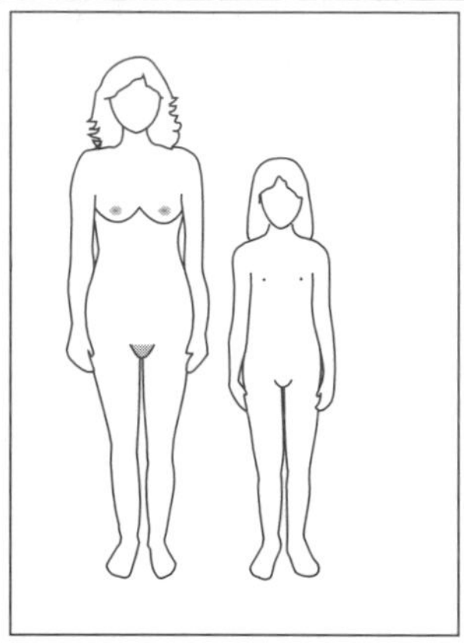
puberty happens at around 14-16 years	puberty happens at around 11-13 years
whole body has a growth spurt	whole body has a growth spurt
body becomes more muscular	hips widen, and buttocks and thighs get fatter
pubic hair grows	pubic hair grows
beard grows	ovaries produce eggs
penis gets larger	periods start
sperm are produced	

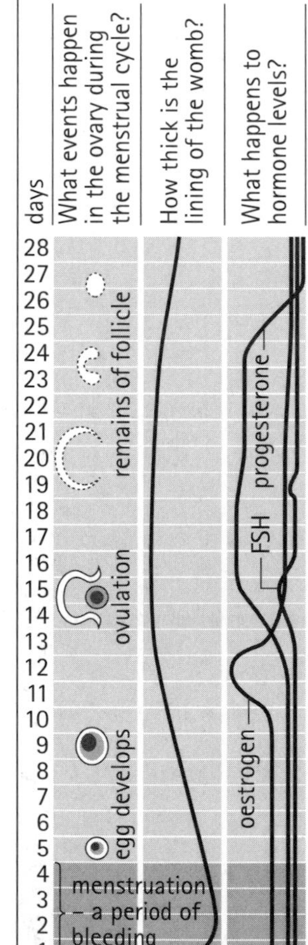

The menstrual cycle

Having a period is called **menstruation**. For most women, menstruation starts at puberty and continues until around 45-50 years of age. The time when periods stop is called the **menopause**. Each menstrual cycle takes 28 days on average and the stages are shown in the picture on the left. You can see that hormones are very important in controlling both when eggs are produced and the changes inside the uterus, where a fertilised egg could develop.

◎ *Work out about how many months altogether a woman is likely to menstruate during her lifetime. Approximately how many eggs would be produced during this time?*

Fertilisation

In humans, **fertilisation** happens inside the female's body, sheltered from hazards in the environment. Fertilisation is when the nucleus of the sperm cell enters the egg, or **ovum**, and fuses with the egg nucleus. These two nuclei contain the DNA, which carries all the information for the new offspring to develop.

> **REMEMBER** Make sure you can work out the likely dates for ovulation and fertilisation in a menstrual cycle.

Increasing fertility

Fertility means how likely it is that fertilisation will occur as a result of mating. There are lots of possible reasons why some people's fertility is low and they have difficulties starting a family. One reason for infertility is that a woman might not produce eggs, or ova. In this case the hormone FSH would be used as a treatment.

What would be the effect of treating with FSH?

Decreasing fertility

Contraception works by preventing an egg being fertilised by a sperm. The picture on the right summarises the main methods of contraception.

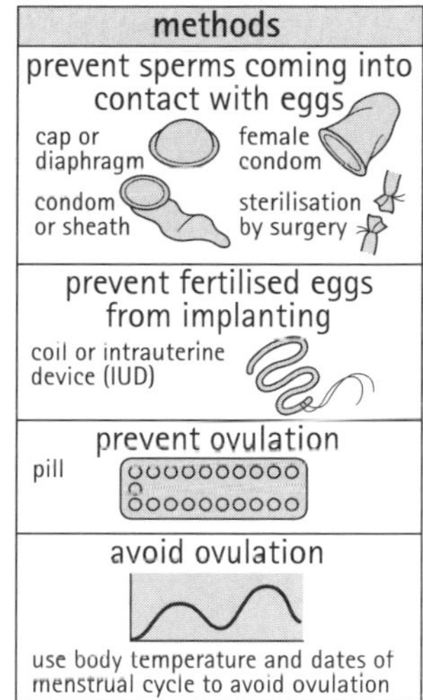

The contraceptive pill contains chemicals similar to hormones, which may:

- stop eggs being released by the ovaries
- make conditions inside the vagina such that sperm are less likely to survive
- make the vaginal mucus thicker so it is more difficult for sperm to swim

Practice Questions - Humans as organisms 9

1 a) Label a diagram like the one below with the key events of the menstrual cycle: a period, lining of the womb thickens, ovulation, fertilisation may occur.

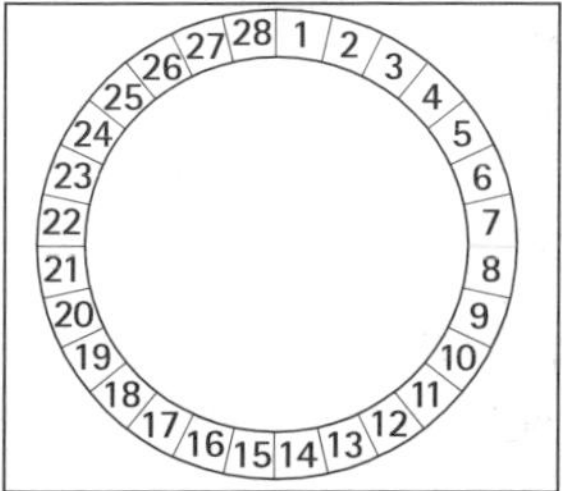

b) If a girl has a period from the 10th-14th of September, when will her next period probably start?

2 Why are the following body changes necessary for a child to grow into an adult?

a) development of breasts in females?

b) widening of hips in females?

c) testes starting to produce sperm in males?

Body systems for reproduction

A reproductive system generally includes:

- a place where female sex cells or eggs are made
- a place where male sex cells or sperm are made
- a way of bringing the male and female sex cells together so that fertilisation occurs

Both male and female sex cells are also called **gametes**.

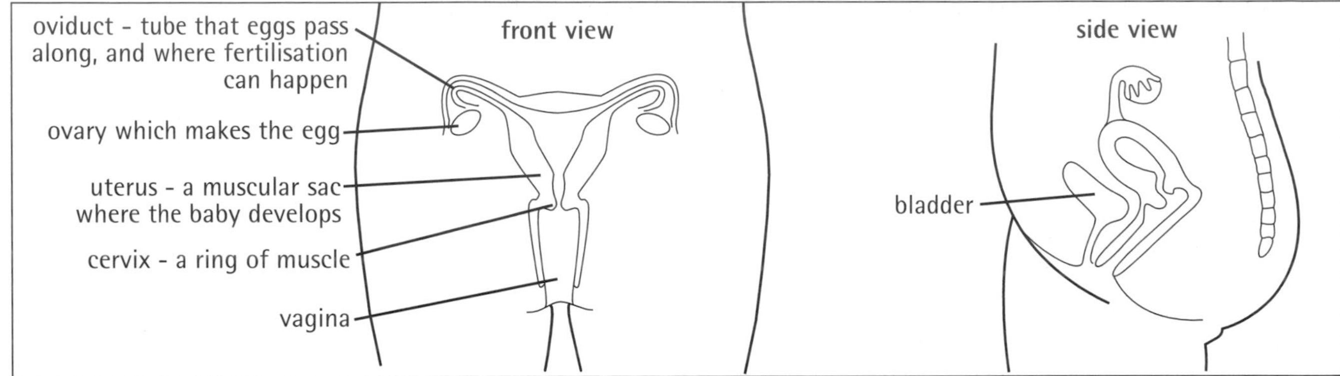

In humans, the female gametes are made in the **ovaries**. One egg (from one or other of the two ovaries) is normally released into an **oviduct** each month. Fertilisation happens in the oviduct as the egg is travelling towards the womb. If an egg is fertilised it sticks to the lining of the **womb** (called **implantation**) and develops there.

What features make the womb a suitable place for the fetus to develop?

- it is protected from injury inside the body
- it is a stable, sheltered environment
- the womb can expand greatly to allow growth
- a special structure called the placenta develops to supply the fetus with nutrition and oxygen

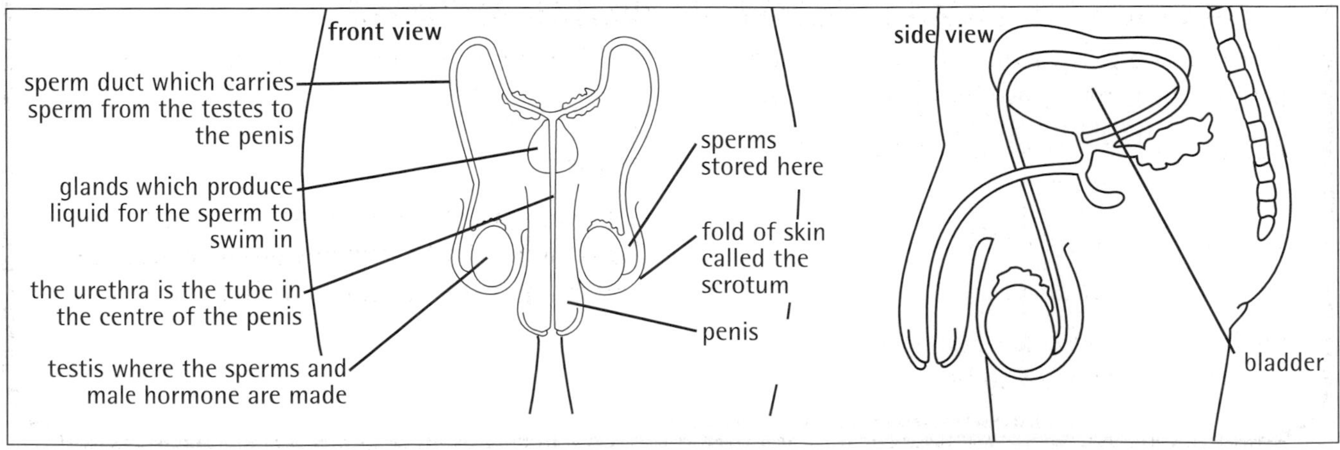

Each testis is continuously making millions of sperm. The penis is used to place the sperm inside the female's body and the glands add liquid for the sperm to swim in. The sperm wriggle their tails to swim through the womb and along the oviducts. Some may come into contact with the egg, but only one sperm can fertilise the egg.

Pregnancy and birth

A human fetus takes thirty-eight weeks to develop in the uterus. During that time the body tissues and organs develop. A few weeks before birth the baby turns into the position shown in the picture below. At birth, a hormone causes the uterus to contract strongly, eventually pushing the baby out through the vagina.

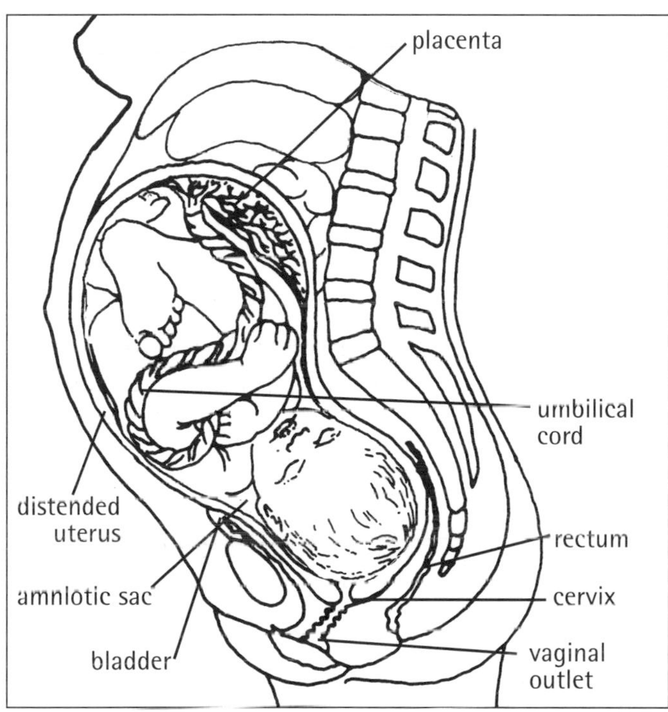

Practice Questions - Humans as organisms 10

1 Match the part of the female reproductive system with the events that happen there:

ovary	a secure place for the fetus to develop
oviduct	sperms enter through here
uterus	produces eggs
vagina	eggs may be fertilised as they pass along here

2 What is the function in reproduction of:

a) the testes?

b) the penis?

3 In humans, fertilisation happens inside the body. Suggest why humans produce very few offspring in comparison to fish or frogs.

Keeping the body in balance

Body cells are very sensitive to change. This is mainly because the chemical reactions that happen in cells are controlled by enzymes, which stop working if the conditions are wrong. Cells work best if the conditions within them stay fairly constant, and this is what is meant by **homeostasis**. The body is sensitive to changes in, among other things:

- temperature
- water and salt content
- pH
- blood sugar levels

The **hypothalamus** in the brain is the control centre for temperature control, or **thermoregulation**, because:

- it is sensitive to the temperature of blood flowing through it (it contains **thermoreceptors**)
- it sends nerve impulses to **effectors** in the skin so temperature is regulated

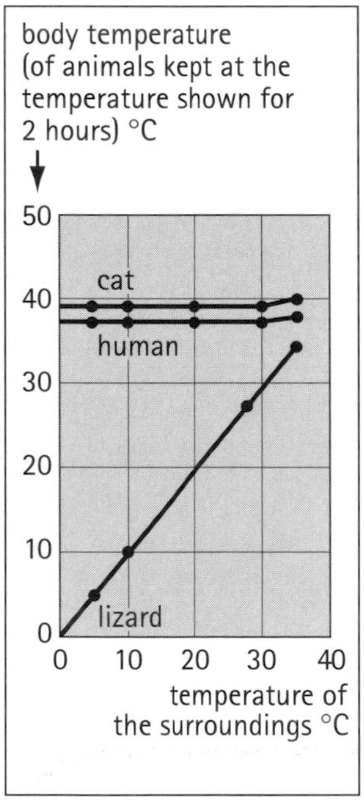

Temperature regulation (thermoregulation)

For some animals, such as insects, the temperature of their surroundings controls their body temperature, how active they are and where they can live. These animals are called **ectotherms**. But humans and other large animals have some control over their body temperature, whatever changes are happening outside. These animals are called **endotherms**. This means that humans can exploit many more environments than would otherwise be possible.

Ways of regulating body temperature

too cold - need to warm the body up	**too hot - need to cool the body down**
sweating decreases	sweating increases
blood circulation near the body surface decreases (**vasoconstriction**)	blood circulation near the body surface increases (**vasodilation**)
by changing behaviour, e.g. wrap up warmly, sit by a fire, go jogging, huddle up in a crowd	by changing behaviour, e.g. moving to a cooler place, taking off a jumper

◎ *Check you know the meaning of receptor and effector.*

The **skin** is a vital organ, because it protects the body from drying out (it's waterproof). It also protects us against infection, excretes waste urea in sweat and regulates body temperature.

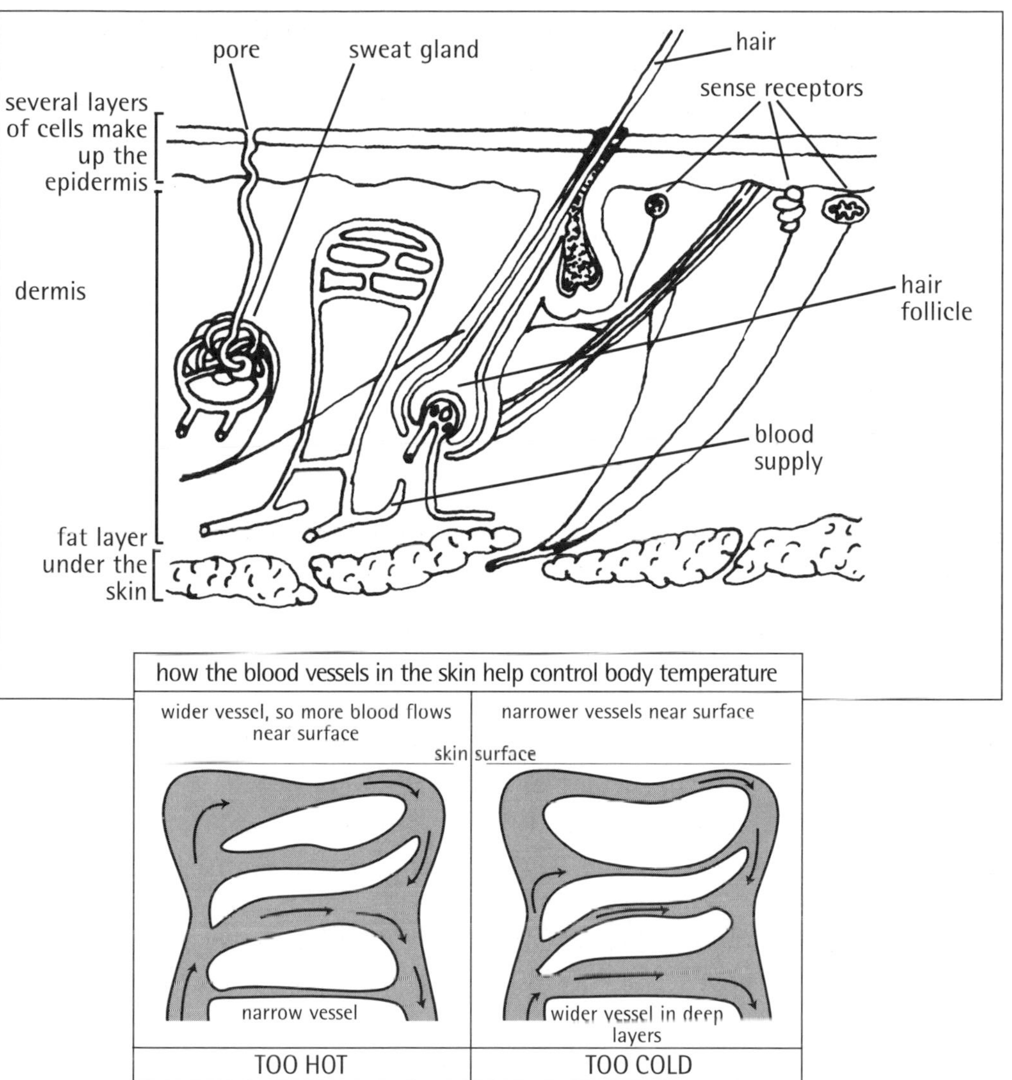

Practice Questions - Humans as organisms 11

1 Compile a table showing the main components of skin and their function, like the one below, adding more rows. The first row has been done for you.

component of skin	function
keratin in surface layers of cells	makes the skin waterproof
sweat glands	

2 What are endotherms and ectotherms?

3 Why is being able to regulate body temperature useful for animals such as humans?

4 Explain how sweating and blood flow help to regulate body temperature.

5 What effect does the Sun's radiation have on the skin?

Balancing water and salts

Living things take in and lose water. They need to be able to balance intake and loss to keep the level of water in the body fairly constant. This process is called **osmoregulation**. For plants and animals that live on land, the challenge is generally to keep enough water in the body. The main ways of doing this are:

- a waterproof covering, e.g. a snail's shell, a waxy cuticle in plants, a slug's slime
- special organs for balancing water content, e.g. the kidneys in humans

The brain is the control centre for osmoregulation. There are **osmoreceptors** in the brain, which are sensitive to how concentrated the blood is. If there is a lack of water, the blood will become too concentrated. If there is too much water in the blood, it will be dilute. The hypothalamus in the brain makes **antidiuretic hormone** (ADH), which reduces the amount of urine the kidneys make (see the picture below).

Water gain and water loss in humans

Water gain (%)		Water loss (%)	
food and drink	86	urine	60
made in the body during respiration	14	sweat	20
		breathing out	16
		faeces	4
		tears	(hardly any)

The human kidneys

The human kidneys have a number of functions. They control water balance and salt balance. They also excrete urea, hormones and medicines in the urine they produce. Finally, they control the pH of our blood.

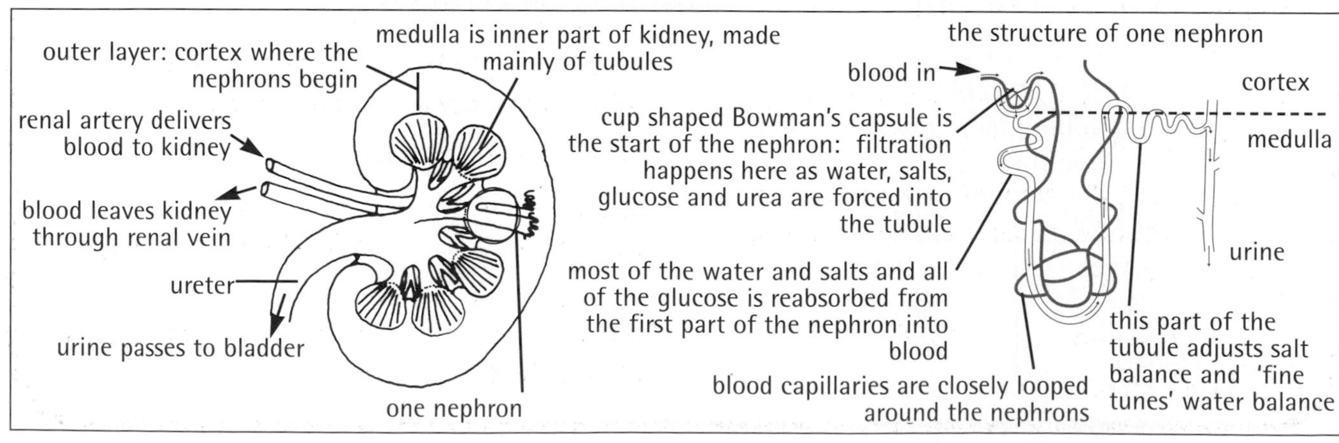

The main points to remember about how a **nephron** works are:

- blood is filtered in the **glomerulus**, due to blood pressure
- useful materials are reabsorbed
- as the filtrate passes along the tubule it becomes more concentrated: the longer the loop of Henle, the less urine is produced and the more concentrated it is
- the second part of the tubule balances salt content and pH

How might drinking several glasses of cola affect water balance in the body? Why do salty meals make you thirsty?

Kidney failure happens when the kidneys stop working. This can happen if the kidneys become infected or are injured. Kidney failure is life-threatening and must be treated. Two approaches are:

- kidney transplant, which is very successful if the tissue type of the donated kidney closely matches that of the patient
- dialysis (see picture below)

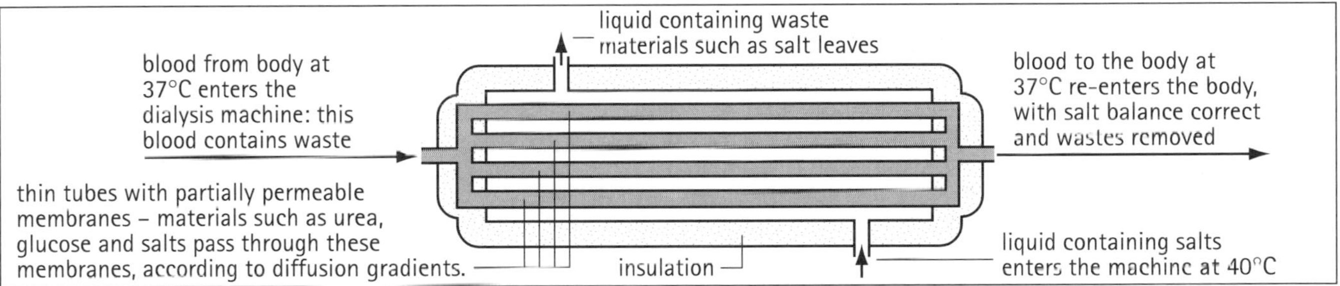

Dialysis can take place for a few hours at a time in hospital or at home with a fixed unit. A newer method involves using the membranes in the abdomen, so dialysis happens within the body while someone is moving about as normal. In many ways a transplant can be more desirable because it is a long-term solution, but there is a lack of donor kidneys.

Practice Questions - Humans as organisms 12

1 a) How do humans take in most of their water?

b) Name **three** factors that might influence how much water is lost as sweat.

c) How might the amount of water lost as sweat affect how much urine you produce?

2 Which part of the kidneys:

a) filter materials out of blood?

b) concentrates the urine?

c) adjusts the pH of blood?

3 The kidneys filter about 180 litres of solution per day out of our blood.

a) What makes filtration happen?

b) Why is the volume of urine much smaller than the volume of liquid filtered each day?

4 Suggest **two** reasons why a kidney transplant may be a better long-term solution than dialysis.

Green plants as organisms

This section is about

- naming the main parts of a plant and their functions
- understanding photosynthesis and the conditions that influence the rate at which it takes place
- naming the main events that occur when a plant transpires, including transport of water and minerals through the plant
- understanding that conditions influence the rate of transpiration
- understanding why water moves by osmosis from one area of a plant to another

What are plants?

Most plants look very different from the way animals look. This is partly because the main parts of plants – stem, leaves and roots – are not the same as animal body parts (such as legs, arms or head).

Another main difference between animals and plants is their colour. Most plants are green in colour, which is a major feature of the way they feed. Plants can make their own food from simple raw materials during the process of photosynthesis, while animals must eat their food. This is why plants are known as producers and animals as consumers. It also means that animals rely directly or indirectly on plants for their food supplies.

Some plants produce flowers, which is where the sex cells or gametes are made. As with animals, the male sex cells must come into close contact with the female sex cells in order for fertilisation to occur. For plants, this means that pollen must travel to an ovule. This happens in many ways, usually involving insects or wind.

Apart from providing food, plants produce many other materials, such as timber, rubber and cotton. What's more, they cover a large part of the Earth's surface and because they exchange gases and produce water vapour, this has an enormous effect on our atmosphere and climate. Gas exchange happens mostly through special pores on the leaf surface.

Plants need sunlight for photosynthesis, so they photosynthesise during the day and respire at night. The net effect is that during the day plants

- give out more oxygen than they take in
- take in more carbon dioxide than they give out
- release water vapour

This section looks at green plants as organisms and how they function.

FactZONE

The plant body

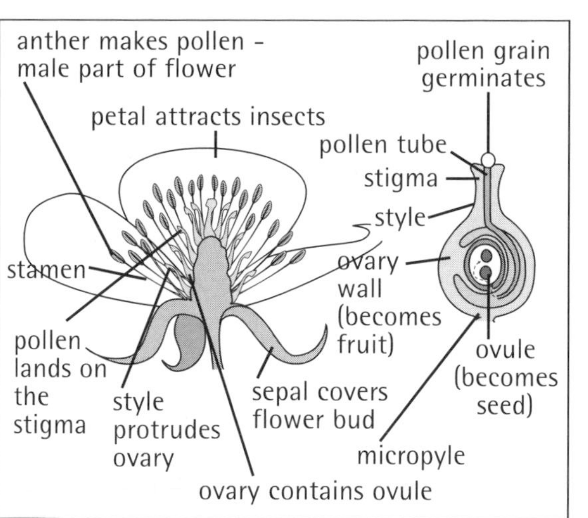

part of a plant	function
leaf	photosynthesis
stem	supports the shoot system, so leaves are in the light; flowers are conspicuous or held higher in the breeze; seeds and fruits are conspicuous to animals; conducts materials up from roots to the shoot and from the shoot to the roots
flower	reproduction
root	uptake of water and minerals, anchors the plant

Photosynthesis

This is a vital process for virtually all living things, because plants produce food, which passes through food chains. Plants also help to keep a balance of gases in the atmosphere:

carbon dioxide + water → glucose + oxygen

energy source is the sun, chlorophyll transfers the energy

(h) $6CO_2 + 6H_2O \rightarrow C_6H_{12}O_6 + O_2$

Photosynthesis is a building-up process that produces glucose, a simple carbohydrate. Some of the glucose is used by the plant as an energy source. Most of the glucose made during photosynthesis is converted directly into starch and stored in the leaves.

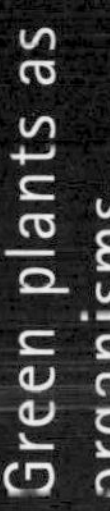

Plant transport systems

Two tissues make up the transport or *vascular* tissues of plants:

- xylem which carries water and minerals from the roots to the shoots
- phloem which carries food materials such as sugar around the plant to wherever it is needed

Water and plants

Water is very important to plants

- as a raw material for photosynthesis
- for transport, as all materials move in solution
- for support. Cells that are full of water make the tissues firm and able to stand upright

Transpiration is the loss of water by evaporation from leaf cells. The water vapour escapes from the leaf through the **stomata**. Transpiration happens fastest when it is warm, breezy and the air outside the leaf is dry.

Plants and photosynthesis

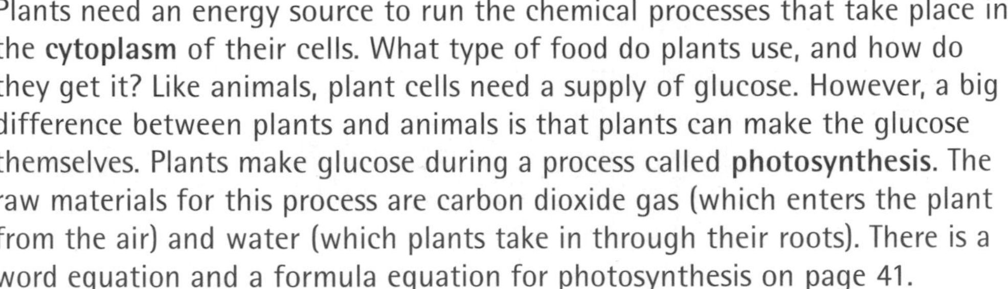

Plants need an energy source to run the chemical processes that take place in the **cytoplasm** of their cells. What type of food do plants use, and how do they get it? Like animals, plant cells need a supply of glucose. However, a big difference between plants and animals is that plants can make the glucose themselves. Plants make glucose during a process called **photosynthesis**. The raw materials for this process are carbon dioxide gas (which enters the plant from the air) and water (which plants take in through their roots). There is a word equation and a formula equation for photosynthesis on page 41.

Practise writing the equation for photosynthesis. The equation for respiration is the opposite to the equation for photosynthesis. Plant cells carry out both processes at the same time during the day. At night, which of these processes stops, and why?

Investigating the rate of photosynthesis

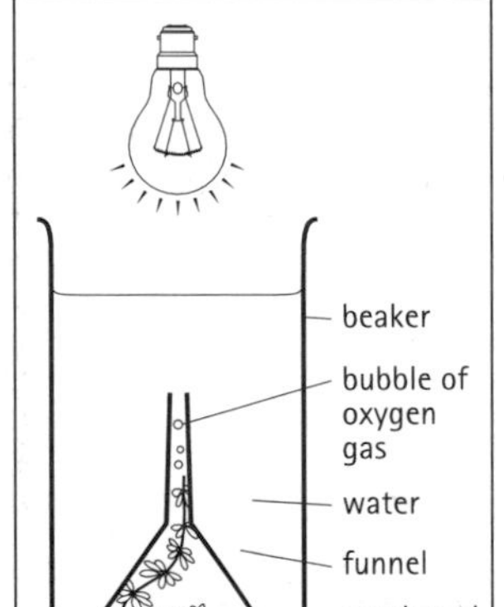

The picture on the left shows one way of estimating the rate of photosynthesis. In this experiment, the rate of oxygen production is used to indicate how fast photosynthesis is happening. This is measured by counting the bubbles of gas that appear in a certain time. You could do this more exactly by collecting the gas and measuring the volume. Other ways of estimating the rate of photosynthesis include measuring how fast carbon dioxide is used or glucose is made.

There are some conditions which have an effect on how fast photosynthesis can happen. They include:

- the availability of light
- the amount of raw materials, particularly carbon dioxide (since all cells contain a lot of water it is less likely to be limited, except in drought conditions)
- the amount of chlorophyll. This might be lacking if a plant does not have enough materials to make it; for example, magnesium is a mineral needed to make chlorophyll
- a suitable temperature, since enzymes only work within certain temperature ranges

How are extra minerals given to plants by plant growers?

Any of these conditions might limit the rate at which photosynthesis can happen, but it is most likely that light or carbon dioxide will be limiting factors. Plant growers can use artificial lights and add extra carbon dioxide to the air inside greenhouses to increase the rate of photosynthesis and how fast plants grow.

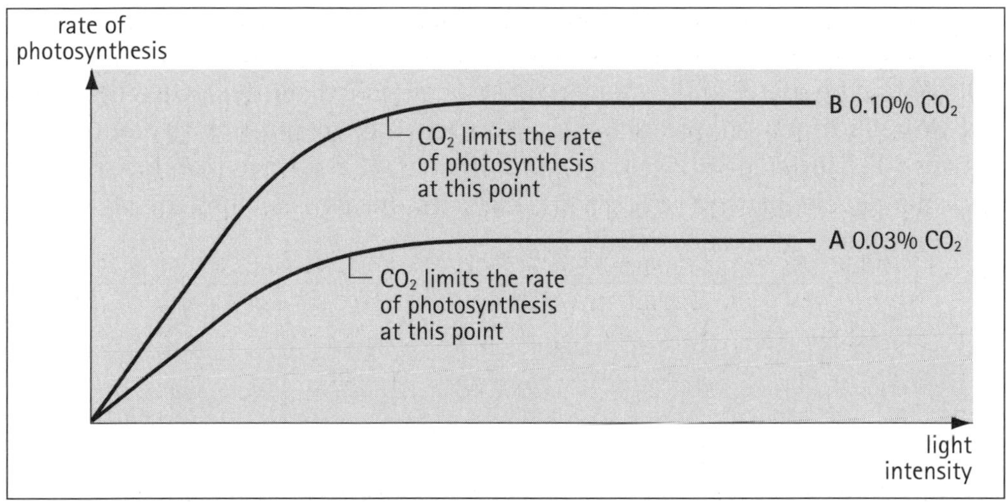

Practice Questions - Green plants as organisms 1

1 a) What are the:

(i) raw materials for photosynthesis?

(ii) products of photosynthesis?

b) Which part of the leaf:

(i) lets air enter and leave the leaf?

(ii) brings water to the leaf?

(iii) takes sugar away from the leaf?

c) Which parts of the plant might be most actively using sugar?

2 Robert set up this experiment to find out how light affects the rate at which plants make their own food.

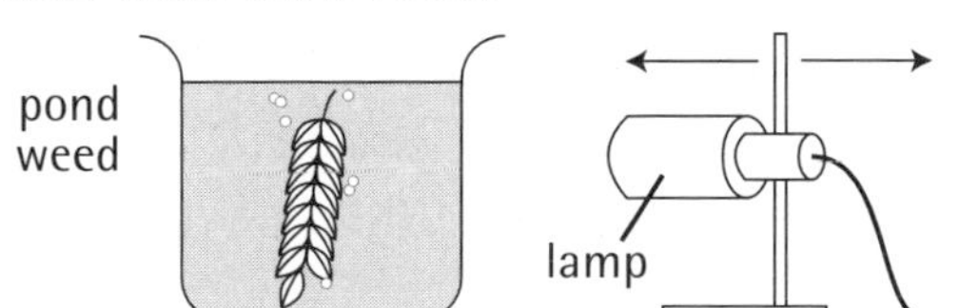

He put the lamp 100 cm away from the plant and counted the number of bubbles made by the plant in one minute. He then moved the lamp nearer to the beaker and counted the bubbles again. The table shows his results.

distance from lamp	no. of bubbles/min
100 cm	10
80 cm	20
60 cm	32
40 cm	37
20 cm	37

a) Plot the points on the grid. One of the points has been done for you.

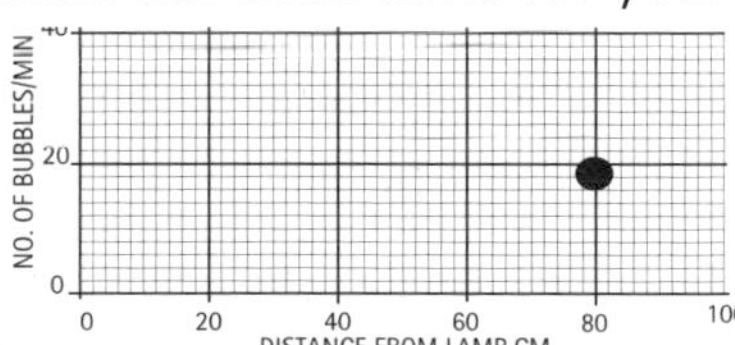

b) Draw the best line on the grid.

c) Predict the number of bubbles per minute if the lamp is placed 10 cm from the plant.

d) How do each of the following affect the rate of photosynthesis in a green plant:

(i) Moving the plant nearer the window?

(ii) Moving it to a colder room?

e) Complete the equation for photosynthesis

______ + ______ → ______ + ______

Transport in plants

Water and plant cells

Plant cells are surrounded by a cell wall, but the **surface membrane** controls what moves in and out of the cell (see page 12). The picture below shows a cell containing water and dissolved substances (called **solutes**). Outside a cell is a very dilute solution. Notice the difference in concentration of solutes between the inside of the cell and surroundings. The surface membrane is semi-permeable, because it lets some particles through, such as the water, but not others, such as the solutes.

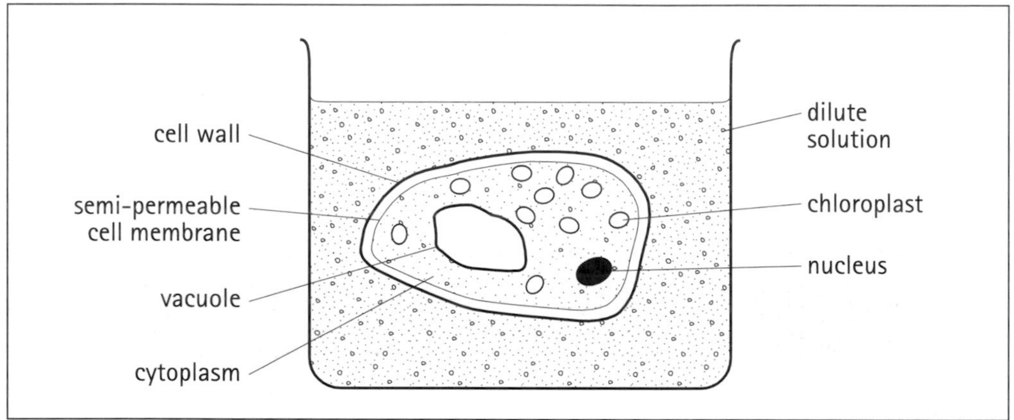

REMEMBER In osmosis, water moves from an area where there is more of it to an area where there is less of it.

Particles move about all the time, bumping into each other and into the surface membrane. Water molecules can pass through the membrane but solutes cannot. As there are more water molecules on one side of the membrane, more tend to move from that side out of the cell than move the other way, as shown in the picture below. This is the process of **osmosis**, which is very important in plants because it causes water movement throughout the plant body.

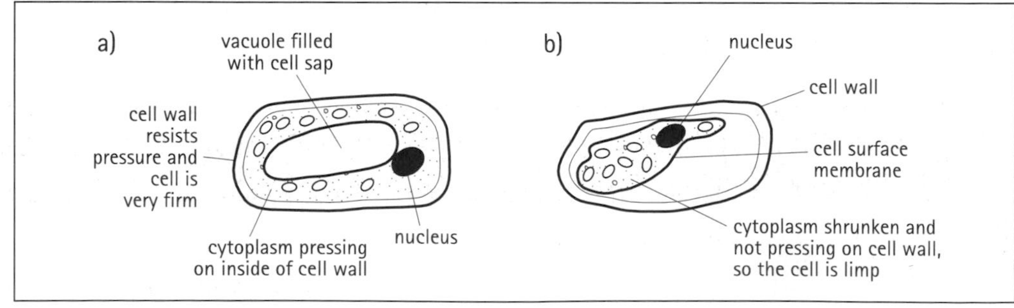

Transpiration and water movement in plants

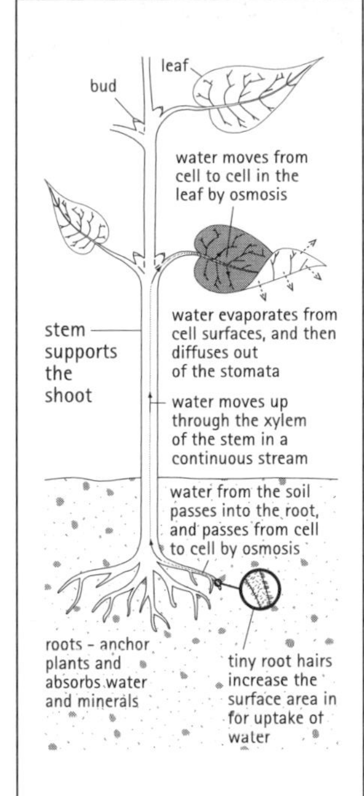

Cell surfaces inside a leaf are moist, and water evaporates from them into the spaces between cells. This water vapour diffuses out of the pores, called **stomata**, on the surface of the leaf. This water loss is called **transpiration**. Cells replace the lost water from the solution inside **xylem vessels**, which pass up through the plant from the roots.

Transpiration increases when:

- the temperature increases, because this makes water molecules evaporate more quickly from cell surfaces and diffuse out of the leaf faster
- it is a windy day, because the moving air moves water vapour away from the leaf surface
- the air around the leaf is dry, because water evaporates more easily

What sort of day makes the washing dry quicker outdoors? Transpiration happens fastest in those conditions too.

The rate of transpiration is also affected by:

- the number of stomata on the leaf surfaces
- the amount of light (because stomata close in the dark)
- the waterproof cuticle, which is usually on the upper surface

Mineral nutrition

Minerals are particles that have dissolved from rock surfaces. They form a solution in the water in the soil and pass into the root by diffusion. Plant growers often add fertilisers to avoid this problem. Organic fertilisers, such as manure and compost, are made from the remains of materials from living things. Inorganic fertilisers (which usually contain potassium, nitrogen and phosphorus) are made from chemicals in a factory. When plants lack minerals their growth is stunted and they do not produce as much fruit as a well-fed plant. Or, like humans, they can also become diseased.

Practice Questions – Green plants as organisms 2

1 a) Why does a plant lose water from its leaves?

b) How does a plant replace water it loses?

2 Some farmers use chemical pesticides on their crops. Give **two** advantages and **two** disadvantages of the use of chemical pesticides.

3 How might:

a) a farmer add minerals to the soil?

b) a gardener add minerals to the soil?

4 How would a plant grower know if adding fertiliser was worthwhile?

Variation and inheritance

This section is about

- how variation can be caused genetically or by the environment
- understanding that a gene codes for a particular characteristic
- knowing the main differences between mitosis and meiosis, and where these two types of cell division happen in the body
- understanding how inheritance occurs during sexual reproduction, according to the model described by Mendel
- interpreting/predicting patterns of inheritance

The nineteenth-century scientists Charles Darwin and Alfred Wallace were both fascinated by the immense variety of plants and animals, and the differences between them. Working independently, they both hit upon the same idea to explain this variety. Their idea is now known as **the theory of evolution by natural selection**.

Charles Darwin had developed his ideas a little earlier than Alfred Wallace, but, possibly concerned about how these ideas conflicted with the idea of Creation set out in the Bible, he had chosen not to publish. In the end they presented their work together at a scientific meeting in London. Much of the evidence Darwin gathered involved fossil remains, which show past life forms that are now extinct.

Variation happens because of environmental factors, such as food supply, and because of the way the genetic material divides up during cell division, when sex cells are formed. New variation also happens when there are sudden changes in the genetic material DNA inside a nucleus. These sudden changes are called **mutations**. They are not very common, and the results can be either harmful or beneficial to the new individual.

Patterns of inheritance can be predicted, using the ideas of another scientist, Gregor Mendel. He carried out a series of experiments breeding plants with different characteristics. What he discovered has helped to explain many aspects of inheritance, and is useful in predicting the inheritance of disease.

FactZONE

There are differences between living things, which is called **variation**. It can be caused by:

- an environmental factor
- a genetic factor

Fossils provide evidence that variation has happened over millions of years, resulting in either a gradual series of changes to living things, known as **evolution**, or sometimes to **extinction**.

The nucleus of a cell contains DNA. The DNA makes up **chromosomes**, which are:

- always in pairs in body cells (including in the fetus). Human body cells have 23 pairs of chromosomes
- always single in sex cells (gametes) within the sex organs. Human gametes have 23 single chromosomes

A **gene** is a short chunk of DNA which codes for a protein. A chromosome contains many genes. An **allele** is one form of a gene.

There are two types of cell division: **mitosis** and **meiosis**. Mitosis results in two identical cells. This type of cell division happens when living things are growing and during **asexual reproduction**. Meiosis happens when gametes are produced during **sexual reproduction**. Meiosis results in four cells, but they are not identical – there is variation in the offspring.

Selective breeding involves breeding from animals that have particularly desirable characteristics in order to produce offspring with the same characteristics.

Genetic engineering involves taking genes from one living thing and inserting them into the DNA of another living thing.

Cloning is a way of producing many identical copies of a living thing.

Variety of life

Variation is the word used to describe the differences between individuals in a group. Imagine a hundred and one dalmations – they are all similar but not the same. Some differences are caused by factors in the environment. For example, if one puppy is fed twice the amount of food that another puppy gets, there will be variation – one will grow bigger than the other. But the difference in the way their fur is spotted will depend on the genetic material they inherited.

What evidence is there for the theory of evolution?

The theory of evolution describes how living things change over many thousands of years, adapting to their environment. Evolution happens because of genetic variation. This can lead to new characteristics that are beneficial to an organism. For example, a mutation in the DNA may mean that a plant becomes resistant to disease. This is an advantage and means that plant will survive and reproduce so that its characteristics pass on to the next generation. Other characteristics may be harmful or even lethal. This can lead to extinction.

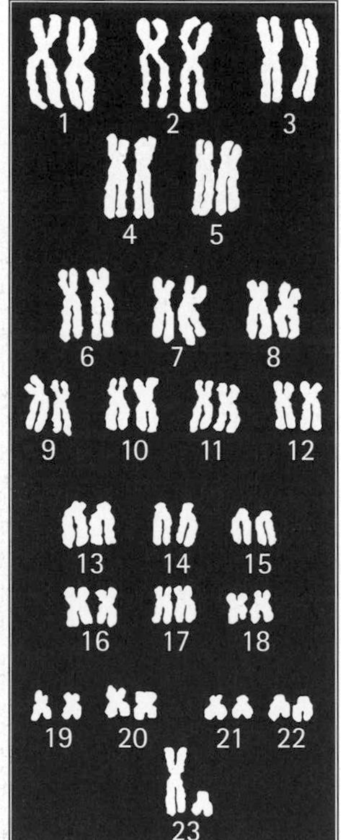

There are 23 pairs of chromosomes in almost every human cell

About genetic material

DNA is a very large molecule. Most of the time it is loosely arranged in the nucleus. But just before cell division the DNA coils up to form chromosomes. The chromosomes in all cells (except sex cells) are in pairs. Each chromosome replicates to form a double thread at the start of cell division.

Mitosis and asexual reproduction

1 DNA is loosely arranged in the nucleus

cell
nucleus
DNA

2 DNA packs up tightly into chromosomes, and replicates so each one is now double – made of two strands

3 the double chromosomes line up at the centre of the cell, and move apart along the spindles giving two sets of chromosomes

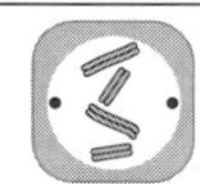

4 the cell divides to form two new cells

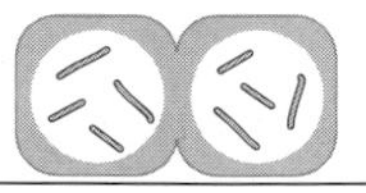

Why are the new cells made during mitosis exactly the same as the parent cell?

Meiosis and sexual reproduction

Meiosis only happens when sex cells are made. One parent cell produces four new cells, each with a different combination of chromosomes. The unusual thing is that the new cells only have single chromosomes. This is because during fertilisation in sexual reproduction the nuclei of two sex cells join, giving pairs of chromosomes in the offspring.

Draw up a table of differences between mitosis and meiosis.

REMEMBER Mitosis is the most common type of cell division and meiosis only happens when sex cells are made.

Choosing characteristics

For many years farmers and gardeners have used selective breeding. They have chosen animals or plants with the best characteristics and bred from them. If the offspring inherit the desirable characteristics, they are bred again. This is a slow and rather unreliable method of getting plants and animals with particular characteristics.

Genetic engineering

Genetic engineering gives an organism DNA from another organism, so it has a new characteristic. It is a very useful way, for example, of getting bacteria to produce substances that can be used in medicine.

Why might some people think that altering the genetic material of an organism is wrong?

Practice Questions – Variation and inheritance 1

1 a) What is variation?

b) Why does variation happen?

c) Explain how variation can lead to both evolution or extinction.

2 A particular type of moth exists in both light and dark forms. Some moths were released in different areas of the UK and recaptured later. The table below shows data for this experiment.

a) What percentage of dark-coloured moths were recaptured in the two areas of the UK?

b) Suggest a reason for the different percentage of light and dark moths recaptured in the two areas.

c) Predict the effect of reducing the soot production in the polluted area on the populations of moths.

area of UK	experiment	no. of light-coloured moths	no. of dark-coloured moths
unpolluted	released	488	485
	recaptured	59	30
heavily polluted with soot	released	62	157
	recaptured	15	83

Inheritance

You can see quite easily that most people look like their parents. This is not surprising, since one gene out of each pair comes from your mother and the other one comes from your father. A gene codes for a particular characteristic, such as eye colour. But there may be more than one form of each gene. For example, if one parent's eyes are brown and the other parent's eyes are blue, the eye colour of the offspring may be brown or blue. The word **allele** is used to describe the different forms of a gene.

There are several ways of showing on paper how inheritance works, using the ideas first set out by Gregor Mendel. This is how it works:

- a new individual always inherits *two* alleles for a particular characteristic
- a **dominant** allele is written with a capital letter, e.g. B for brown eyes, and the **recessive** allele is written with a lower case letter, e.g. b for blue eyes.
- a dominant allele will hide the appearance of the recessive allele even if there is only one of them. For example Bb will give brown eyes because the B (brown eye colour) hides the b (blue). BB will also give brown eyes. Only bb will give blue eyes.

See how this works in example 1.

Example 1: The inheritance of eye colour

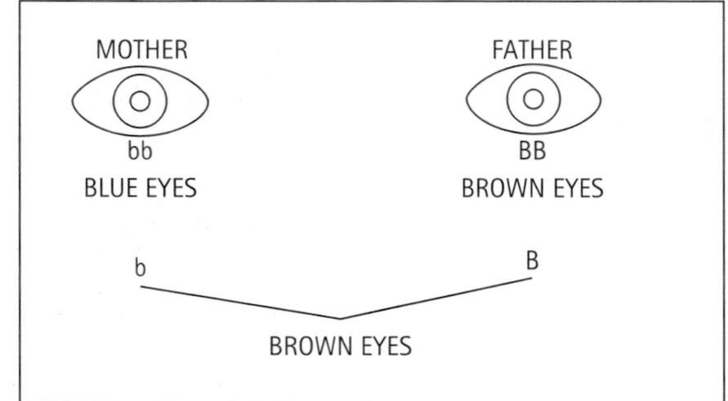

REMEMBER The word gene means the DNA that codes for a particular characteristic. In a question on inheritance, use the word allele to refer to different forms of a gene.

Example 2: The inheritance of freckles

This example shows how to use a checkerboard. Write each allele from the parents along the side of the checkerboard.

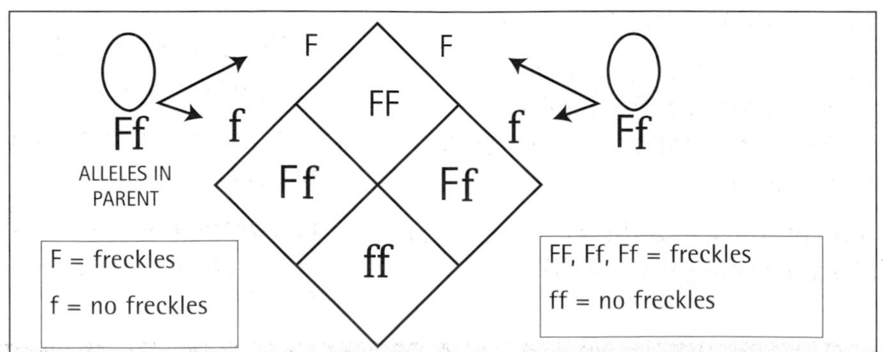

Example 3: The inheritance of sex

Around 50% of the human births each year are male and 50% are female. Why this happens is shown in the picture below.

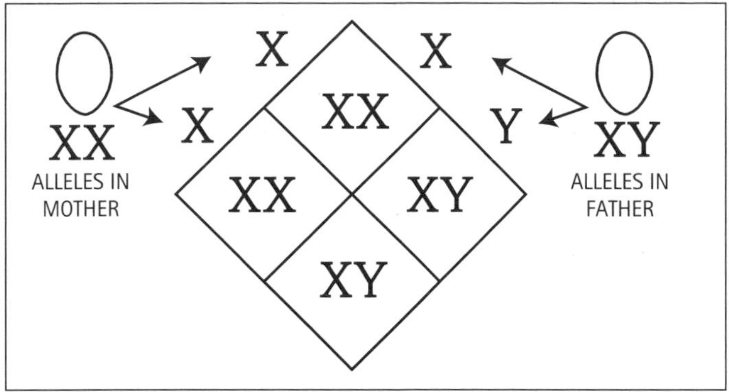

Example 4: An inherited disease: cystic fibrosis

Around 5% of Europeans carry one allele for cystic fibrosis. But since this is a recessive allele, they suffer no effects at all. If a child inherits two of the recessive cystic fibrosis alleles, they produce sticky mucus in the lungs and gut. Because of this thick mucus, the lungs get blocked up easily and digestion is difficult. You can use a checkerboard to predict how likely it is that someone will have a child with cystic fibrosis.

REMEMBER You need to know examples of genetic diseases for the exam. Check which examples you need for your exam board.

Practice Questions - Variation and inheritance 2

1 In humans some people have different shaped ear lobes

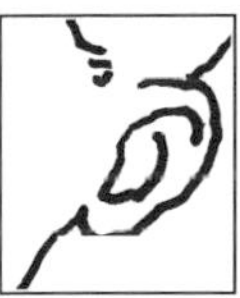

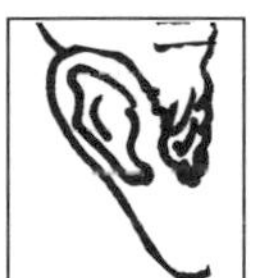

ear lobes droop	ear lobes slope to face
(called 'free')	(called 'attached')
dominant allele D	recessive allele d

What are the chances of Ben and Judy having children with attached ear lobes, if Judy has the alleles dd and Ben has alleles Dd?

2 The allele for freckles (F) is dominant to the allele for no freckles (f). The family tree on the right shows the inheritance of freckles for a particular family.

a) How do you know that Rumina must have two alleles the same for freckles?

b) How can you tell from his children that Tariq probably has two alleles FF for freckles?

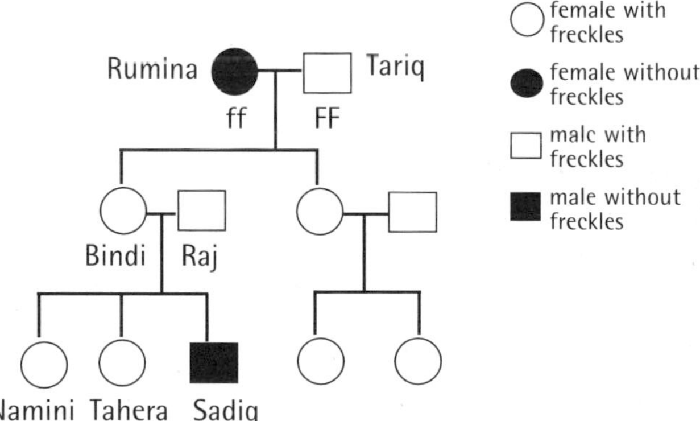

c) What other combination of alleles might Tariq possibly have?

d) What alleles did Sadiq inherit for the presence or lack of freckles?

e) Explain why Bindi and Raj must both have inherited the alleles Ff for the presence of freckles.

Living things in their environment

This section is about

- competition for resources such as food
- adaptation of living things to their environment
- predator/prey population graphs and pyramid of numbers and pyramid of biomass drawings
- energy transfer through food chains and how good farming practices aim at improving energy transfer
- the effect of human activities on the environment
- the role of microbes and other organisms in recycling nutrients such as carbon and nitrogen

Biodiversity is a word that describes the huge variety of living things. There are many millions of species, exploiting nearly every habitat the Earth has to offer. An **ecosystem** consists of living things and the way they interact with the environment.

Tropical rainforest is an example of an ecosystem with enormous biodiversity. Its destruction is tragic because no one knows how to rebuild this ecosystem, so it is lost for ever. As well as the loss of habitat, there are far-reaching effects, such as climate change.

All living things have an impact on the environment. Humans exploit the environment more than any other species, which is why our activities must be carefully monitored and controlled. For example, moving species from their natural habitat and introducing them into another ecosystem can have very upredictable results, causing problems. Understanding ecology can provide solutions for problems that have come about because of human activities. Our lifetimes are very short compared to the life of Earth, yet we leave a legacy for the future.

Energy and materials flow through an ecosystem. The source of energy is the sun, and this energy is transferred from one living thing to another at each level in a **food chain**. A food chain shows which living things are food for others, and food chains often overlap. It is easy to overlook tiny living things, yet they are vital pieces of the ecosystem 'jigsaw'.

The Earth's resources can easily feed the world's fast-growing population, but even so people still die of starvation. It's a matter of producing enough of the right *types* of food, and getting it to where it's needed. This doesn't just happen by chance, which is why scientists, farmers and politicians are involved in managing the production and distribution of food supplies. At the same time there is a great concern that in producing enough food, we do not destroy the environment.

FactZONE

An ecosystem is made up of living things, the environment they live in and the interactions between them. The Earth is the largest ecosystem, called the **biosphere**. The climate and shape of the land varies around the world, giving several major ecosystems including:

- desert
- dry tropical grassland (savannah)
- tropical rainforest
- temperate forest (such as mixed woodlands in Europe)
- pine forest

Each of these ecosystems supports a different variety of living things. Within an ecosystem the living things compete for space and food.

The number of different things living in an environment is called the **species diversity**. Species diversity is often reduced by human activities, such as:

- farming
- industry
- the growth of cities
- removing rainforest

A food chain describes the feeding relationships between living things. Plants are called **producers**, because they make their own food, and they are at the start of the food chain. **Consumers** are animals which eat just plants (called **herbivores**), plants and animals (called **omnivores**), or just animals (called carnivores). Materials and energy flow through a food chain.

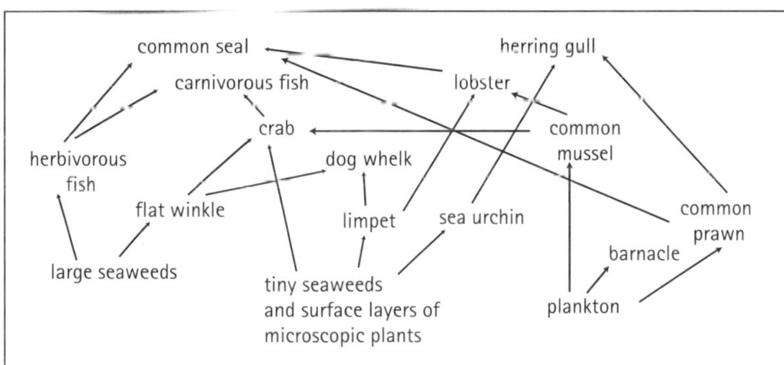

Food chains link in a food web.

Microbes, such as bacteria and fungi, as well as invertebrates such as insects, are very important in food chains as **decomposers**. Decomposers bring about the natural recycling of materials by causing decay or rot. Many synthetic materials, such as plastics, do not rot, and are called **non-biodegradable.**

We must make important choices about how we use the Earth's resources. Often there are competing priorities because different things are important to different groups of people.

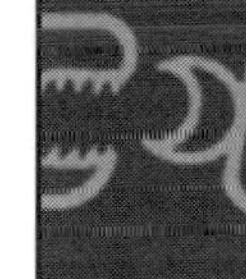

Surviving

Survival involves getting the basic needs of life, which include a suitable space to live in, a food supply, and shelter from natural enemies and climate. Many examination questions ask about what happens if one of these factors changes. Look at the food web in the picture below.

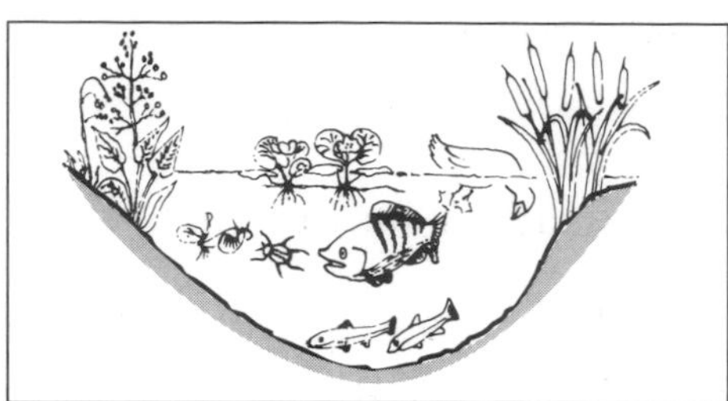

- *Name two producers. What are the factors important for the growth of the producers in the pond?*
- *Pick out two foodchains. Do the links in the food chains overlap at all?*
- *Imagine that pollution kills most of the water beetle population. What would happen to the other organisms in the food chains that include water beetles? Try to work out the 'knock-on' effects.*

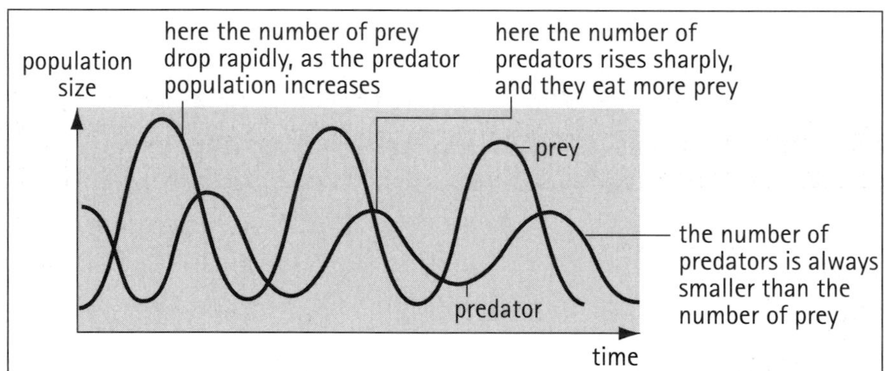

A predator is an animal that eats another, and the prey is the animal which is eaten. The size of the population for the predator and prey are dependent on each other.

- *Find out about myxomatosis and its effect on the rabbit population.*

Sometimes there are changes in an environment which reduce the population or even wipe out a particular species. For example, the DNA of a virus might change, giving a new type of virus that causes disease in squirrels. Many squirrels might catch the disease and die. Yet a few will reproduce and pass on genes for resistance to disease. Over a period of time the squirrel population will start to increase again. This is an example of how living things continually adapt to survive changes in their environment.

Fishing for food?

One of the Earth's richest food stores is the sea. For many years people have fished successfully, e.g. in the North Sea, and around the Grand Banks off northern Canada. But over the last few decades more and more fish have been taken out, particularly species like cod. Despite controls, the cod stocks had sunk to a very low level by the early 1990s. Now there is a ban on fishing cod on the Grand Banks. Scientists hope this will give the remaining fish time to grow and reproduce, so replenishing the stocks.

Can you think how else this food supply could be managed?

One way of managing it might be by finding alternatives, for example:

- fish farming, e.g. salmon and trout are successfully farmed
- growing protein rich plants, such as pulses and beans, to use as an alternative food source to fish

REMEMBER Read all the exam questions very carefully, because they contain the clues to the answers. You are not expected to know every example off by heart, but you have to be able to interpret the information.

Practice Questions – Living things in their environment 1

1

a) Comment on how the crop plants in the picture above are growing.

b) List **three** factors that the crop plants are competing for.

c) Suggest an environmental factor that might explain the growth pattern seen in this field of wheat.

2 A rabbit and a fox both live in woodland on the edge of open countryside.

a) Which of these is the predator?

b) A farmer kills many of the rabbits at the start of one summer. What effect will the reduction in rabbit population have on the fox population?

3 a) What type of pollution mostly causes acid rain?

b) Why is acid rain damaging to:
(i) waterways
(ii) forests?

c) Suggest a reason why forest in Sweden may now be grown in soil that is covered by plastic sheeting.

Food chains and energy flow

A **food chain** describes the feeding relationships between living things. The picture below shows a food chain from a woodland ecosystem.

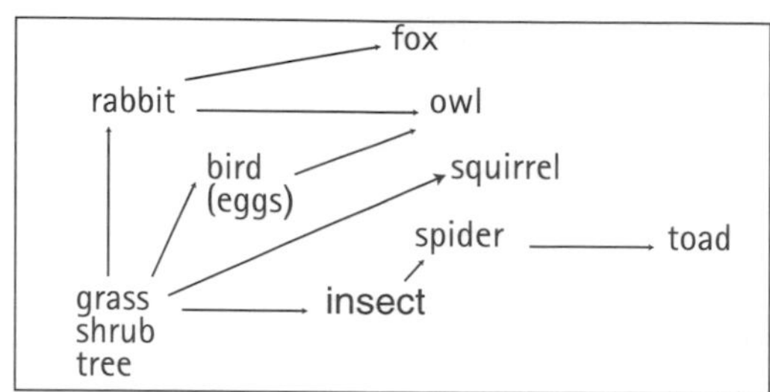

How might a scientist investigate how many organisms there are at each level in a food chain?

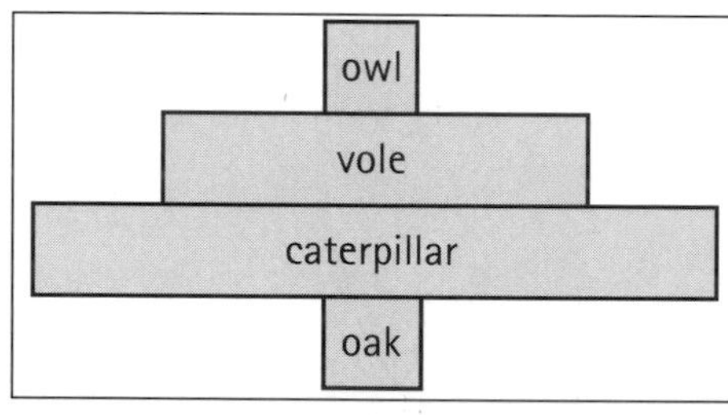

REMEMBER Examination questions often ask why there is a difference in shape between a pyramid of numbers and a pyramid of biomass.

The pyramid of numbers shown above is drawn to scale according to the number of organisms at each level in the food chain. This method does not take account of how big each plant or animal is.

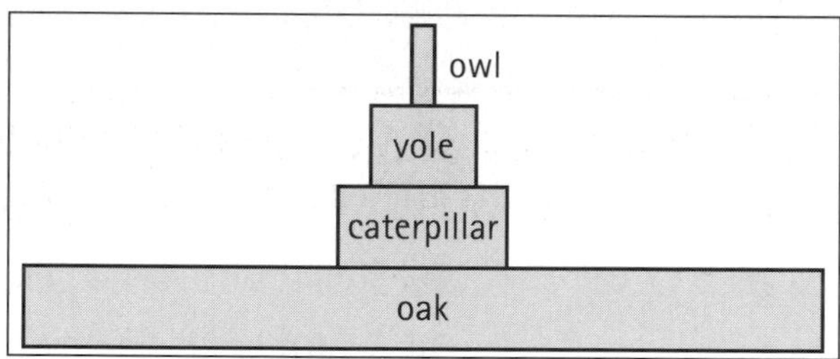

The pyramid of biomass shown above is a useful way of drawing a food chain because it gives information about the amount of living material that can survive at each level in a food chain.

Energy transfers

Light or solar energy is radiation from the sun. Plants use this energy source and transfer it to food materials within their leaves during photosynthesis (see page 42). When an animal eats a plant food, materials from the plant are built into the body of the animal. At the same time, energy transfers between them. But not all of the energy in the food which is eaten actually gets built into the body of the animal that eats it. This is true at each stage of a food chain, so the energy transfers are not very efficient.

What happens to the energy from food that does not get built into the consumer's body?

Some of it:

- transfers to the surroundings in waste materials, such as urine and faeces
- is used in respiration

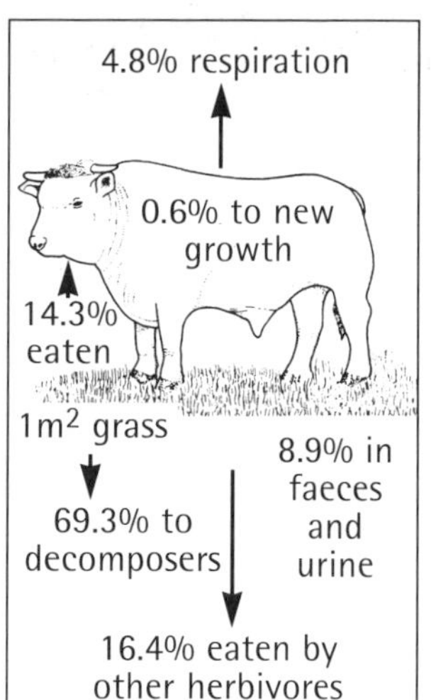

Improving energy flow

The amount of energy that flows through a food chain depends on the plants and animals involved. In terms of the energy transferred to the next living thing in a food chain and the amount of protein available in the food, it is more efficient to farm crop plants rather than animals. Materials that build the bodies of living things are used more than once – they recycle in nature.

Energy transfers through food chains

Food chain	Example	Energy yield to humans
Crop → human	Monoculture of wheat	7,800–11,000 $kJ.10^{-3}ha$
Crop → livestock → human	Barley fed beef	745–1,423
Intensive grassland → livestock → human	Intensive beef or dairy herd on grassland	Meat: 339 Milk: 3,813
Grassland and crops → livestock → human	Mixed dairy farm	1,356

Practice Questions – Living things in their environment 2

1 Study the food web for an ecosystem below.

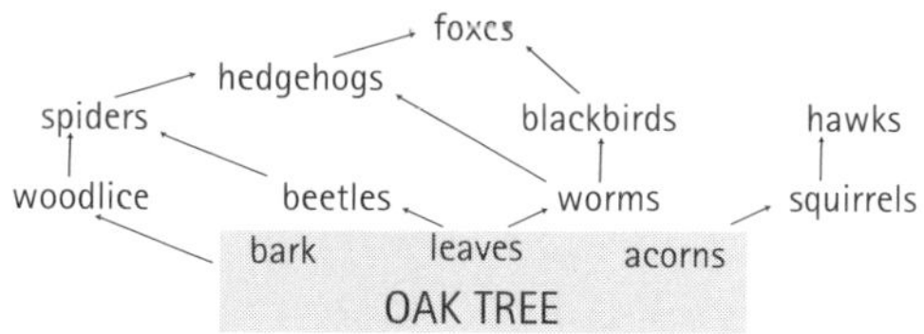

a) Complete this food chain:

leaves →________ → ________ → *foxes.*

b) (i) What is meant by 'producer' and 'consumer'? (ii) Give examples from this web.

c) Foxes are predators, they kill other animals for food. Name another predator in this web.

d) Suggest and explain one effect on the food web if a disease killed all the spiders.

2 Plankton are small plants and animals near the sea surface. The animals eat the plants. Scientists found that plants in each square metre absorbed 8500 kJ of energy from the Sun each day and used 100 kJ to make cells. The rest was transferred to the surroundings.

a) The animal plankton gained 25 kJ of energy and used 10 kJ for making cells and 12 kJ for movement. How much do they transfer to the surrounding per square metre per day?

b) Fish feeding on animal plankton gained 0.2% of the total energy entering the ecosystem. How much of the total energy is gained by the secondary consumers?

Elements and compounds

This section is about

- elements, compounds and mixtures
- solubility and dissolving
- ways of separating mixtures

Substances (elements or compounds) that are mixed together are called mixtures. Some of these substances dissolve in each other, such as salt in water, and others do not, such as oil and water or sand and water.

Substances that do not dissolve are called **insoluble.** Substances that do dissolve are called **soluble**. You will need to think about how particles dissolve.

For salt or sugar dissolving in water, the particles of salt or sugar have to fit in between the water particles. How easily the particles fit in between depends on their size.

In the picture on the right, water is called the **solvent**, the liquid which does the dissolving, and the salt or sugar is called the **solute**, the substance being dissolved. When no moreparticles can fit in between the solution, it is called a **saturated** solution – no more of the substance will dissolve.

What happens when substances dissolve

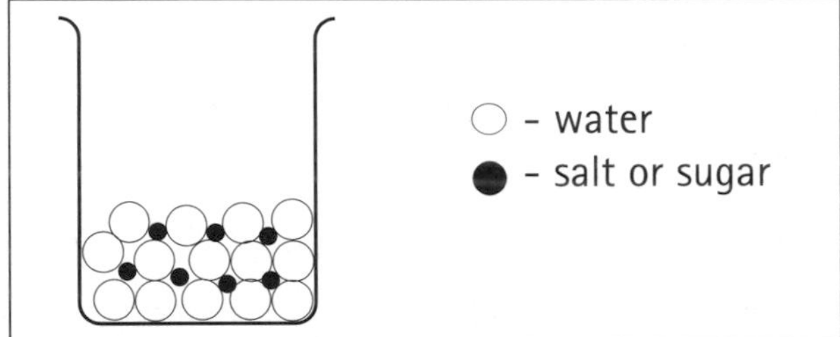

Mixtures often need to be separated. There are a number of methods of separation which can be used depending on whether you need to separate solid from liquids or liquids from liquids. It also depends if they are soluble.

FactZONE

An element is a substance made up of identical atoms. All known elements are found in the periodic table. Examples are iron, oxygen and aluminium.

A compound is a substance containing two or more elements that are bonded together. They are difficult to separate. Examples are water, sodium chloride and calcium carbonate.

A mixture is when two or more substances (elements and compounds) are mixed together. They can usually be separated easily. Examples are air (nitrogen, oxygen, carbon dioxide, etc.) and oil (petrol, paraffin, bitumen, etc.).

Methods of separation

There are a number of different ways of separating elements and compounds:

- filtering: used to separate insoluble solids from liquids
- evaporation: used to separate a soluble solid from a liquid
- distillation: used to separate a liquid from a soluble solid or two liquids with different boiling points
- chromatography: used to separate soluble solids

Usually the first question on the chemistry section is based on your knowledge and understanding of this.

You need to know examples of mixtures that are separated using different methods:

- filtering: sand and water/mud and water
- evaporation: salt (sodium chloride) and water
- distillation: alcohol and water (they have different boiling points)
- chromatography: coloured ink/any type of colouring

You need to be able to recognise and label diagrams showing the different separation methods.

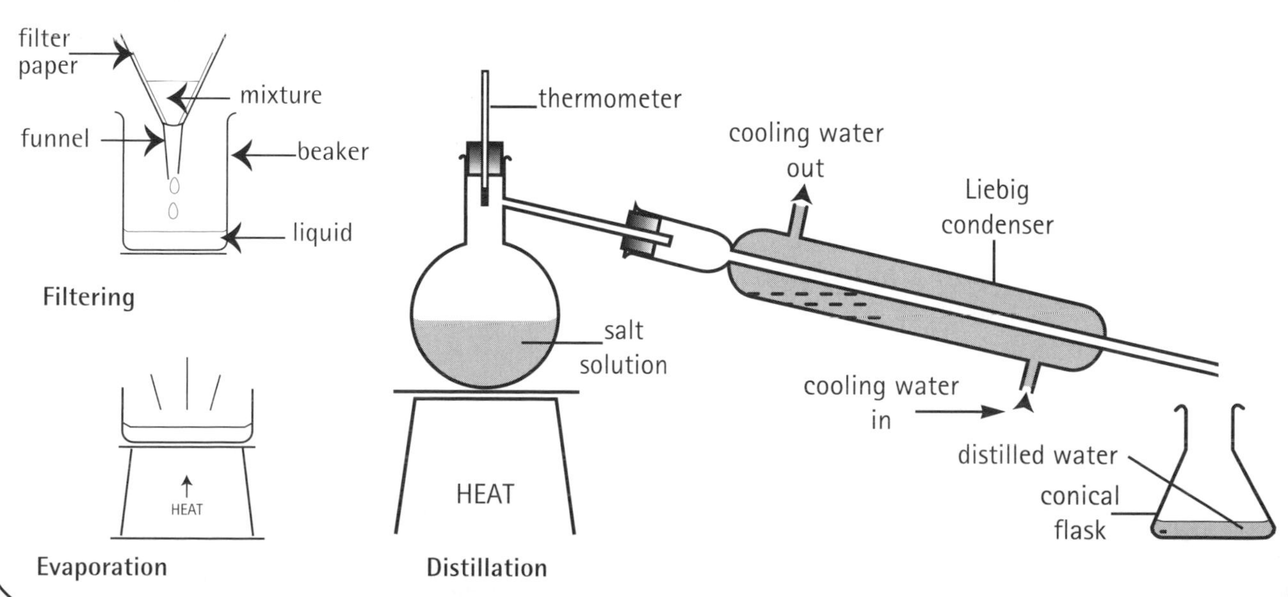

Chemical reactions and rates

This section is about

- types of chemical reactions
- how to write chemical equations for the reactions
- how the rate of reaction can be changed by varying temperature, concentration, surface area and adding a catalyst
- the collision theory to explain rates
- reactions involving enzymes
- properties and reactions of acids and bases
- the pH scale
- neutralisation

Chemical reactions are happening all the time. In every chemical reaction something new is formed and there is a temperature change. For example, burning wood is a chemical reaction. The temperature increases and a black powder (carbon) is left (a new product).

There are a number of different types of reactions, e.g. oxidation, combustion, neutralisation (reactions of acids and bases). For every reaction you can write an equation. Some may be simpler than others, but you always write the names/formulae of the reactants (the starting substances) on the left-hand side of the equation and the products (the substances formed) on the right-hand side of the equation.

A reaction happens in a certain amount of time. Some reactions are fast, e.g. a firework exploding, and some are slow, e.g. iron rusting. The rate is a measure of how fast a reaction takes place. The rate of reactions can be changed by changing the reaction conditions.

Chemical equations can be written in words or you can use the chemical formulae. You need to be able to:

- write equations and balance them
- use state symbols
- (h) use ionic equations

To be an expert at writing equations you need to remember the rules and get as much practice as you possibly can.

For all equations the reactants are written on the left and the products are written on the right, for example:

reactant + reactant = product

FactZONE

If a chemical reaction gives out heat it is called an **exothermic** reaction. 'Exo' means 'go out' and 'thermic' means 'heat'.

If a chemical reaction takes in heat it is called an **endothermic** reaction. 'Endo' means 'take in'.

Most reactions are exothermic.

Types of reactions

- combustion: this is the reaction of a substance which burns in oxygen

e.g. methane + oxygen = carbon dioxide + water

Methane is the gas used in a Bunsen burner.

- oxidation: this has three definitions:
  1. a reaction where a substance combines with oxygen, so combustion is also oxidation
  2. a reaction where electrons are removed
  3. a reaction where hydrogen is removed from a substance
- reduction: this has three definitions:
  1. a reaction where oxygen is removed from a substance
  2. a reaction where electrons are gained
  3. a reaction where hydrogen is gained by a substance

Oxidation and reduction are opposite types of reaction.

- decomposition: this is where substances are decomposed, or broken down. There are three main types:
  1. thermal decomposition – substances broken down by heat
  2. electrolyic decomposition – substances broken down by electric current
  3. catalytic decomposition – substances broken down by a catalyst
- displacement: this is where one part of a compound is replaced during a chemical reaction, e.g. metals or halogens:

magnesium + copper sulphate → magnesium sulphate + copper

In the above equation magnesium 'displaces' copper because it is more reactive than copper (see section on metals and reactivity on page 82 for more information).

Chemical equations

Word equations

You'll often be asked to write the word equation to represent a chemical reaction. It's also useful to write down the word equation first if you're asked to write the equation in symbols. For example:

magnesium + oxygen = magnesium oxide

REMEMBER Know the pattern for the reactions of acids, metals and hydrocarbons. They are the most popular in exam questions.

◎ *Complete the following equations: zinc + copper sulphate = ________; magnesium + hydrochloric acid = ________; methane + oxygen = ________.*

Writing formulae for compounds

Each element has a combining power, which tells you the number of electrons it needs to lose, share or gain when it forms a compound. When elements combine, the combining powers of both elements in the compound must be equal. To work out the formula for magnesium chloride:

	Mg	Cl
combining power	2	(8 – 7) = 1

to make the combining powers equal, you need 2 x Cl. The number of each type of atom is put after the symbol. So, one atom of Mg combines with two atoms of Cl, giving the formula $MgCl_2$.

REMEMBER Use the periodic table to work out the combining power.

Groups I to IV = number of group

Groups V to VIII = 8 – number of group

◎ *Write the formulae for sodium fluoride, calcium oxide and potassium sulphide.*

Writing equations and balancing them

Step 1: Write out the word equation

calcium + oxygen = calcium oxide

Step 2: Work out the formulae

$Ca + O_2 = CaO$

O_2: formula for oxygen gas

Ca in CaO: combining power = 2

O in CaO: combining power = (8 – 6) = 2

The combining powers are equal, so one atom of Ca combines with one atom of oxygen.

Step 3: Balance the equation

To balance the equation you need to make sure there are the same number of atoms of each element on both sides of the equals sign. When you are balancing, the number goes in front of the symbols.

Ca +	O_2	=	CaO	
1'Ca'	2'O'		1'Ca', 1'O'	not balanced, need 2 'O' on RHS
Ca +	O_2	=	2CaO	
1'Ca'	2'O'		2'Ca', 2'O'	not balanced, need 2 'Ca' on LHS
2Ca +	O_2	=	2CaO	
2'Ca'	2'O'		2'Ca', 2'O'	balanced

REMEMBER If you have a transition element the combining power is put in brackets after the element e.g. Iron (III) chloride.

Step 4: Put in the state symbols

The state symbols show whether the substance is solid, liquid or gas (what 'state' the substance is).

2Ca(s) + O_2(g) = 2CaO(s)

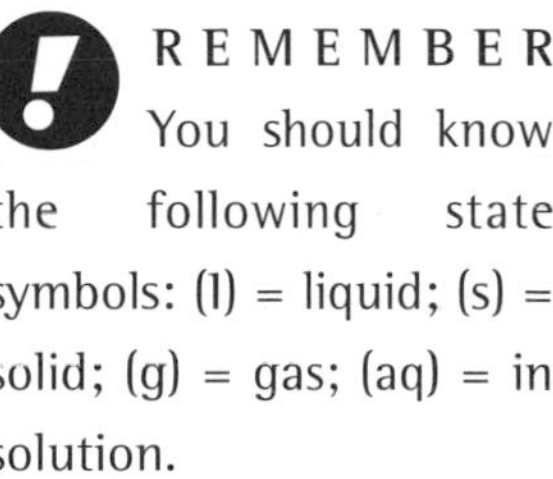

REMEMBER You should know the following state symbols: (l) = liquid; (s) = solid; (g) = gas; (aq) = in solution.

◎ *Write a balanced equation to show the reaction between sodium and chlorine to produce sodium chloride. The word equation is done for you:*
sodium + chlorine = sodium chloride

(h) Ionic equations

In ionic equations you use only the important ions involved. For example:

sodium hydroxide + hydrochloric acid = sodium chloride + water

All ions present:

Na^+OH^- + H^+Cl^- = Na^+Cl^- + H_2O

Cross out the ions that are the same on both sides to give:
OH^- + H^+ = H_2O

Practice Questions – Chemical reactions and rates 1

1 How many different kinds of atoms there are in hydrogen peroxide, H_2O_2?

2 Balance the following equations:

a) $CaCO_3$ → CaO + CO_2

b) H_2 + O_2 → H_2O

c) (h) Na + H_2O → NaOH + H_2

3 Write balanced equations for the following word equations:

a) copper (II) oxide + magnesium → magnesium oxide + copper

b) (h) iron + chlorine → iron (III) chloride

Rates of reaction

Rate is a measure of change that happens with time:

- an increase in temperature increases the rate
- an increase in concentration increases the rate
- an increase in surface area increases the rate
- a catalyst increases the rate but does not take part in the reaction

The collision theory

The collision theory says that when particles of substances collide with one another there is a reaction. The more collisions, the faster the reaction or the more energy the particles have the faster the reaction.

Enzymes are substances that act as biological catalysts. Each enzyme works most effectively at a certain temperature, called the 'optimum temperature'. You can learn more about enzymes on page 19 in the Biology section.

Enzymes are used in baking bread, brewing beer and making yoghurt.

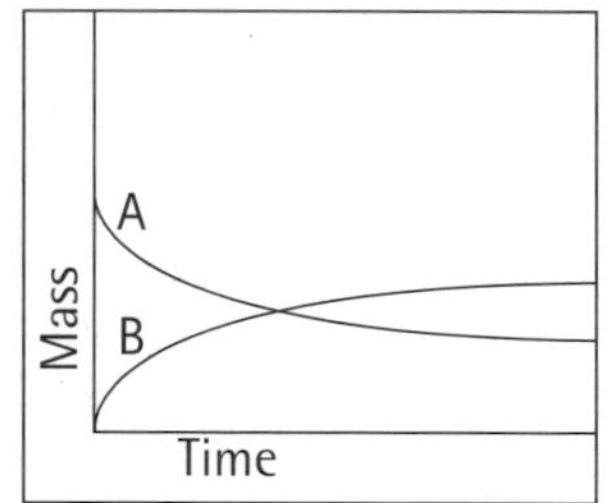

Using graphs to show rates of reactions

In the picture on the left, A represents the shape of a graph of amount of reactants changing with time and B represents the shape of a graph of amount of product changing with time.

◎ *Using the theory that particles need to collide to react, try to explain why an increase in temperature causes an increase in rate; an increase in concentration causes an increase in rate; an increase in surface area causes an increase in rate.*

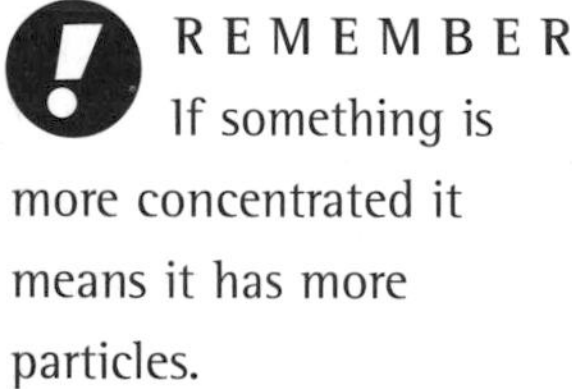

If something is more concentrated it means it has more particles.

A **catalyst** speeds up a reaction because it lowers the **activation energy**, which is the amount of energy needed for a successful collision. From the graph below you can see that more particles will have the lower activation energy so more successful collisions.

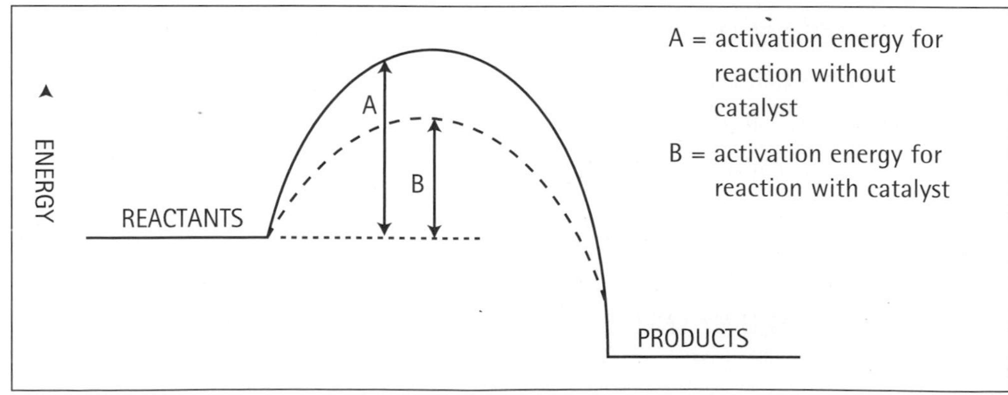

How to interpret information from graphs

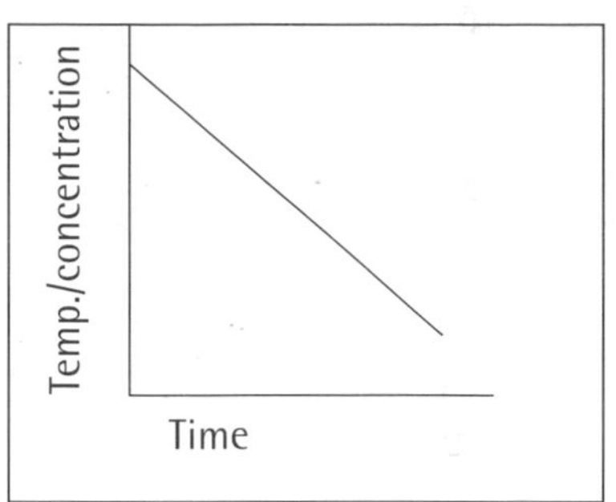

The graph above shows how rate changes with temperature or concentration. This shape of graph shows that as temperature or concentration increases, rate increases.

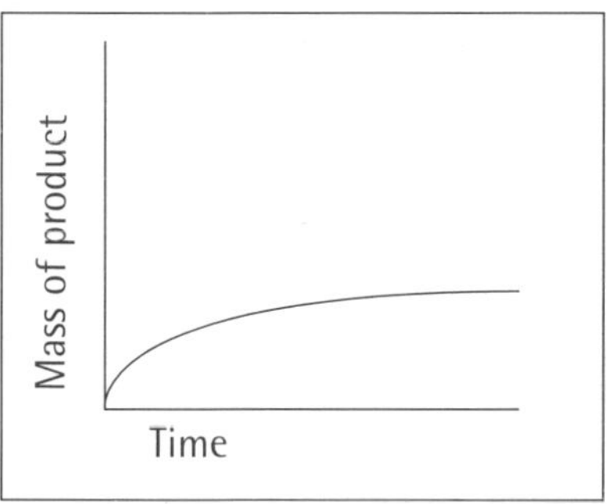

This graph above shows that the rate decreases with time for any reaction. When the line levels off the reaction is complete.

REMEMBER Exam questions on rate often include graphs. Make sure you can draw line graphs and interpret the information.

Practice Questions – Chemical reactions and rates 2

1 A solution of hydrogen peroxide (H_2O_2) decomposes slowly to form water and oxygen.

a) Complete the word equation for this reaction:

Hydrogen peroxide → ________ +

________.

b) This reaction is speeded up by adding manganese (IV) oxide. What name is given to a substance that speeds up a reaction without being used up?

c) Tina found the mass of hydrogen peroxide at various times, then worked out the loss in mass. Her results are shown in the following table.

Time (minutes)	Mass (g)	Loss in mass (g)
0	40.1	0.0
2	39.5	0.6
4	39.3	0.8
6	39.2	0.9
8	39.1	1.0
10	39.1	1.0
12	39.1	1.0

Using graph paper and the information in Tina's table, plot the points and draw a line graph of loss in mass against time.

d) Explain in one sentence why the reaction slowed down.

Acids and bases

REMEMBER pH is measured on a scale of 1 to 14. Acids have pHs below 7.

pH is a measure to indicate whether a solution is **acid, alkali** or **neutral.** Universal indicator is used to indicate pH. It is measured on a scale of 1 to 14, and the indicator changes colour according to the pH, as shown below.

pH scale													
1	2	3	4	5	6	7	8	9	10	11	12	13	14
Strong acid					Weak acid			Weak alkali					Strong alkali
						Neutral							
Red		*Orange*		*Yellow*		*Green*		*Blue*				*Purple*	

Acids react with:

- metals to form a salt and hydrogen
- metal carbonates to form a salt, carbon dioxide and water
- metal hydroxide and oxides to form salt and water
- ammonia to form ammonium salts

(h) Acids produce hydrogen ions, H^+, when added to water.

Bases are metal hydroxides, oxides and carbonates. Bases that dissolve in water are called alkalis. Bases neutralise acids to produce salts and water.

REMEMBER Bases neutralise acids to produce salts and water. An everyday example of this reaction is indigestion medicine, which neutralises acid from the stomach.

(h) Alkalis form hydroxide ions, OH^-, when added to water.

Neutralisation is the reaction between an acid and a base. It is used in everyday life to cure indigestion and for treating soil.

(h) The ionic equation for neutralisation is shown below:

$H^+(aq)$	+	$OH^-(aq)$	=	$H_2O(l)$
from acid		from alkali		water

The following are examples of household substances of differing pH:

- weak acid – lemon juice/vinegar
- neutral – water
- alkalis – soap, oven cleaner, washing powder

Practise writing word and symbol equations for reactions of acids.

Here is an example:

potassium hydroxide + sulphuric acid = potassium sulphate + water

$$2KOH(aq) + H_2SO_4(aq) = K_2SO_4(aq) + 2H_2O(l)$$

sodium carbonate + *hydrochloric acid* = ________ + ________

+ ________

magnesium + *sulphuric acid* = ________ + ________

sodium hydroxide + *hydrochloric acid* = ________ + ________

The salts formed when acids react with metals are given the following names:

- hydrochloric acid – metal chlorides
- sulphuric acid – metal sulphates
- nitric acid – metal nitrates

Dilute and concentrated is a measure of the amount of water added to the acid. The more water you add to it, the more dilute it is.

Strong and weak is about the number of hydrogen ions produced in the water. Strong acids produce many hydrogen ions, e.g. hydrochloric acid. Weak acids produce few hydrogen ions, e.g. citric acid.

REMEMBER You need to know the difference between strong and weak acids and dilute and concentrated acids.

Practice Questions – Chemical reactions and rates 3

1 What element is contained in all acids?

2 a) What is neutralisation?

b) Give an example of neutralisation that is used in everyday life.

3 a) Vinegar is a weak acid and sulphuric acid is a strong acid. Explain what this means.

b) What is the difference between concentrated and dilute hydrochloric acid?

Materials and their properties

This section is about

- the structure of atoms
- how atoms bond, ionically and covalently
- some of the properties of substances

How a material behaves depends on its properties. For example, glass has the following properties:

- it is hard
- it has a high melting point
- it is not reactive
- it is transparent

Its properties make it suitable for particular purposes, such as for use in windows.

Certain types of materials are **composites**, that is, they are made of two or more materials which makes them more suitable for a job. For example, car tyres are made of rubber reinforced with metal threads, so that they are strong but also flexible when going on bumpy surfaces.

On an atomic scale it is important to find out how the electrons are arranged and how they combine with other atoms to form elements.

For example, diamond and graphite are both made of carbon, but they have different structures.

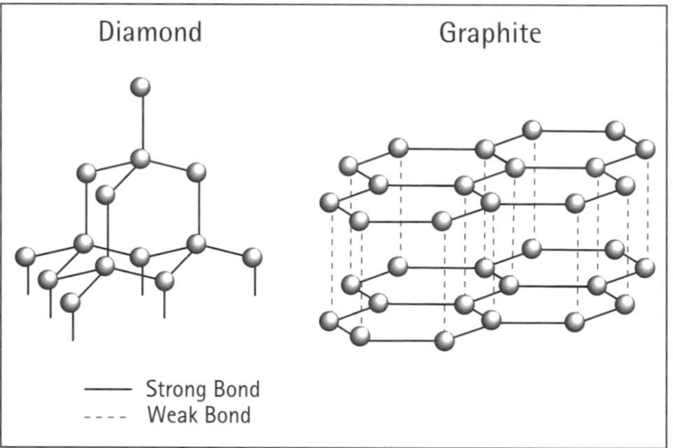

Diamond is hard and strong because each carbon atom has four strong covalent bonds. Graphite has a layered structure and the forces between the layers are weak, which makes it soft, and great to use in pencils! As you write the layers come off.

FactZONE

The table below shows the main groups of materials.

Material group	Example	Typical properties	Raw material used
metals	iron, steel, lead, copper, brass	hard, strong, high density, good conductors of heat and electricity, malleable (can be beaten into thin sheets), ductile (can be drawn into fine wires), usually burn on heating, high melting points	metal ores in Earth's crust
plastics	poly(ethene), polystyrene rubber	flexible, low density, easily moulded, poor conductors of heat and electricity, often transparent, melt and often burn on heating	crude oil, sap of rubber trees
ceramics (pottery)	china, concrete, bricks, tiles	hard, brittle, medium density, very high melting point, non-conductors of heat and electricity, very unreactive, do not burn	clay, sand and other minerals
glasses	Pyrex, lead crystal, soft soda glass	same properties as ceramics, often transparent	sand, limestone and other minerals
fibres	cotton, wool, paper, nylon, polyester	flexible, low density, may burn on heating, long stringy strands	natural fibres from plants and animals, crude oil

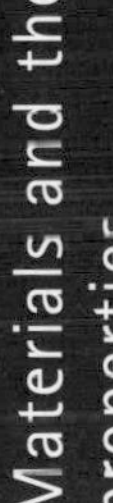

Atomic structure

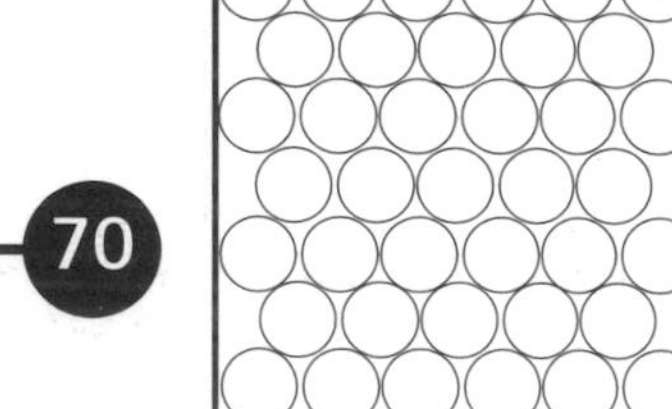

SOLID

Atomic structure is concerned with how particles are arranged in solids, liquids and gases, and how atoms themselves are structured, including the arrangement of the electrons.

Arrangement of particles

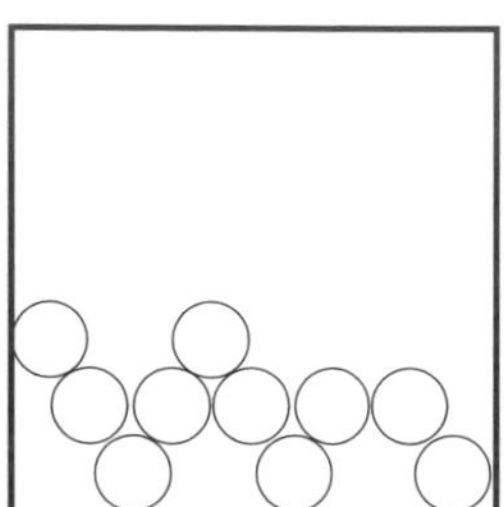

LIQUID

All matter can exist in three states: solid, liquid and gas. The states can be changed from one to another by changing the temperature. The temperature at which a pure solid changes from a solid to a liquid is called the **melting point** and the temperature at which it changes from a liquid to a gas is called its **boiling point**. The arrangement of particles in solids, liquids and gases is shown in the pictures on the left.

Kinetic theory

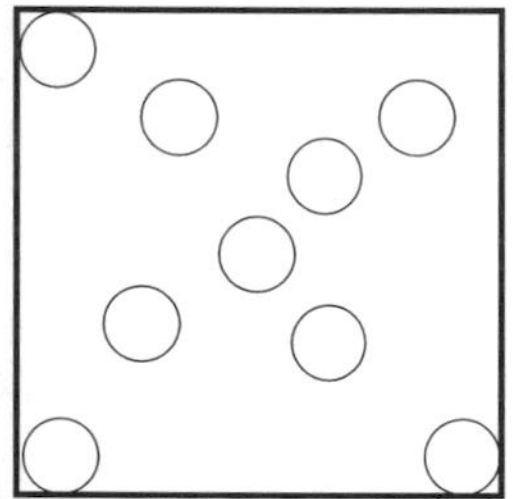

GAS

The main points of the kinetic theory are that:

- everything is made of tiny particles that move all the time
- the higher the temperature the faster the particles move
- heavier particles move more slowly than light ones at a given temperature

The theory can be used to explain:

- the difference between solids, liquids and gases
- changes of state – melting, boiling, freezing, etc.
- dissolving
- diffusion – movement of particles from a high concentration to a low concentration
- Brownian motion – to show that particles are moving and colliding with each other
- expansion of solids and liquids

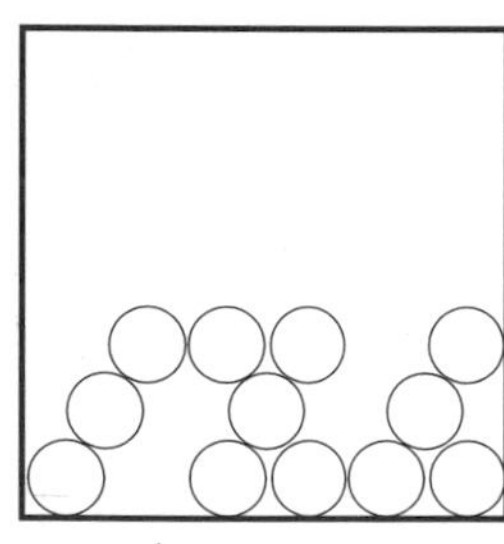

correct

When asked to draw particles in a liquid remember that there is some connection between the particles, as shown in the pictures on the left.

Atomic structure

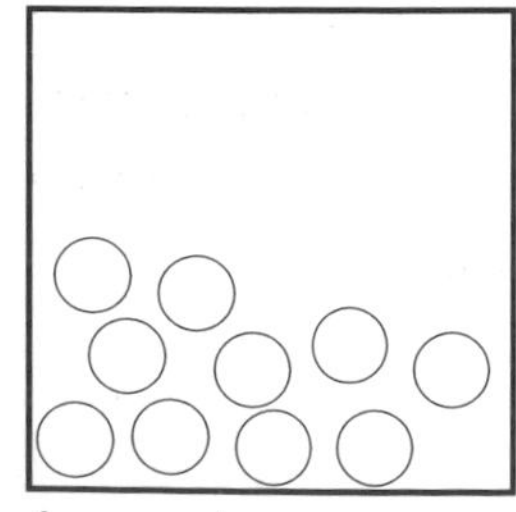

incorrect

An atom consists of a small heavy nucleus containing **protons** and **neutrons** surrounded by **electrons**. The forces that hold the particles in an atom together are electrostatic, which is the attraction between the positive and negative charges:

- protons have a charge of +1 and a relative mass of 1

- electrons have a charge of –1 and almost no mass (1/1840)
- neutrons have no charge and a mass of 1

The atomic number is the number of protons in an atom and the atomic mass is the number of protons plus the number of neutrons.

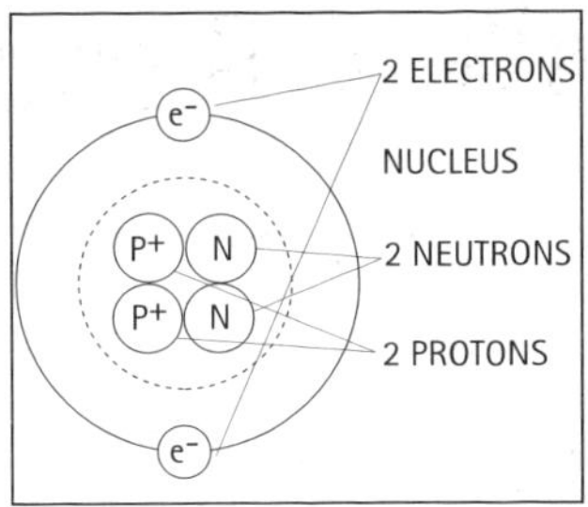

Atomic structure of helium

The picture on the right shows the atomic structure of helium. If you know the atomic number and atomic mass of an element you can work out how many protons, electrons and neutrons it has.

Number of protons or electrons = atomic number

Number of neutrons = atomic mass – atomic number

◎ Work out the number of protons, electrons and neutrons for $^{11}_{23}Na$, $^{6}_{12}C$, $^{19}_{9}F$, $^{1}_{1}H$ and $^{26}_{56}Fe$.

Isotopes

All the atoms of an element have the same atomic number, but they can have different mass numbers because the number of neutrons can vary. Atoms of the same element that have different numbers of neutrons are called **isotopes**. For example:

$^{17}_{35}Cl$	$^{17}_{37}Cl$
17 protons, 18 neutrons	17 protons,20 neutrons

The two isotopes of chlorine shown above have the same atomic number and the same number of protons, but different atomic masses and different numbers of neutrons.

◎ *Work out the number of protons and neutrons for the three hydrogen isotopes $^{1}_{1}H$, $^{1}_{2}H$ and $^{1}_{3}H$.*

Electron arrangement in atoms

Electrons are grouped within an atom in regions of space called **shells** or **energy** levels. Each shell can hold a maximum number of electrons.

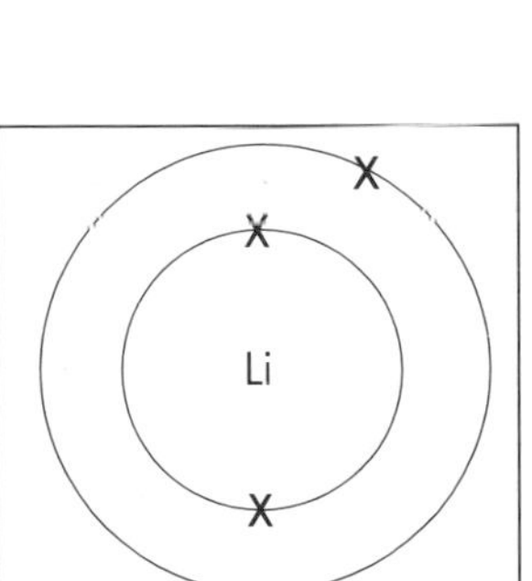

- the first shell can hold 2 electrons
- the second shell can hold 8 electrons
- the third shell can hold 8 electrons

The electrons in an element arrange themselves to fill up the shells in order. For example, lithium (^{3}Li) has three electrons. Two fill the first shell and there is one in the second shell. This is written Li 2.1 and it can be shown in a diagram like the one on the right.

REMEMBER You need to know the electron arrangement of the first twenty elements.

◎ *Work out the electron arrangements for ^{12}Mg, ^{9}F, ^{20}Ca, ^{17}Cl and ^{6}C.*

When elements react they want to be stable. They want full shells. For example, ^{11}Na has the electron arrangement 2.8.1. It wants to have the stable arrangement 2.8, and to do this it must lose one electron and become Na^+.

Bonding

When elements join together to form compounds they do this by bonding. The properties of the compounds that are formed depend on the type of bonding that has taken place.

Atoms attract one another. The force of attraction between atoms is called a bond. Atoms bond together in different ways:

- by sharing electrons between atoms. This is called **covalent bonding** and is usually between non-metals
- by transferring electrons from one atom to another. This is called **ionic bonding**, and these bonds usually form between a metal and a non-metal

In all cases atoms bond to achieve full shells of electrons.

In forming an ionic bond the atoms lose and gain electrons. If they lose electrons they form a positive ion (**cation**), these are usually metals. If they gain electrons, they form a negative ion (**anion**), these are usually non-metals.

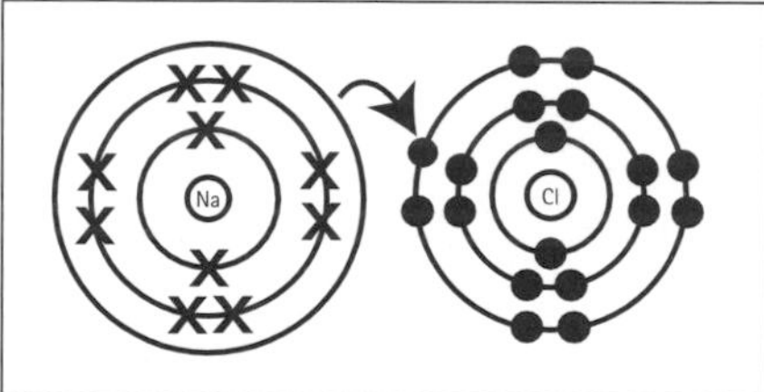

Dot and cross diagram for formation of sodium chloride

Ions are charged particles. If they lose electrons they become positively charged. If they gain electrons they become negatively charged. The number of electrons lost or gained is the number on the charge.

What charges will the ions of ^{12}Mg, ^{8}O and ^{13}Al have in a compound?

REMEMBER When elements combine they want full outer shells.

The properties of ionically bonded compounds are:

- hard
- conducts heat and electricity when melted or in solution
- high melting points

The properties of covalently bonded compounds are:

- low melting point
- insulator of electricity

REMEMBER Use dot and cross diagrams to show the formation of compounds.

When atoms bond together covalently, the particle they form is called a **molecule**.

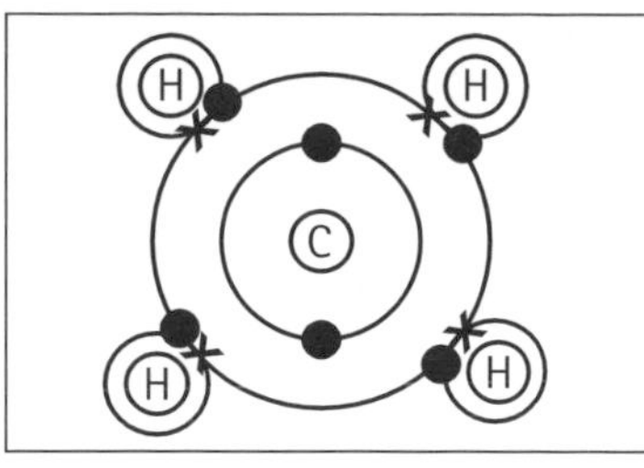

Diagram to show how methane is formed from carbon and hydrogen (CH_4)

Structure

Ionic compounds form giant structures in a lattice, as shown in the picture below. There is a strong electrostatic attraction between the positively charged sodium ions (Na^+) and the negatively charged chloride ions (Cl^-).

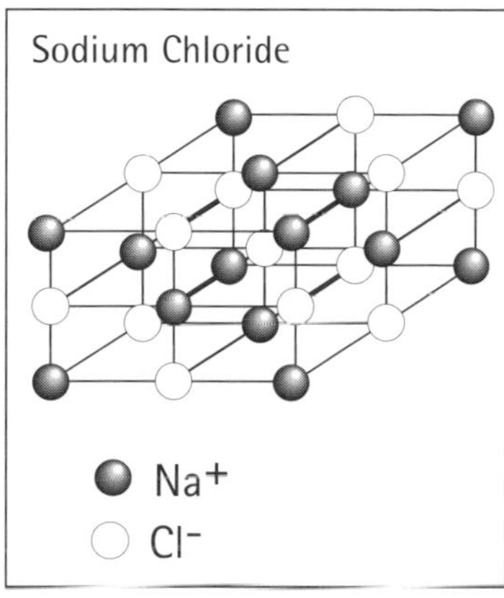

If two electrons are shared by the same element the bond is called a double bond.

Practice Questions – Materials and their properties 1

1 Lithium reacts with fluorine to form a substance called lithium fluoride.

a) The diagram below shows the outer electrons in an atom of lithium and in an atom of fluorine.

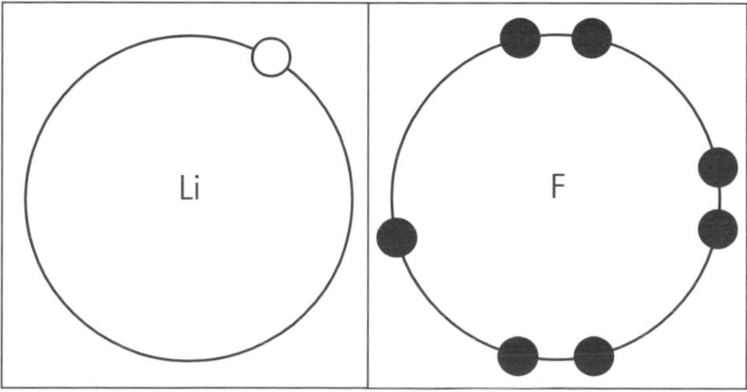

Draw an arrow on this diagram to show what happens to the electrons when lithium reacts with fluorine.

b) Draw the way the electrons are arranged in lithium fluoride. Show on your diagram the charges on the substances formed.

c) What type of bonding is present in lithium fluoride?

The periodic table

This section is about

- how the periodic table is arranged
- how it can be used to work out the properties of the elements
- alkali metals, Group I
- halogens, Group VII
- Noble gases, Group 0/Group VIII
- transition elements
- metals and their reactivity
- quantitative chemistry - amounts in chemistry

The periodic table is an essential tool to predict how elements will react and their properties. All you need to do is to see and apply patterns.

The periodic table is arranged into **groups**, which are the columns that go down, and **periods**, which are the rows that go across. Elements in the same group have similar properties because they have the same number of electrons in their outer shell. Their group number is the same as the number of electrons in their last shell. For example, elements in Group III have three electrons in their last shell.

The number of electrons in the outermost shell gives information on the properties and reactions of the elements.

How reactive elements are depends on:

- how many electrons they need to lose, gain or share
- how easy it is for them to lose or gain electrons

Elements want to be stable when they react. That is, they want to have full shells of electrons. The easier it is for the element to do this, the more reactive it is. Group 0/Group VIII elements are unreactive because they have full outer shells of electrons.

The period indicates which shell of electrons is filling up. Period 1 has two elements, because the first shell can hold two electrons. Period 2 has eight elements, because the second shell can hold eight electrons, and so on.

FactZONE

The periodic table contains all known elements in order of atomic number, starting with hydrogen, which has atomic number 1.

	I	II											III	IV	V	VI	VII	VIII/0
								H Hydrogen 1										He Helium 2
2	Li Lithium 3	Be Beryllium 4											B Boron 5	C Carbon 6	N Nitrogen 7	O Oxygen 8	F Fluorine 3	Ne Neon 4
3	Na Sodium 11	Mg Magnesium 12											Al Aluminium 13	Si Silicon 14	P Phosphorus 15	S Sulphur 16	Cl Chlorine 17	Ar Argon 18
4	K Potassium 19	Ca Calcium 20	Sc Scandium 21	Ti Titanium 22	V Vanadium 23	Cr Chromium 24	Mn Manganese 25	Fe Iron 26	Co Cobalt 27	Ni Nickel 28	Cu Copper 29	Zn Zinc 30	Ga Potassium 31	Ge Germanium 32	As Arsenic 33	Se Selenium 34	Br Bromine 35	Kr Krypton 36
5	Rb Rubidium 37	Sr Strontium 38	Y Yttrium 39	Zr Zirconium 40	Nb Niobium 41	Mo Molybdenum 42	Tc Technetium 43	Ru Rubidium 44	Rh Rhodium 45	Pd Palladium 46	Ag Silver 47	Cd Cadmium 48	Rb Rubidium 49	Sn Strontium 50	Sb Antimony 51	Te Strontium 52	I Iodine 53	Xe Xenon 54
6	Cs Caesium 55	Ba Barium 56	La Lanthanum 57	Hf Hafnium 72	Ta Tantalum 73	W Barium 74	Re Rhenium 75	Os Osmium 76	Ir Iridium 77	Pt Platinum 78	Au Gold 79	Hg Mercury 80	Tl Caesium 55	Pb Barium 56	Bi Bismuth 83	Po Polonium 84	At Astatine 85	Rn Radon 86
7	Fr Francium 87	Ra Racium 88	Ac Actinium 89															

TRANSITION ELEMENTS

magnetic metals

These are the most reactive metals

This line divides the metals from the non-metals

These are the most reactive non-metals. They are called the **halogens**

These are very unreactive gases (the **noble** gases)

Alkali metals (Group I)

The alkali metals are the elements in Group I of the periodic table. The reactivity of the elements increases as you go down the group.

Electron arrangements

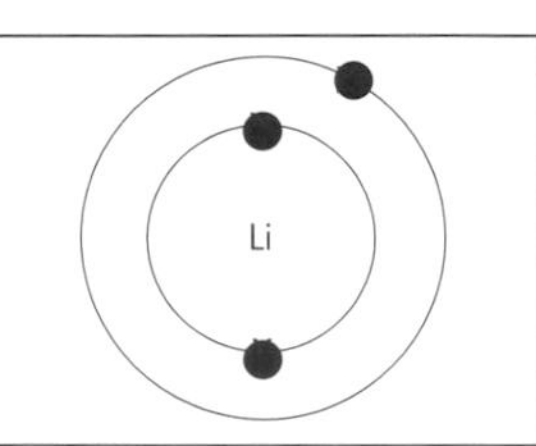

Lithium ^{3}Li 2.1

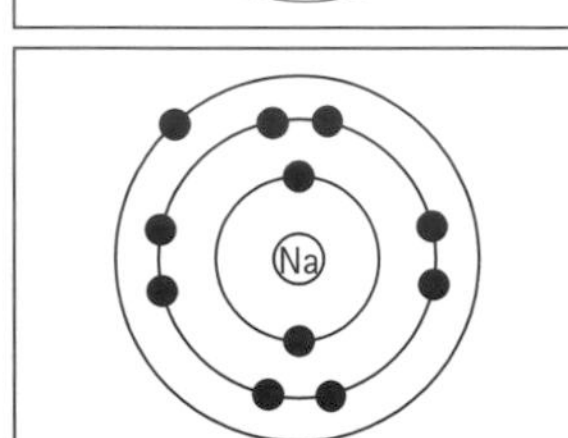

Sodium ^{11}Na 2.8.1

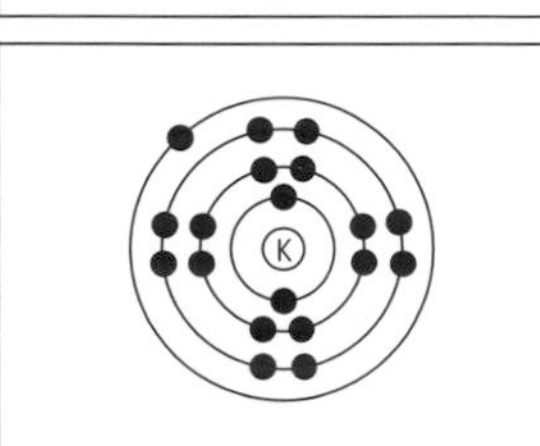

Potassium ^{19}K 2.8.8.1

Why is it easier for K to lose one electron than Li?

Think about the attraction between the positive nucleus and the outer shell electron. As you go down Group I the reactivity increases because the outer shell electron gets further away from the positive nucleus and is easier to lose.

Group I elements are more reactive than Group II elements. Is it easier to lose one electron or two electrons?

Alkali metals

Group I metals are less dense and have lower melting points than other metals.

They react with water to form metal hydroxides and water:

$2M(s) + 2H_2O(l) \rightarrow 2MOH(aq) + H_2(g)$

where M = metal.

They react with halogens to form metal halides and oxygen to form metal oxides. All of these are ionic solids:

$2M(s) + X_2(g) \rightarrow 2MCl(s)$

where X = halogens

$4M(s) + O_2(g) \rightarrow 2M_2O(s)$

Alkali metal compounds

All alkali metal compounds are ionic and will dissolve in water to form metal hydroxides.

Metal hydroxides are ionic. They form OH^- ions which means they are bases.

When sodium chloride solution is electrolysed, chlorine is formed at the anode. Hydrogen is formed at the cathode.

lithium + oxygen = ____________

The alkali metals form salts when they react with the halogens. For example:

potassium + iodine = potassium iodide

Fill in the word equations for fluorine and bromine:

sodium + fluorine → ____________

lithium + bromine → ____________

You should know the ions that the alkali metals form. For example:

$NaOH \rightarrow Na^{+}\ OH^{-}$

$K_2O \rightarrow 2K^{+}\ O^{2-}$

What ions do NaF, KOH and LiO form?

REMEMBER You should know the general formula for reactions of the alkali metals.

Practice Questions – The periodic table 1

1 Why do Group 1 elements have similar chemical properties?

2 a) Name the two products formed when potassium reacts with water.

b) Write down two observations that you would see.

c) The reaction causes the pH of the solution to change. Explain why this happens.

Halogens (Group VII)

The halogens are the elements in GroupVII of the periodic table. The reactivity of the elements decreases as you go down the group.

Electron arrangements

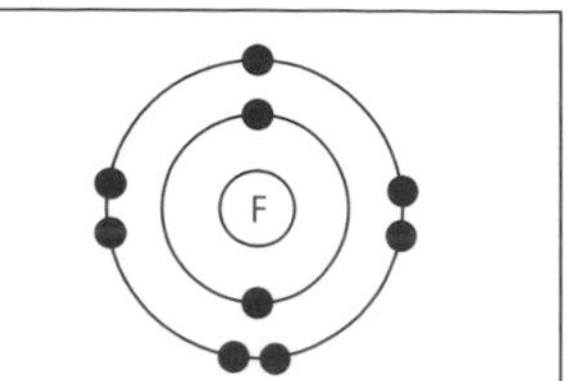

Fluorine ^{9}F 2.7

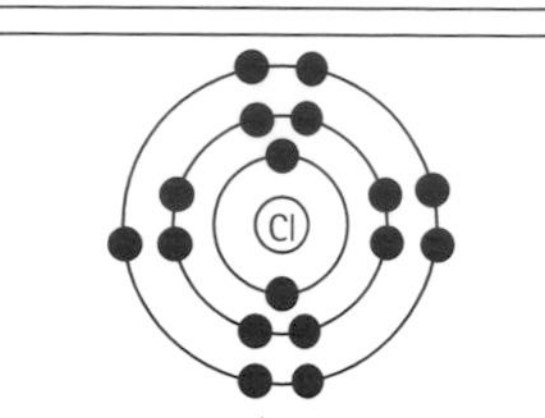

Chlorine ^{17}Cl 2.8.7

Why is it easier for F to gain one electron than Cl?

Think about the attraction between the positive nucleus and the outer shell electron. As you go down Group VII the reactivity decreases because it is more difficult to gain an extra electron the further the outer shell is from the positive nucleus.

Group VII elements are more reactive than Group VI. Is it easier to gain one electron or two electrons?

REMEMBER Chlorine is a gas, its melting and boiling points will be below 20°C.

Chlorine, bromine and iodine

- chlorine is a green/yellow gas
- bromine is a dark red liquid
- iodine is a purple solid

REMEMBER Bromine is a liquid, its melting point will be below 20°C.

The halogens are diatomic molecules. They are molecules of two atoms joined together by a single covalent bond, and are written Cl_2, Br_2, I_2.

The melting points and boiling points increase as you go down Group VII.

Chlorine has many uses, including as a bleaching agent, for sterilising water and in the manufacture of hydrochloric acid.

REMEMBER Iodine is a solid, its melting and boiling points will be above 20°C.

Halogen compounds

A more reactive halogen will displace a less reactive halogen.

Halogens react with hydrogen to form hydrogen halides, which are covalently bonded compounds:

$H_2(g) + X_2(g) \rightarrow 2HX(g)$

where X = halogen.

These hydrogen halides, that is hydrogen chloride, bromide and iodide form, an acidic solution in water.

(h) They form $H^+(aq)$ ions in water, which makes them acidic.

The reactions of hydrogen and the halogen show how their reactivity decreases down the group.

(h) ◎ *Chlorine will displace ________ and ________.*

Bromine will displace ________.

◎ *Write complete word equations for the following:*

chlorine + potassium bromide =

bromine + potassium iodide =

Practice Questions – The periodic table 2

1 The table below gives some information about the elements in Group VII of the periodic table.

element	symbol	atomic number	melting point (°C)	boiling point (°C)	reaction with sodium
fluorine	F	9	–220	–188	reacts explosively when heated gently
chlorine	Cl	17	–101	–35	reacts rapidly when heated gently
bromine	Br	35	–7	+57	reacts slowly when heated very gently
iodine	I	53		+184	reacts very slowly when heated gently

a) Suggest a value for the melting point of iodine.

b) Suggest how the size of the atoms of these elements change down the Group from fluorine to iodine. Explain your answer.

c) (h) In chemical reactions, each atom of these elements gains an electron to form an ion.

Suggest and explain the pattern when these elements react with sodium.

d) (h) Suggest what products are formed when chlorine reacts with a solution of potassium bromide in water.

e) Astatine is another member of Group VII of the periodic table. Predict one physical property of astatine.

Noble gases

The Noble gases are the elements in Group 0/GroupVIII of the periodic table. They are helium (He), neon (Ne), argon (Ar), krypton (Kr), xenon (Xe) and radon (Rn). The gases are unreactive because they have full outer shells of electrons, so are stable.

The Noble gases have a variety of uses, for example:

- helium is used for airships
- neon is used for colour in advertising signs (lights)
- argon is the gas used in light bulbs

Watch the video section on the periodic table, then explain the pattern of densities for Group 0/Group VIII.

REMEMBER Most questions on Noble gases ask you to explain why they are not reactive and to list their uses.

Practice Questions - The periodic table 3

1 Group 0/Group VIII elements do not react. Explain why.

2 Draw a diagram to show the electron arrangement of a neon atom (atomic number = 10).

Transition elements

The transition elements are those elements in the block between Group II and Group III. They are metals with high melting points and high densities. They are often used as catalysts, as are their compounds, which are often coloured.

The transition elements have a variety of uses, for example:

- copper is used for electrical wiring and domestic hot water pipes
- zinc is used for galvanising iron
- iron is used as a catalyst in the manufacture of ammonia
- manganese is used as a catalyst

There are many transition elements, but you will not be expected to know all of them. Make sure you can name some examples of, for example:

- coloured compounds – copper sulphate ($CuSO_4$), blue
- catalysts – manganese dioxide/iron/vanadium

REMEMBER The transition element iron is the only metal that rusts. You should know what causes rusting and how to prevent iron from rusting.

Practice Questions – The periodic table 4

1 Name four transition elements.

2 Name three properties associated with the transition elements.

Metals and reactivity

The metals are arranged in a list of decreasing reactivity, shown below. This is called the Reactivity Series.

Potassium	K	Most reactive
Sodium	Na	
Calcium	Ca	
Magnesium	Mg	
Aluminium	Al	
Zinc	Zn	
Iron	Fe	
Hydrogen	H	
Lead	Pb	
Copper	Cu	
Silver	Ag	
Gold	Au	Least reactive

REMEMBER You should learn the order of metals in the Reactivity Series.

Any metal will displace a metal below it in the Reactivity Series from its solution.

The table below shows how the metals in the Reactivity Series react with air, water and dilute acids.

Metal	Reaction with air	Reaction with water	Reaction with dilute acids
Potassium	Burns in air easily to form oxide	Set alight with cold water	Very violent reaction
Sodium		Reacts quickly with cold water	
Calcium		Reacts slowly with water	
Magnesium		Reacts very slowly with cold water, fast with steam	Fairly fast reaction but gets slower as you go down the list
Aluminium	Reacts	Layers of oxide stop reaction	
Zinc		Reacts quickly with steam	
Iron		Reversible reaction with steam	
Copper		No reaction	No reaction
Gold	No reaction		

Displacement

You need to know the rule for the displacement reaction: **If the metal is higher in the series than the metal in the compound, displacement takes place.**

The higher the metal in the series the more difficult it is to extract.

Use the displacement rule to predict whether reactions will take place between the following metals and compounds:

magnesium + copper sulphate

iron + aluminium oxide

calcium + zinc sulphate

It might help you to know that in two of them there will be reactions and in one there won't be a reaction.

Write equations for the reactions which take place.

General equations

There are a number of general equations involving metals:

metal + oxygen = metal oxide

metal + water = metal hydroxide + hydrogen

metal + acid = salt + hydrogen

See page 62 for more information on writing chemical equations.

What would you observe during the reaction shown in the picture on the right?

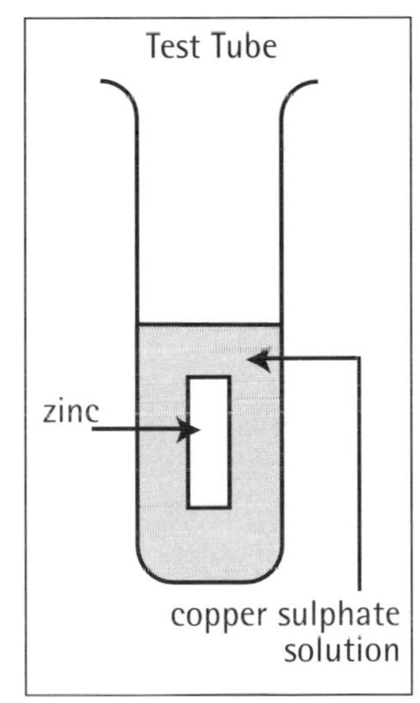

There would be two marks for a question like this in the exam. Make sure you write down what you observe, not what happens:

- you can guarantee it will 'fizz' (1 mark)
- usually there will be a 'colour change'. For this reaction there are two: blue copper sulphate fades and an orange layer forms (1 mark for either observation)

Practice Questions – The periodic table 5

1 What would you observe if magnesium was added to dilute hydrochloric acid?

2 What would you observe if potassium was added to cold water?

Quantitative chemistry

The unit of measuring quantities of atoms and molecules is called the **mole.** A mole of any substance contains 6×10^{23} particles (this is called Avogadro's number).

Elements

For elements, a mole (6×10^{23}) of atoms or molecules always has the same mass as its relative atomic mass (called RAM or A_R for short) in grams. For example, iron has a relative atomic mass of 56, so one mole of iron weighs exactly 56 g, and carbon has a relative atomic mass of 12, so one mole of carbon weighs exactly 12 g.

Compounds

For compounds, a mole has the same mass as the relative formula mass in grams. An example is given below for calcium carbonate, $CaCO_3$:

> **REMEMBER** You will always be given the relative atomic masses in the exam.

RAM of Ca = 40

RAM of C = 12

RAM of O = 16

$CaCO_3 = 40 + 12 + (16 \times 3) = 100$ g

Gases

For all gases one mole occupies a volume of 24 dm^3. For example, nitrogen has a relative atomic mass of 14, so one mole of nitrogen gas (N_2) has a mass of 28 g (2 x 14) and a volume of 24 dm^3.

Concentration

Concentration is measured in moles per litre (mole/l). A solution with a concentration of one mole per litre would contain the relative formula mass of the compound in 1 dm^3 of water. For example, for a 1 mole/l sodium chloride solution:

relative formula mass of sodium chloride (NaCl) = 23 (Na) + 35.5 (Cl)

one mole/l solution of NaCl = 58.5 g in 1dm^3 of water

Calculations

Example 1

How many moles are there in 20 g of calcium? (Relative atomic mass of Ca = 40) number of moles = $\frac{\text{mass (of material)}}{\text{mass of 1 mole}} = \frac{20}{40} =$ 0.5 moles

How many moles are there in 230 g of sodium? (Relative atomic mass of Na = 23)

REMEMBER You should know and be able to use the formulae for calculations.

Example 2

What mass of sulphur contains 0.1 moles? (Relative atomic mass of S = 32)

mass = number of moles x mass of 1 mole

= 0.1 x 32

= 3.2 g

What mass of sodium chloride contains 2 moles? (Relative atomic mass of Na = 23, Cl = 35.5)

The more complicated calculations involve working out the mass of a product of reactant in a balanced equation.

What mass of magnesium is needed to make 80 g of magnesium oxide? (Relative atomic mass of Mg = 24, O = 16)

Step 1: Chemical equation 2Mg + O2 = 2MgO

2 moles 1 mole 2 moles

Step 2: Work out the number of moles of MgO in 80 g (use the equation in example 1, above):

mass = 80 g

mass of 1 mole = 24 + 16 = 40 g

Mg O

number of moles = $\frac{80}{40}$ = 2 moles

Step 3: Use chemical equation to work out number of moles of magnesium needed to produce 2 moles of magnesium oxide:

2 moles of magnesium produces 2 moles of magnesium oxide.

Step 4: Work out the mass of 2 moles of magnesium (use equation 2 above):

mass = 2 x 24 = 48 g

These types of calculations are difficult, but remember even if you don't get all of it right it is usually worth 3 or 4 marks. So persevere.

REMEMBER Exam questions often ask for your answer in tonnes, so keep the calculations in tonnes.

Practice Questions – The periodic table 6

1 How many tonnes of calcium oxide is produced if 50 tonnes of calcium carbonate is heated?

Equation: $CaCO_3 \rightarrow CaO + CO_2$ (relative atomic mass of Ca = 40, C = 12, O = 16).

Industrial processes

This section is about

- manufacturing processes
- manufacture of ammonia from nitrogen and hydrogen
- manufacture of fertilisers
- oil formation and separation into useful products
- polymers
- extraction of metals - aluminium and iron
- reversible reactions and equilibrium

Industrial processes are concerned with chemical reactions taking place on a large scale. It is important to understand the reaction taking place, but there are also other considerations:

1. Choice of site in the process. The chemical plant should be situated within easy access of its raw materials and/or near road, rail or sea routes for transportation.

2. Using the minimum amount of energy. All industrial processes give us a product which is useful, but the company needs to make a profit. Therefore to keep costs down, the product needs to be made without using too much heat or electrical power. Also, if the reaction is exothermic, the heat produced can be used to increase production.

3. Continuity of the process. In some industrial processes not all the reactants are turned immediately into products, so the unused reactants need to be recycled efficiently so that they can be put through the process again.

4. Production of valuable by-products. With some chemical reactions there is often more than one product. If this is the case in an industrial process, it is very economical and useful to make use of any extra products.

5. Pollution. Most industrial plants are very large and can often spoil the look of the landscape. It is essential that the amount of pollution produced by the process is kept to a minimum.

FactZONE

A chemical plant is where the process takes place. The important industrial processes you need to know are:

- TV Manufacture of ammonia from nitrogen and hydrogen

$N_2(g) + 3H_2(g) \rightleftharpoons 2NH_3(g)$

This is a reversible reaction.

- Manufacture of fertilisers from ammonia. The two main fertilisers are ammonium nitrate (NH_4NO_3) and ammonium sulphate ($(NH_4)_2SO_4$).
- TV Fractional distillation of oil to produce petrol/kerosene/butane etc.
- TV Formation of polymers. For example, the production of polythene from ethene, pictured below

```
 [ H       H ]           [   H   H   H   H   H       ]
 [  \     /  ]           [   |   |   |   |   |       ]
 [   C = C   ]   ---->   [ - C - C - C - C - C - ... ]
 [  /     \  ]           [   |   |   |   |   |       ]
 [ H       H ]n          [   H   H   H   H   H       ]
```

where n is a large number.

- Extraction of metals, such as aluminium by electrolysis and iron by reduction with carbon.

In all these processes, you need to know the conditions for manufacture and the equations of the explanation of how it happens. If you know them, easy marks can be gained.

Make flow charts and/or key fact cards for each process. Remember to incorporate the other considerations in making the process economical.

Useful products from air

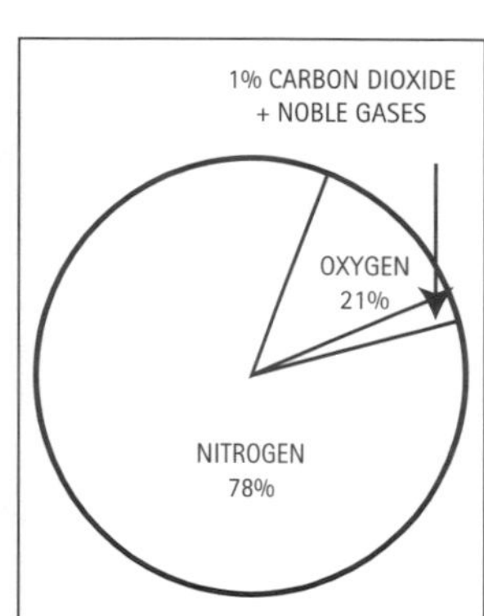

Air is made up of:

- oxygen (21%)
- nitrogen (78%)
- carbon dioxide + noble gases (1%)

It is used in a number of industrial processes, for example, in the manufacture of ammonia and fertilisers.

Manufacture of ammonia

 *Watch the section on the manufacture of ammonia then complete the flow diagram below.*

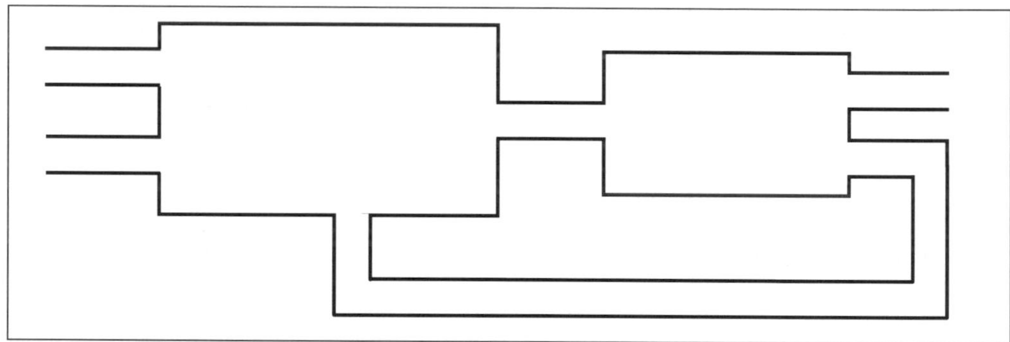

Ammonia is manufactured from nitrogen and hydrogen:

$N_2(g) + 3H_2(g) \rightleftharpoons 2NH_3(g)$

This is a reversible reaction.

Optimum conditions means the right amount for the right cost.

Manufacture of fertilisers

Fertilisers are ammonium salts. The two most common are ammonium nitrate (NH_4NO_3) and ammonium sulphate $(NH_4)_2SO_4$. They both contain nitrogen and they are both soluble in water.

Ammonium nitrate is made by reacting ammonia and nitric acid:

$NH_3(g) + HNO_3(aq) \rightarrow NH_4NO_3(aq)$

Ammonium sulphate is made by reacting ammonia and sulphuric acid important:

$2NH_3(g) + H_2SO_4(aq) \rightarrow (NH_4)_2SO_4(aq)$

Effect of fertilisers on plant growth

Use the nitrogen cycle in biology to help you understand the flow diagram below:

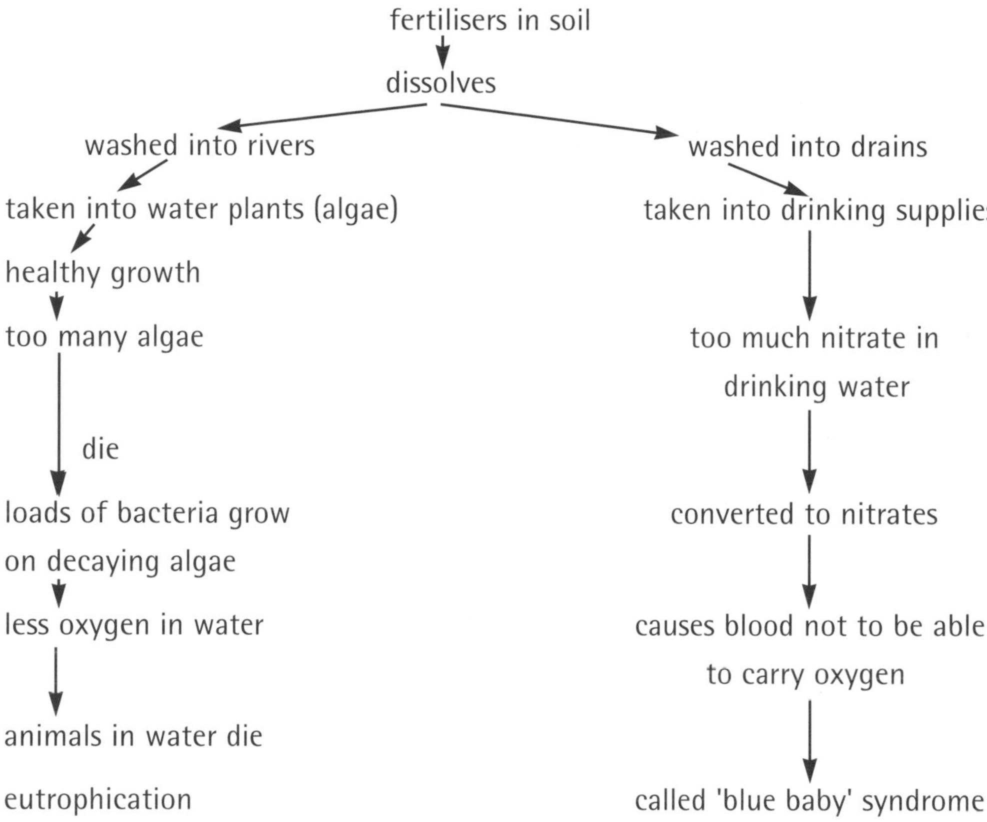

Practice Questions – Industrial processes 1

1 Ammonium nitrate is a salt which is an important fertiliser.

a) (i) Which one of the following would you add to ammonia solution to make ammonium nitrate?

ammonia ammonium sulphate nitric acid potassium chloride sulphuric acid water

(ii) What type of reaction takes place when ammonium nitrate is formed?

b) Using too much nitrogenous fertiliser like ammonium can cause water pollution.

(i) How can the fertiliser put on to fields get into river water?

(ii) What property of ammonium nitrate enables this to happen?

(iii) What effect might the nitrogenous fertiliser have on the algae in the river?

(iv) Explain how this results in fish dying in the river.

Useful products from oil

Oil was formed from organic materials (dead sea creatures) which were trapped in between sediment over millions of years. It contains a mixture of products, mainly hydrocarbons, which have many uses, but before it can be used it has to be separated by fractional distillation. This method separates the different substances because they have different boiling points.

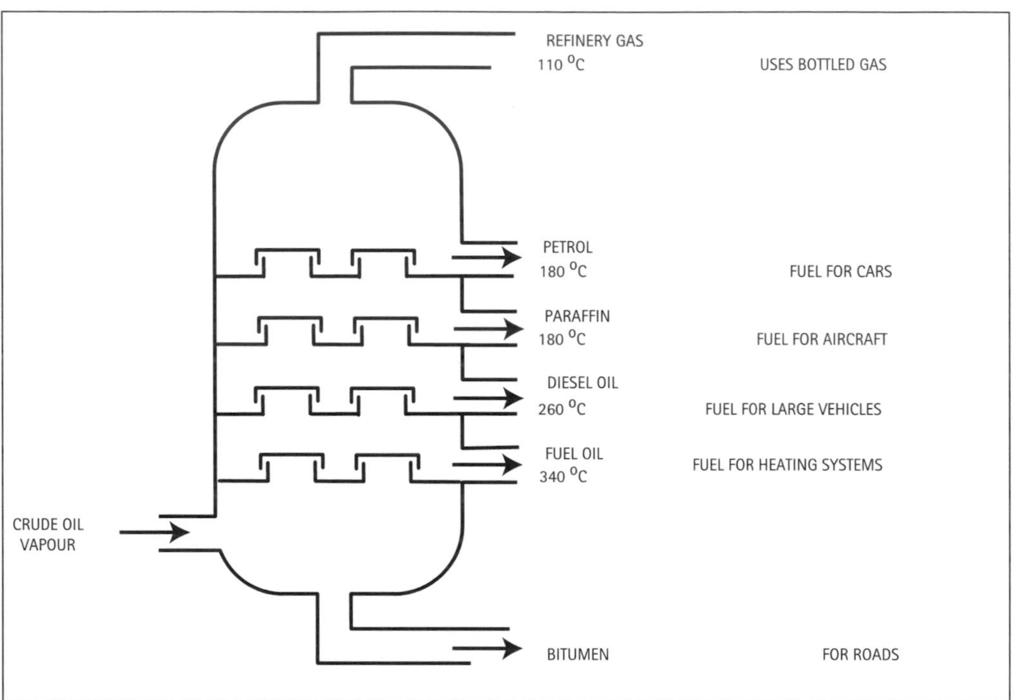

Diagram to show how properties change

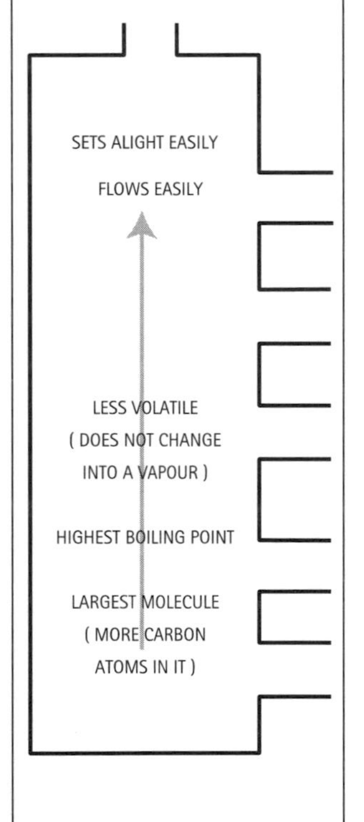

Hydrocarbons are compounds that contain only carbon and hydrogen. When they are burnt in oxygen they produce water and carbon dioxide.

hydrocarbon + oxygen = carbon dioxide + water

Crude oil is a good energy source, but is non-renewable and therefore it will run out.

Refinery gas:

- sets alight easily
- flows easily
- is volatile
- has a low boiling point
- has small molecule

What would you expect fuel oil to be like?

REMEMBER You need to know patterns in properties of hydrocarbons found in crude oil.

Equations

The equation for the complete combustion of hydrocarbons is:

$CH_4(g) + 2O_2(g) \rightarrow CO_2(g) + 2H_2O(l)$

Complete the following equations:

$C_2H_6 + O_2 \rightarrow$ ________ + ________

$C_6H_{12} + O_2 \rightarrow$ ________ + ________

Look at section on equations (page 62) if you find it difficult.

What would be formed if there was not enough oxygen?

Practice Questions – Industrial processes 2

1 How is crude oil formed?

2 How is it separated into useful products?

More useful products from oil

 Hydrocarbons may be either saturated (called **alkanes**) or unsaturated (called **alkenes**). They may be broken down into smaller molecules, which is called **cracking**, or joined together to form larger molecules, which is called **polymerisation**.

Alkanes

Alkanes are **saturated** hydrocarbons. This means that each carbon has four bonds to other atoms. Examples include:

- methane, CH_4
- ethane, C_2H_6
- propane, C_3H_8

Their names always end in '-ane'.

The structures of alkanes are shown in the picture below.

```
        H   H                     H   H   H
        |   |                     |   |   |
    H - C - C - H             H - C - C - C - H
        |   |                         |   |
        H   H                     H   H   H
```

ethane (C_2H_6)

propane (C_3H_8)

REMEMBER To check the structure of hydrocarbons make sure there are four lines from each C and one from each H.

Alkenes

Alkenes are unsaturated hydrocarbons. This means that there is one double bond between two carbon atoms. Examples include:

- ethene, C_2H_4
- propane, C_3H_6

Their names always end in '-ene'.

The structures of alkenes are shown in the picture below.

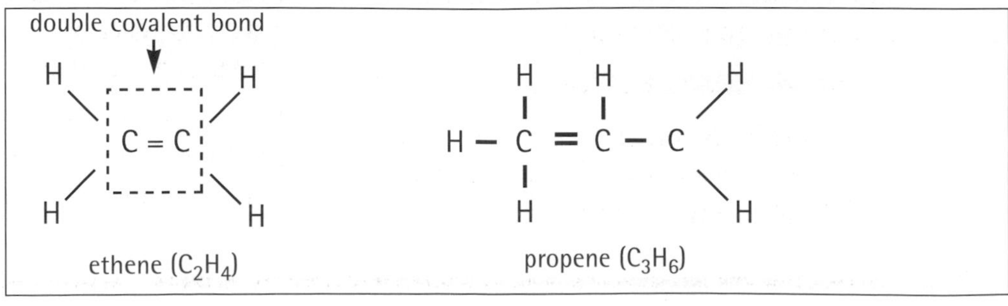

ethene (C_2H_4)

propene (C_3H_6)

◎ *Finish drawing the structure of propene that has been started below*

C–C=C

Ⓗ There is a simple test to tell the difference between alkanes and alkenes using bromine water. Alkenes take away the brown colour from bromine water; alkanes do nothing.

Cracking and polymerisation

Cracking is the process when a larger molecule is broken into (cracked) smaller molecules using a **catalyst**. When alkanes are cracked they gain a double bond and form alkenes and smaller alkanes.

Polymerisation is the reaction where monomers (mono means one) join together to form polymers (poly means many).

Ⓗ In addition polymerisation many ethene molecules are added together to form polythene. See diagram in FactZone on page 87.

Monomers for addition polymerisation must contain a double bond so that the bond can break and the monomers add on.

Polymers and their uses include:

- polythene, used for plastic bags and bottles
- Ⓗ polypropene, used for crates and ropes

◎ *Complete the following word equation to show polymerisation of propene:*

	heat/pressure	
propene	⟶	______
monomer	*catalyst*	*polymer*

Practice Questions – Industrial processes 3

1 a) (i) Methane is a hydrocarbon. What does the word hydrocarbon mean?

(ii) Write the formula of methane.

b) (i) Methane is the main constituent of an important domestic fuel. By what name is this fuel generally known?

(ii) When this fuel burns in air, heat is released. What name is given to reactions which give out heat?

(iii) Name and write the formula of each of the two products formed when methane burns in a plentiful supply of air.

Extracting metals from ores

Ores are usually metal oxides found in the earth. The metal can be extracted and purified. The method of extraction depends on the position of the metal in the Reactivity Series.

Extraction

Metals above zinc in the Reactivity Series are extracted using electrolysis. The picture below illustrates the extraction of aluminium from its ore. Aluminium ore is aluminium oxide, which is called bauxite.

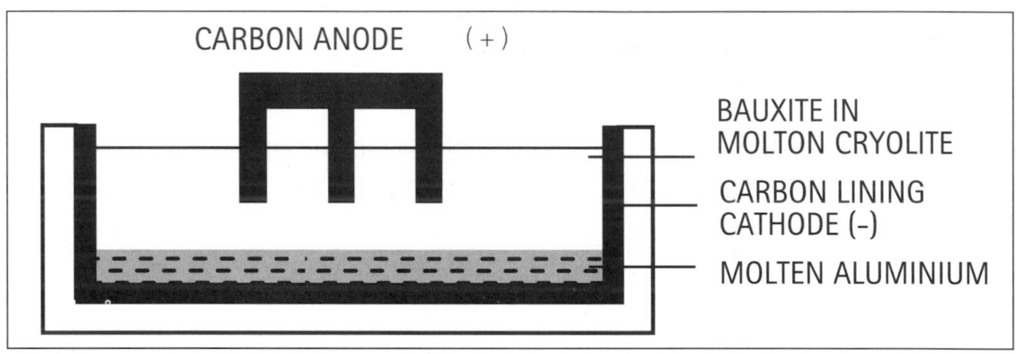

Cathode (–) reaction: positive aluminium ion gains electron to form aluminium.

h $Al^{3+} + 3e^{-} \rightarrow Al$ (cathode)

Anode (+) reaction: negative oxide ions lose electrons to form oxygen.

h $2O^{2-} - 4e^{-} \rightarrow 2O_2$ (anode)

REMEMBER The blast furnace is a favourite topic with examiners.

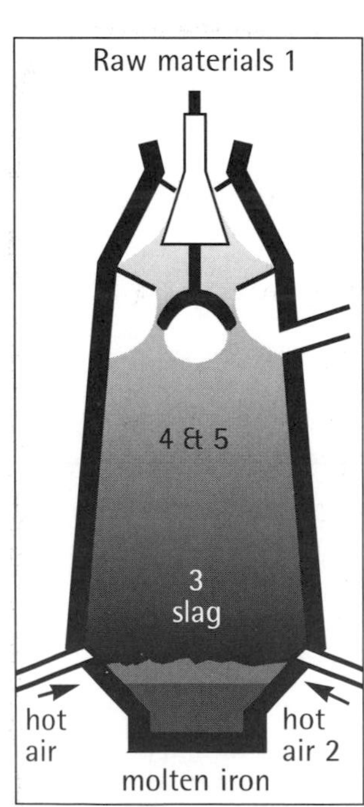

Metals below zinc in the Reactivity Series are extracted by reduction using carbon or carbon dioxide. The picture on the left illustrates the extraction of iron from its ore. Iron ore is iron oxide, usually called haematite.

1 The raw materials (limestone, coke, iron ore) are put into the blast furnace.

2 The 'blast' is hot air, and the important part is oxygen.

The equations below show the process:

3 air reacts with coke

carbon + oxygen = carbon dioxide

4 carbon dioxide reacts with more coke

carbon dioxide + coke = carbon monoxide (reducing agent)

5 iron ore + carbon monoxide = iron + carbon dioxide

limestone reacts with impurities to produce 'slag'

Purification

Some metals can be purified by electrolysis. The picture below shows the purification of copper.

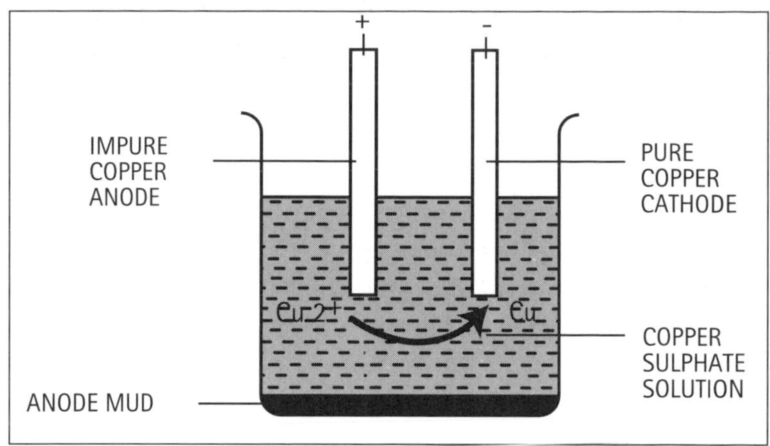

> **REMEMBER** In the purification of metals by electrolysis, at the anode there is a change from metal atoms to ions.

Anode reaction: copper atoms → copper ions

$$Cu(s) - 2e^- \rightarrow Cu^{2+}(aq)$$

Cathode reaction: copper ions → copper atom

$$Cu^{2+}(aq) + 2e^- \rightarrow Cu(s)$$

Silver is also purified by electrolysis and a similar method is used for 'plating' metals.

You will not need to be able to draw the diagrams, but you must know the processes and equations for the extraction and purification of metals.

Practice Questions – Industrial processes 4

1 Iron is made from haematite in a blast furnace. The raw materials used in the process include coke, limestone and air. The diagram below shows a blast furnace.

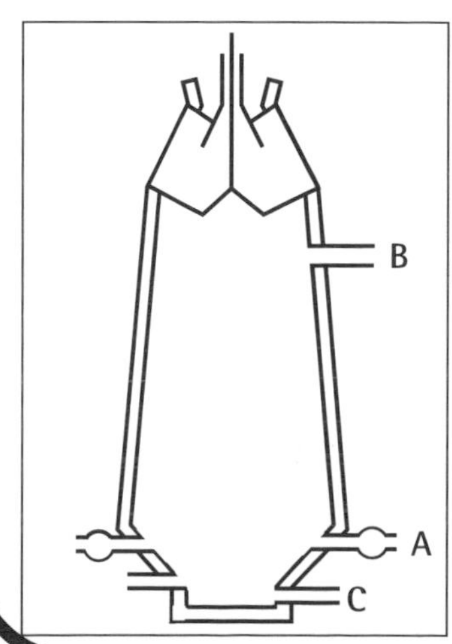

a) Name the raw materials put into the hopper.

b) Name the raw material that enters at A.

c) Name the product taken out at C.

d) The mixture of gases leaving at B contains nitrogen and sulphur dioxide. Suggest how each of these gases came to be present.

e) The temperature inside the furnace is over 1000°C. Suggest one source of heat which keeps the contents at this temperature.

Reversible reactions

Reversible reactions are reactions that can go both ways. This means that the reactants are converted to products and the products can be converted back to the original reactants.

$$\text{reactants} \underset{\text{back reaction}}{\overset{\text{forward reaction}}{\rightleftharpoons}} \text{products}$$

An example of a reversible reaction is the thermal decomposition of hydrated copper sulphate to anhydrous copper sulphate:

$CuSO_4(s) + H_2O(l) \rightleftharpoons CuSO_4.5H_2O(aq)$

anhydrous hydrated

If the rate of the forward reaction is equal to the rate of the back reaction then the reaction is in **equilibrium**. Nothing appears to be happening. To help understand this, imagine trying to walk up an escalator that is going down. If you are going up at the same speed as the escalator is moving down, you will not appear to be moving.

The production of ammonia is a reaction that is in equilibrium. The conditions for the process need to favour the forward reaction. Watch the video section on the production of ammonia to help you understand this better.

Effect of temperature and pressure on equilibrium

An increase in temperature is favoured by the endothermic reaction. In a reversible reaction, the reaction one way is endothermic and the reaction the other way is exothermic. If the temperature is increased the rate of the endothermic reaction will be increased.

In the thermal decomposition of hydrated copper sulphate to anhydrous copper sulphate the forward reaction is exothermic. Will the forward or backward reaction be faster if the temperature is increased?

The only substances that are affected by change of pressure are gases.

The reaction for the manufacture of ammonia is:

$N_2(g) + 3H_2(g) \rightleftharpoons 2NH_3(g)$

4 volumes 2 volumes

Which reaction will be favoured by an increase in pressure?

Remember that an increase in pressure favours a decrease in volume. Read about Boyle's law on page 118 in the Physics section to understand this further.

Le Chatelier's principle

If you make a change to a system in equilibrium, the system will cancel the change. For example, if you increase the temperature the system will try to decrease the temperature.

REMEMBER Questions on the effect of temperature and pressure on equilibrium are a favourite on higher exam papers, usually combined with the industrial process of ammonia manufacture.

Practice Questions – Industrial processes 5

1 Give an example of a reversible reaction. Explain how the reaction can be reversed and write an equation for it.

2 The reaction between nitrogen and hydrogen to form ammonia can be in equilibrium. What does equilibrium mean?

(h) 3 In the following reversible reaction, the forward reaction is exothermic.

$$CuSO_4(s) + H_2O(l) \rightleftharpoons CuSO_4.5H_2O(aq)$$

If the temperature was increased what would happen to the position of equilibrium?

Earth and air

This section is about

- the structure of the Earth and the theory of plate tectonics
- rocks and the rock cycle
- changes in the atmosphere around the Earth

All the changes that take place in the Earth's structure are linked to the constant forming, breaking up and reforming of rocks. During these changes volcanoes erupt, earthquakes take place, new mountains are made and different types of rocks are formed (igneous, sedimentary and metamorphic). These rocks change from one type to another as shown in the rock cycle.

All the changes take place because the Earth is made up of plates, which are constantly moving. The plates can move in three ways, which have different effects on the Earth:

- they can slide past each other, causing earthquakes
- they can move away from each other, which usually happens on the ocean floor, causing a new ocean floor to be formed – often called 'ocean floor spreading'
- they can collide with each other, which can cause volcanoes and can cause fold mountains to form

The atmosphere surrounding the Earth has been almost constant for the past 200 million years. It has a delicate balance, and too much or too little of the compounds in the atmosphere can have a long-term effect on the environment. For example, too much carbon dioxide causes global warming.

There are three main cycles that are important in maintaining the Earth's present atmosphere: the carbon cycle, the water cycle and the nitrogen cycle (for more information see page 56 in Biology section).

FactZONE

Plate tectonics

Plates can do three things:

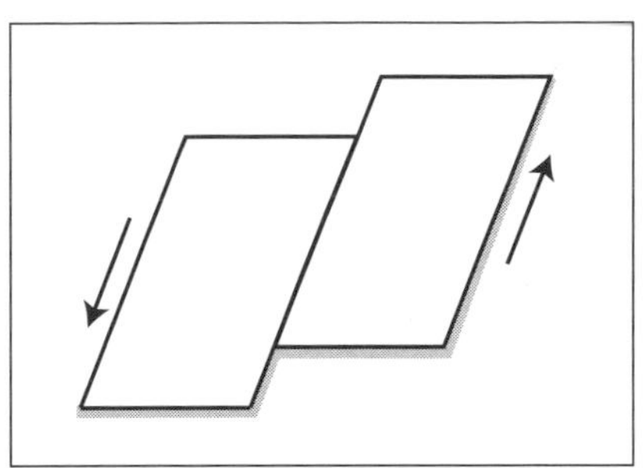

plates sliding

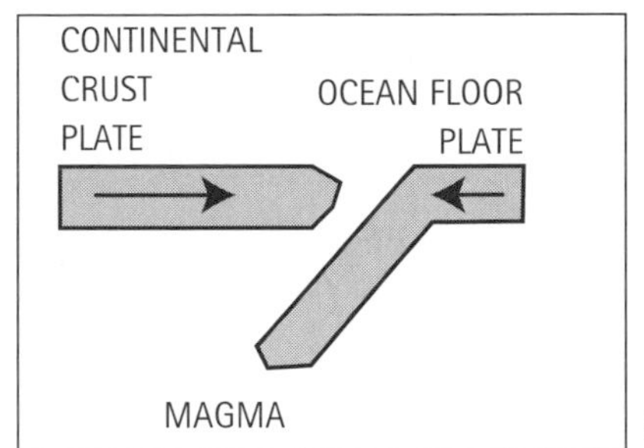

plates colliding

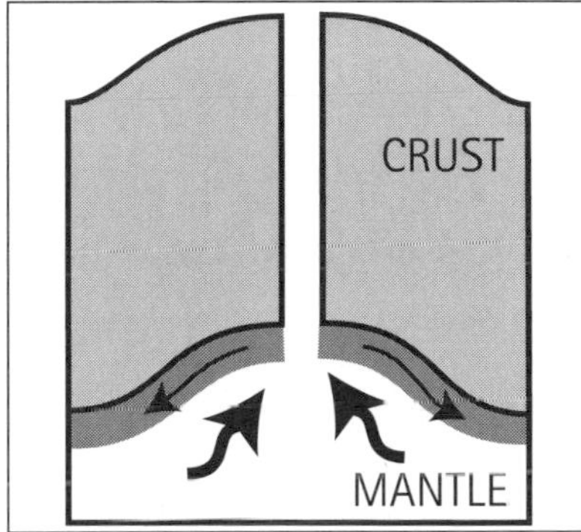

plates moving away

The video explains earthquakes, plate tectonics and the difference between S and P waves.

Rock cycle

The rock cycle shows how rocks are constantly being formed and broken down.

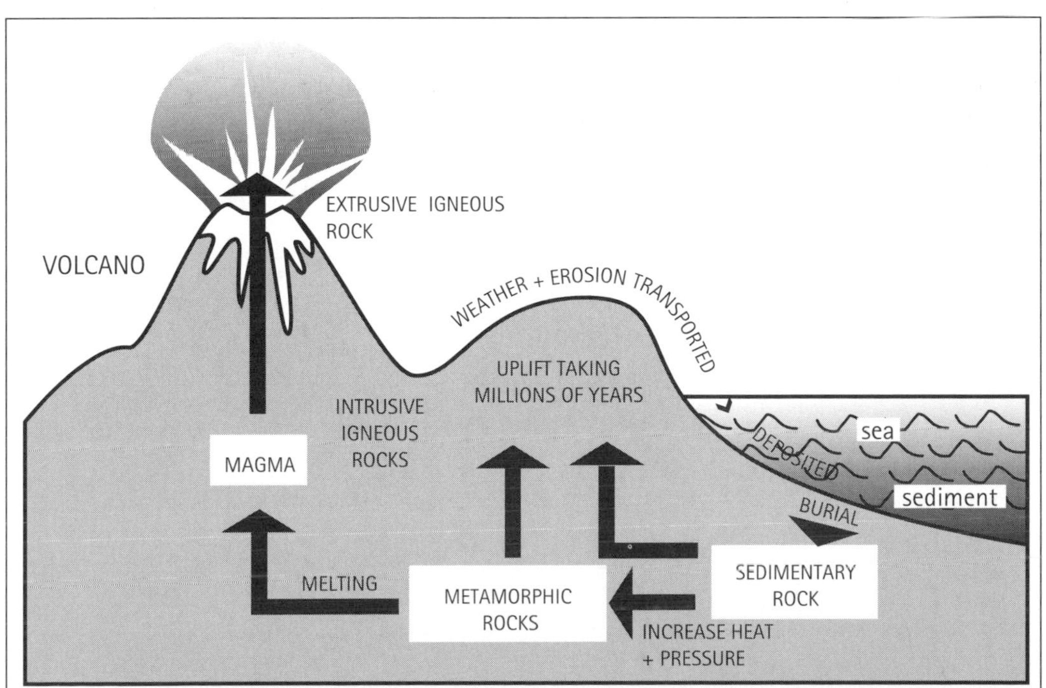

Plate tectonics

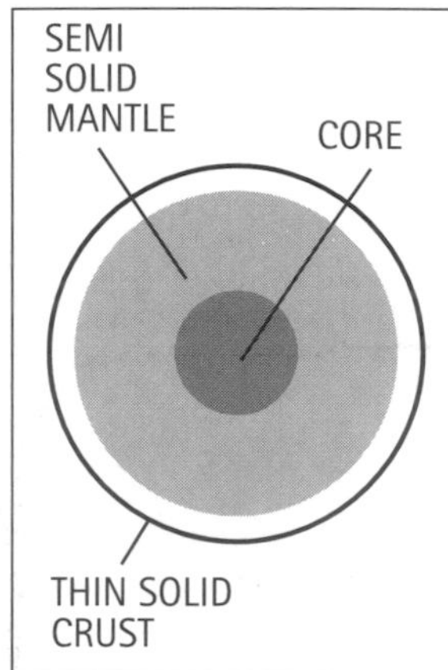

The Earth is a layered structure, as shown in the picture on the left.

The Earth's crust is a set of adjacent, slow-moving plates called **tectonic plates**. These are shown in the picture below.

The plates move as a result of convection currents within the Earth's mantle.

h The energy required for these convection currents comes from radioactive decay within the Earth.

The plates can move in three different ways, which have different effects on the Earth:

- when plates slide past each other earthquakes occur
- when plates move apart (constructive plate margins) hot molten rock from the magma forms new rock
- when plates collide (destructive plate margins) mountains fold and often volcanoes and earthquakes occur

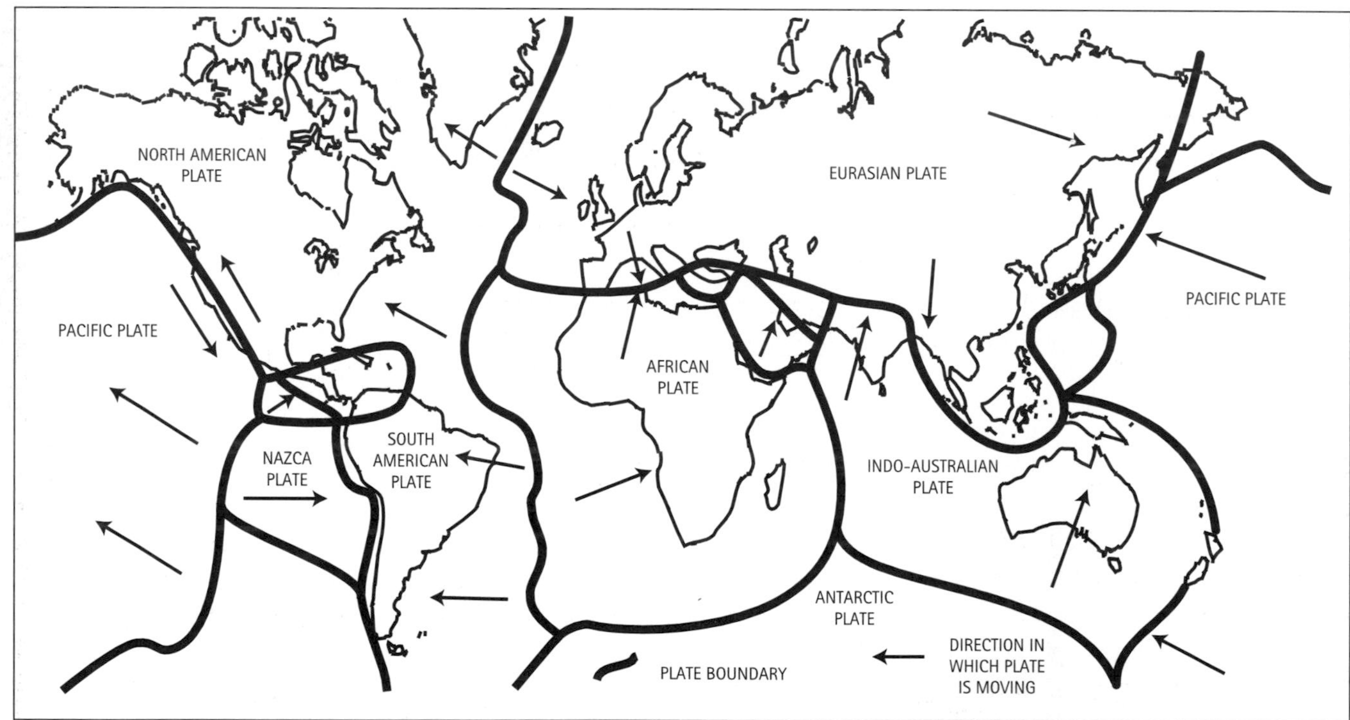

Practice Questions – Earth and air 1

1 a) Convection currents occur in the molten mantle of the Earth. The diagram below represents the structure of the inside of the Earth.

(i) Describe what you might expect to find at **Y**.

(ii) Suggest **two** effects that the convection currents would have on the ocean plates.

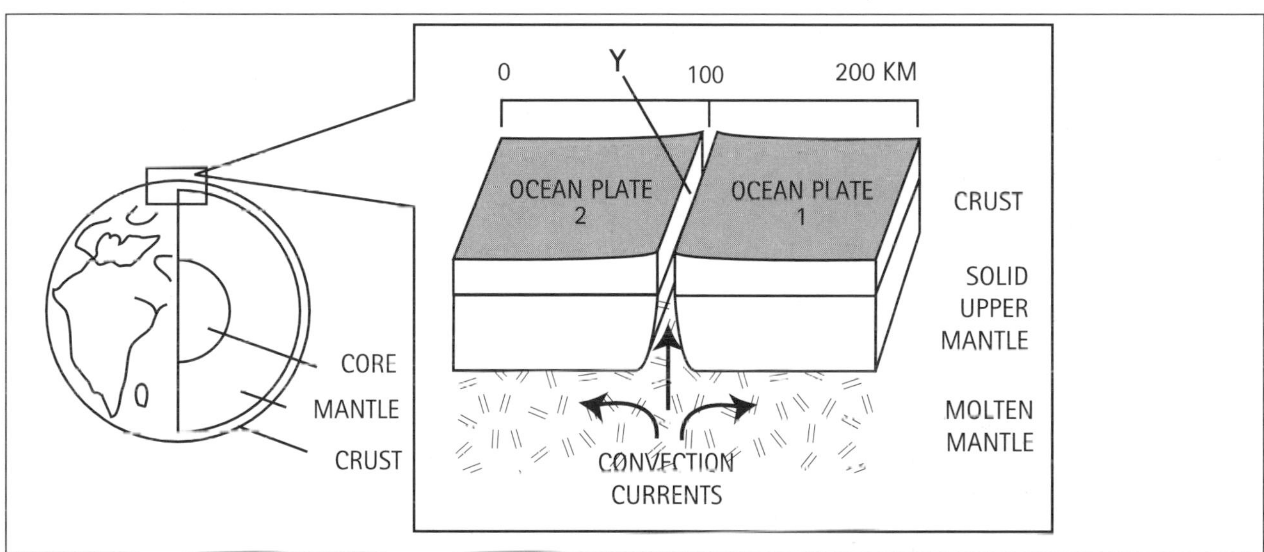

b) The diagrams below show how the map of the Earth has changed over the past 200 million years.

Suggest how this change could have happened and what might happen to the continents during the next 200 million years.

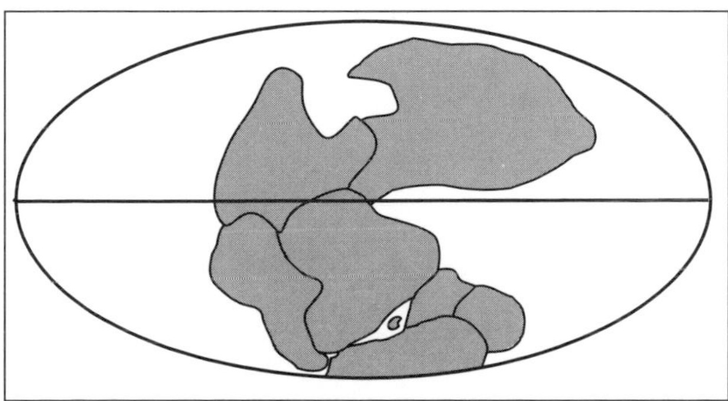

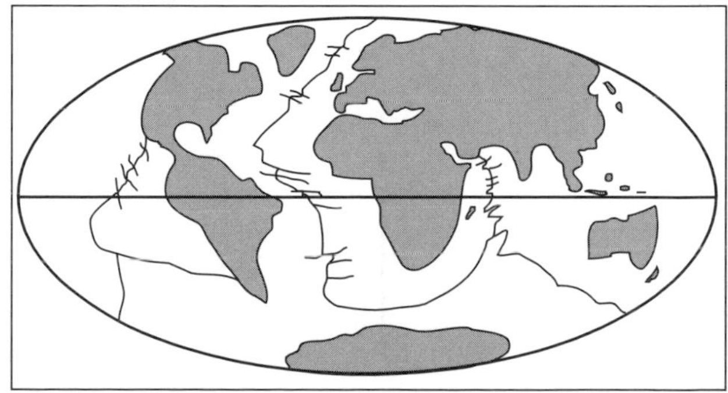

Rocks

There are three types of rocks: **igneous**, **sedimentary** and **metamorphic**.

Igneous rocks

Igneous rocks are formed by molten rock (**magma**) which is then cooled. The slower the rock cools, the bigger the crystals that are formed. Extrusive igneous rock is formed outside the Earth's crust and intrusive igneous rock is formed within the Earth's crust. Examples of igneous rocks include basalt (extrusive) and granite (intrusive).

> **REMEMBER** Extrusive rock is formed **out**side the Earth's crust and **in**trusive rock is formed with**in** the Earth's crust.

Does basalt or granite have the biggest crystals? Why?

Sedimentary rocks

Sedimentary rocks are formed by rock fragments being deposited (sediments) and compressed together. There are many stages in the formation of a sedimentary rock:

- weathering, which breaks up rocks. There are three types of weathering, which are the same as the three main areas of science: physical, chemical and biological
- erosion, which wears away the rocks
- transportation, which moves the rock fragments from one place to another
- deposition, when the rock fragments are deposited and layers form
- burial, as the layers move deeper into the Earth

Examples of sedimentary rocks include mudstone, limestone and sandstone. Fossils are found in sedimentary rocks.

In the picture below, which rock is the oldest?

> **REMEMBER** You should know examples of different types of rocks.

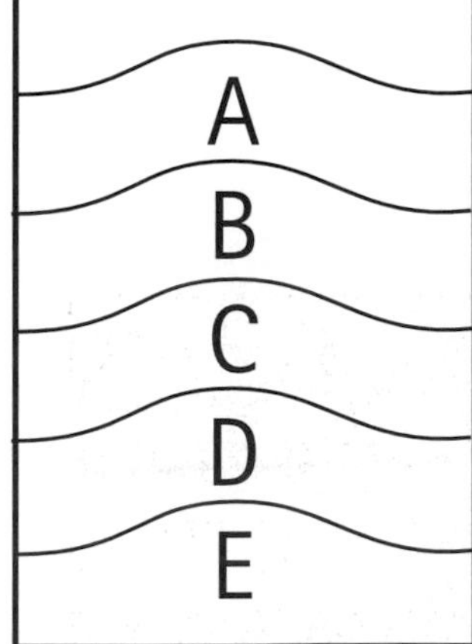

Metamorphic rocks

Metamorphic rocks are formed when rocks are changed by heat or pressure. For example, slate is formed from mudstone and marble is formed from limestone.

Rocks are used for building and for making statues.

Practice Questions – Earth and air 2

1 The diagram below gives an outline of how rocks are formed.

a) Name the types of rocks formed at **A** and **B**.

b) How is the sediment changed into sedimentary rock?

c) Suggest how the mountain may have been formed.

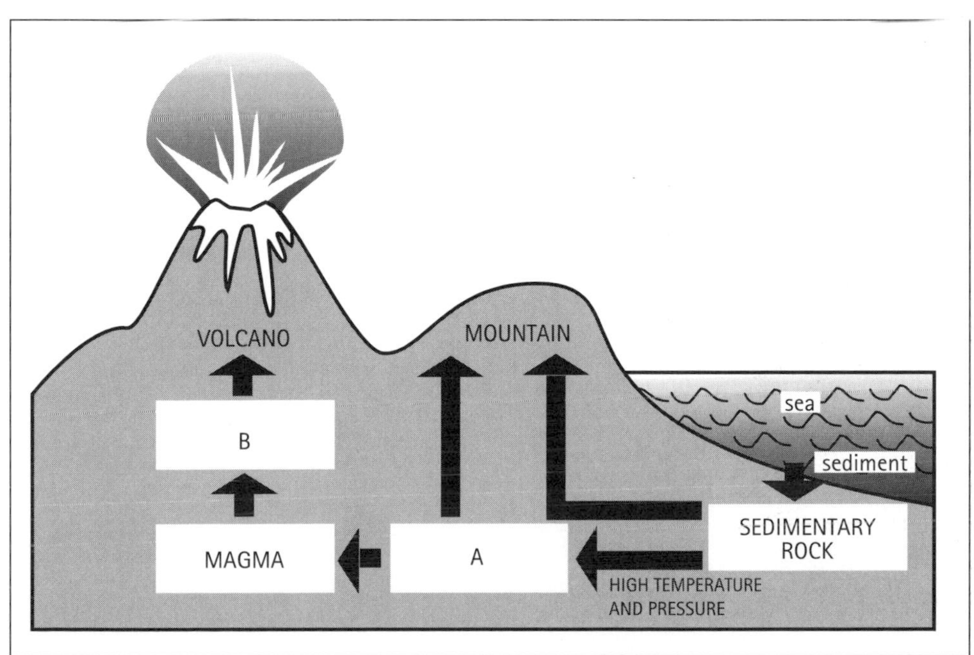

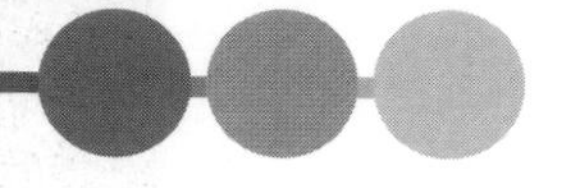

Changes in the atmosphere

The Earth was formed about 4500 million years ago. When it first formed, the atmosphere was very different to our atmosphere today, which evolved gradually over many millions of years.

Evolution of atmosphere

When the Earth's surface solidified, there were many volcanoes erupting, which gave off carbon dioxide, methane and ammonia gas.

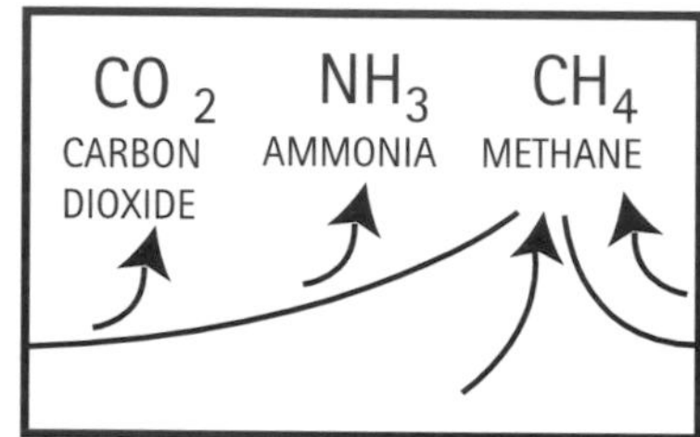

The water vapour that was formed condensed as the Earth cooled to form the oceans and seas.

By 500 million years ago plants had started to give out oxygen, which reacted with methane, and nitrifying microbes were producing nitrogen from ammonia.

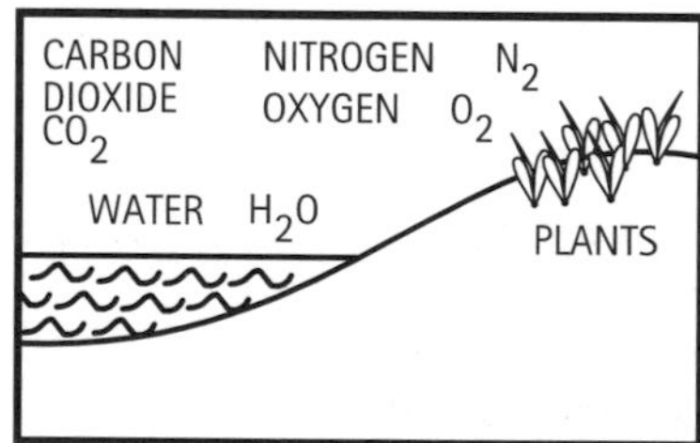

By 200 million years ago the Earth's atmosphere was as it is today.

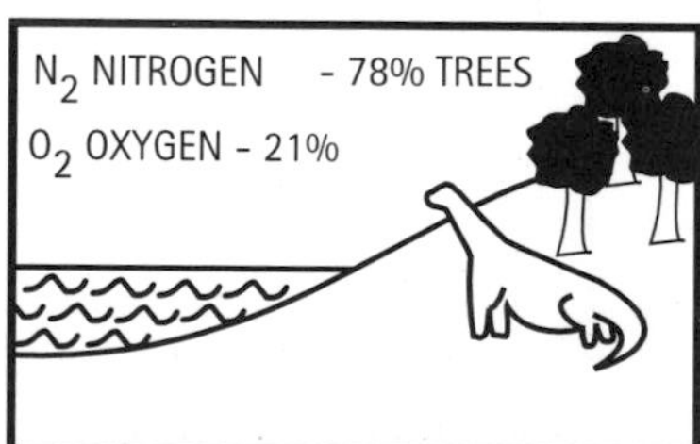

(h) Carbon dioxide gas is reduced by dissolving in the oceans to form carbonate.

(h) Nitrifying bacteria removed ammonia from the early atmosphere.

(TV) ◎ *Summarise in a time line like the one shown on the right the evolution of the atmosphere.*

400
300
200
100
1
MILLIONS OF YEARS AGO

The carbon cycle

The carbon cycle, which is illustrated below, helps to maintain the basic balance of the atmosphere.

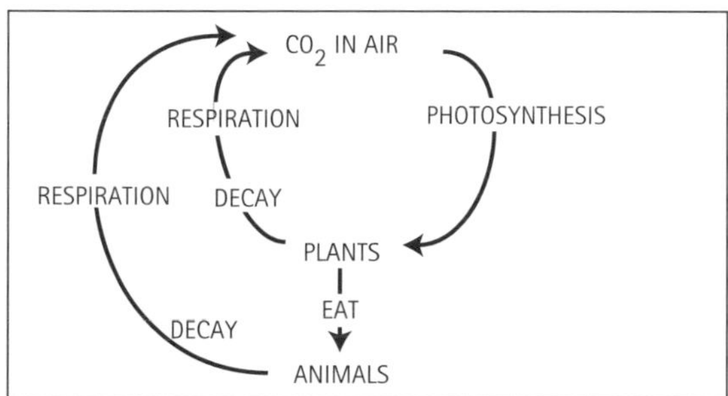

There is more information on photosynthesis on page 42 and on respiration on page 26.

(TV) The amount of carbon dioxide in the atmosphere must be balanced. If it's not there will be **global warming**.

◎ *Summarise the greenhouse effect, focusing on the effect on the carbon cycle.*

Practice Questions – Earth and air 3

1 The diagram below shows the carbon cycle.

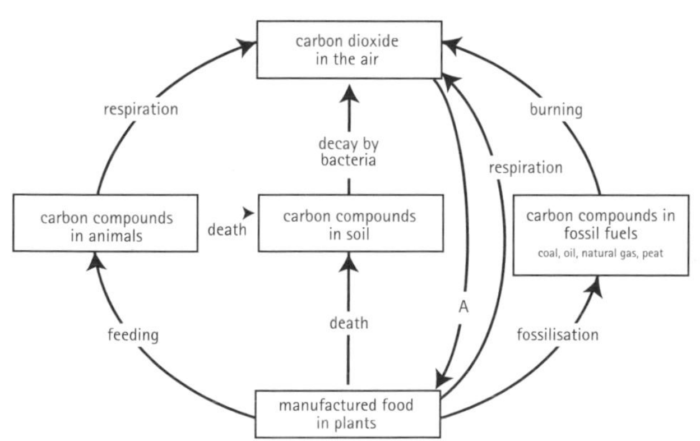

a) Use the diagram to write down **three** ways in which carbon dioxide is put back into the atmosphere.

b) Find the arrow labelled A.

(i) What is this process called?

(ii) What does it do to the amount of carbon dioxide in the atmosphere?

c) Over the past 100 years more fossil fuels have been burned.

(i) What change might this make to the amount of carbon dioxide in the air?

(ii) Some scientists are worried about a change in climate this might cause. What change in climate do they think might take place?

Electricity and magnetism

This section is about

- current, voltage and resistance in circuits
- electric charge and electrostatics
- electricity, energy and power
- using electricity
- electromagnetism
- generation and transmission of electricity

Electric current is a flow of charged particles around an electric circuit. The charges transfer energy from a battery or other power supply to the components in the circuit. Changing the resistance in a circuit changes the current. An electric current passes through a component when there is a voltage across the ends. The current through the component depends on the voltage across it.

When materials are rubbed together electrons are transferred from one material to the other, leaving one material positively charged and the other, which now has extra electrons, negatively charged. We can show by experiment that this charge is the same as the charge that creates an electric current.

The current from batteries is direct current (d.c.). It always flows in the same direction. The current from the mains is alternating current (a.c.). It changes direction 50 times a second.

Power is transmitted around the country along power lines. The power lines have resistance and get warm as the current passes through them. The energy lost in the power lines depends on the current and the resistance of the lines. Transformers are used to step up the voltage for transmission, so that the current is lower. When the power lines reach the community they serve, transformers step down the voltage to safer levels suitable for domestic electricity.

When an electric current flows in a wire, a magnetic field is created around the wire. This effect is used in electric motors, electric generators and transformers.

Although electricity is immensely useful, and it would be difficult to imagine a world without it, it can also be dangerous. A small electric current passing across the heart is enough to kill.

You must always take care when you are using electricity, particularly mains electricity, which can deliver high currents at fairly high voltages. Fuses and residual current devices are designed to protect the user and also to prevent damage to the device if there is a fault in the circuit.

FactZONE

You should know these circuit symbols

cell

power supply

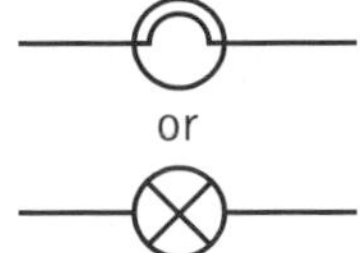

or

lamp

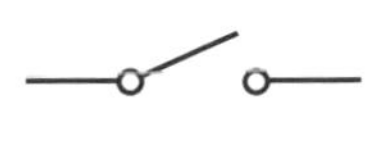

switch

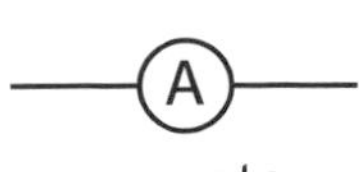

ammeter

voltmeter

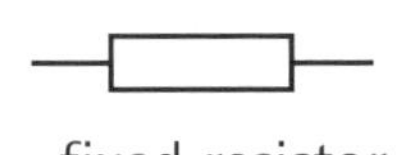

fixed resistor

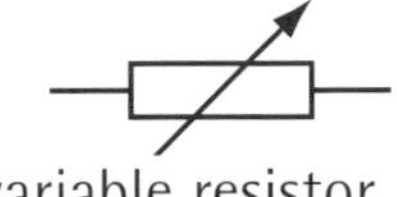

variable resistor

It is useful to know these symbols too

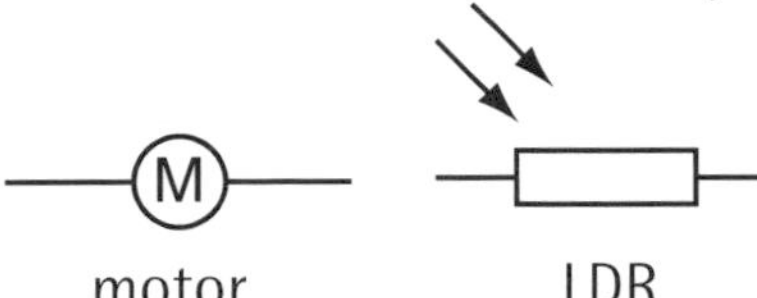

motor LDR

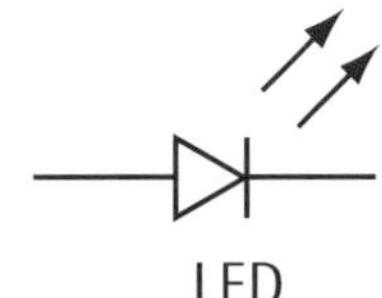

LED

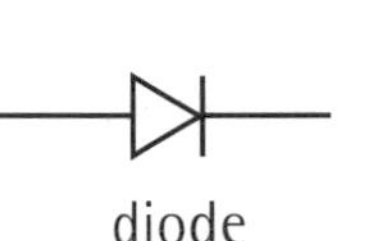

diode

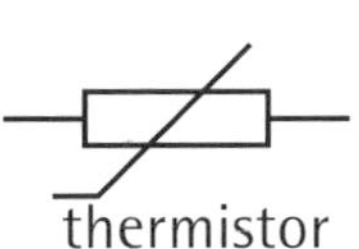

thermistor

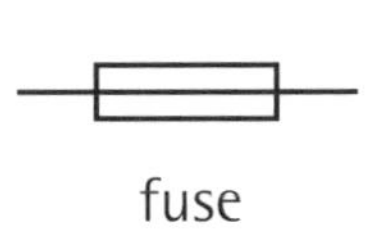

fuse

Units for measuring electrical quantities

electric current is measured in **amps** (A). The current is measured with an **ammeter**

voltage (potential difference) is measured in **volts** (V). Voltage is measured with a **voltmeter**

resistance is measured in **ohms** (Ω)

power is measured in **watts** (W)

(h) electric charge is measured in **coulombs** (C)

You need to know these relationships

voltage (volts) = current (amps) × resistance (ohms) $V = IR$

electrical power (watts) = voltage (volts) × current (amps) $P = VI$

energy (kilowatt-hours, kWh) = power (kilowatts, kW) × time (hours)

(h) $\text{voltage (volt)} = \dfrac{\text{energy (joule)}}{\text{charge (coulomb)}}$

(h) charge (coulombs) = current (amps) × time (seconds)

(h) for a transformer $\dfrac{\text{voltage across coil 1}}{\text{voltage across coil 2}} = \dfrac{\text{number of turns in coil 1}}{\text{number of turns in coil 2}}$

Electric current and voltage

An electric current transfers energy from the power supply to the components in the circuit. The current is a flow of electric charge. The same current leaves the power supply as returns to the supply.

An ammeter is placed in **series** in the circuit.

Series circuit

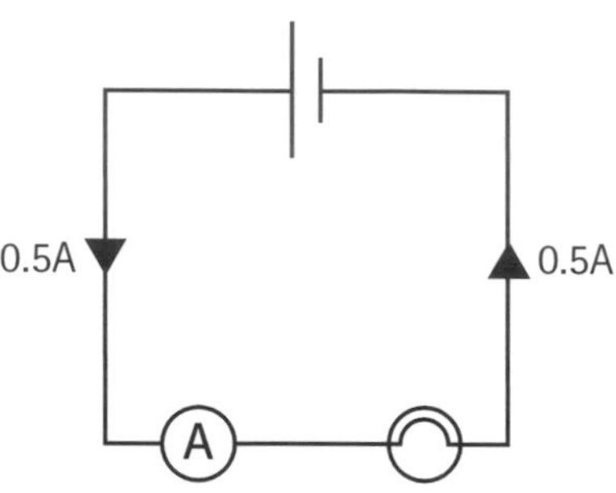

The current is the same all round the series circuit.

Parallel circuit

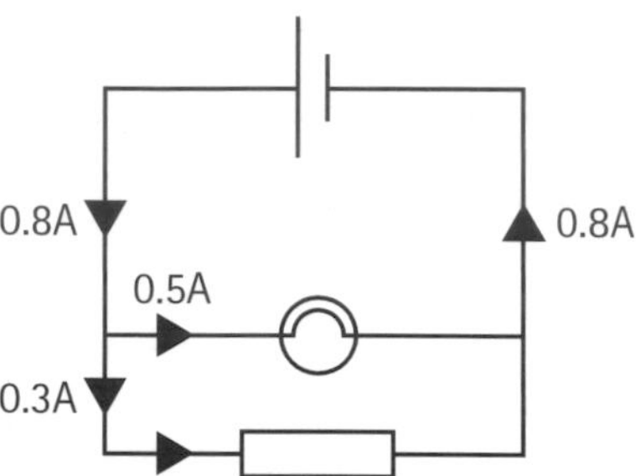

In a **parallel** circuit the currents flowing into a junction add up to the current going out.

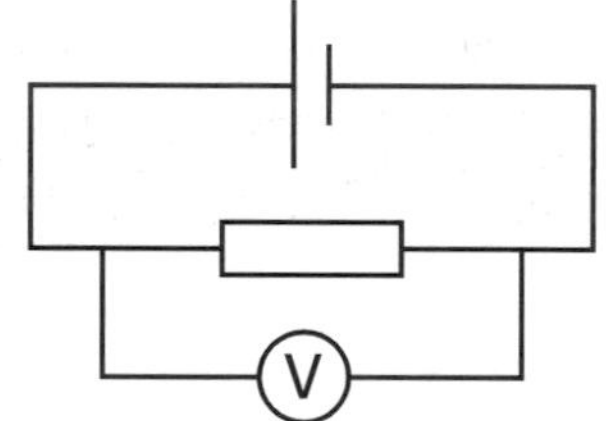

Can you name all the components in the circuit?

A current only passes through a component or wire if there is a voltage across it.

The bigger the voltage across a component the bigger the current through the component.

The smaller the voltage across a component the ________ the current through the component.

We connect a voltmeter across the component to measure the voltage.

REMEMBER Questions often ask where the ammeter or voltmeter should go in a circuit.

Resistance

Changing the **resistance** in a circuit changes the current. Most components have some resistance, but connecting wires have a low resistance.

The bigger the resistance the smaller the current (if the voltage does not change).

Some wires are designed to have resistance, we call them resistance wires. They are used to make variable resistors. The longer the resistance wire, the bigger the resistance.

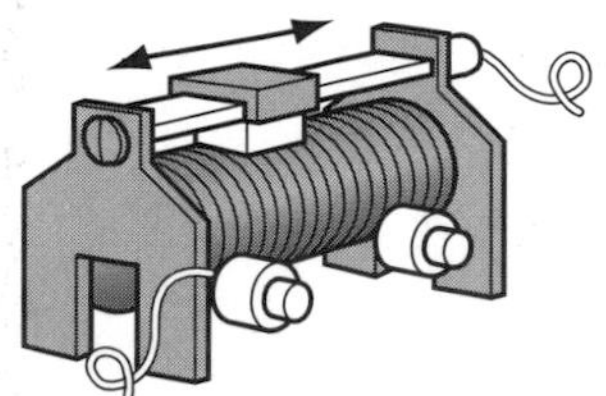

This is a variable resistor – what is the symbol?

Variable resistors can be used to control the current in a circuit. The longer the wire, the greater the resistance and the smaller the current. A lamp in the circuit will glow less brightly.

◎ *The shorter wire the __________ the resistance and the _________ the current. A lamp in the circuit will glow ________________.*

Resistors get hot when a current passes through them. The filament in a lamp is a very thin wire which gets hot when a current passes. The same effect heats the element in an electric fire or a hair drier.

The following equation relates voltage, current and resistance:

voltage (volts) = current (amps) × resistance (ohms)

Resistance can be worked out using:

$$\text{resistance (ohms)} = \frac{\text{voltage (volts)}}{\text{current (amps)}}$$

> **REMEMBER** You need to know this equation and be able to use it: V = IR

Practice Questions – Electricity and magnetism 1

1 Identify these circuit symbols:

a
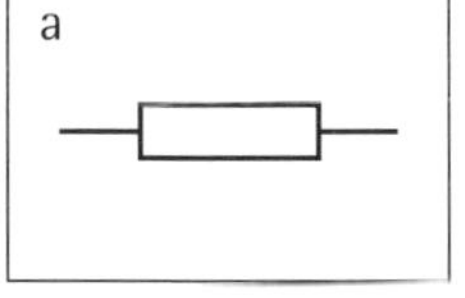

b
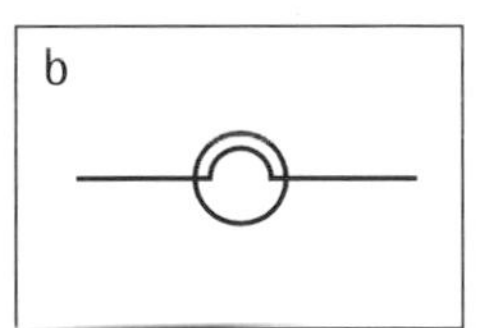
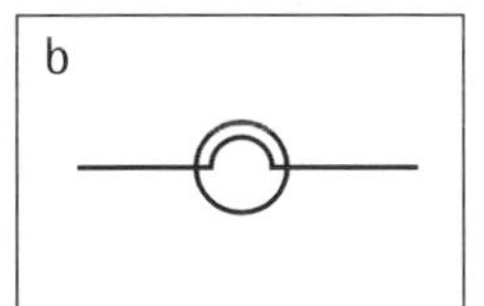

c
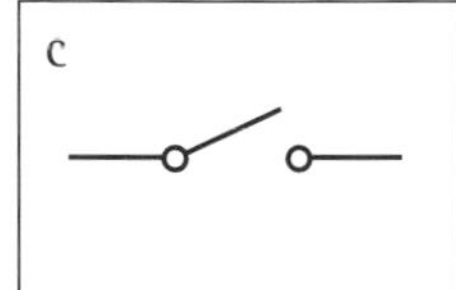

d
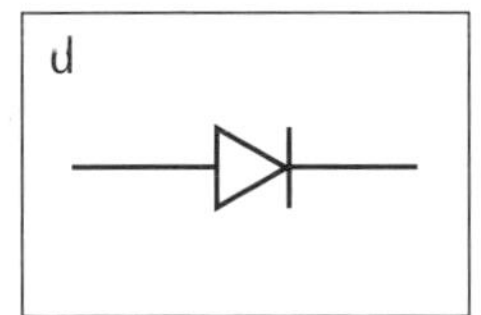
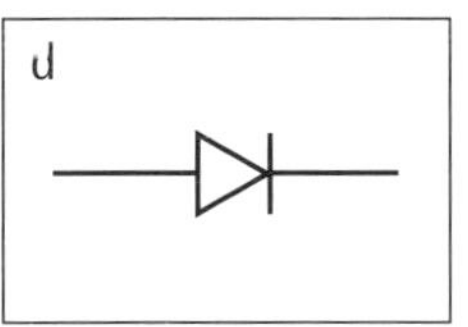

e
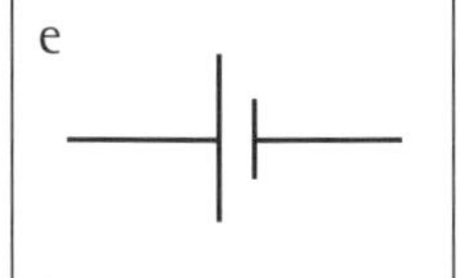

f
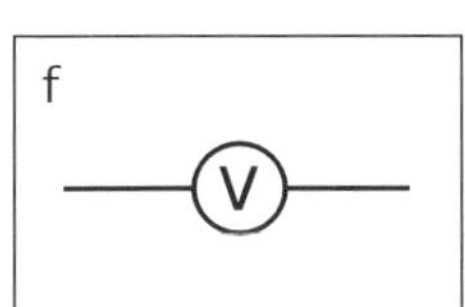
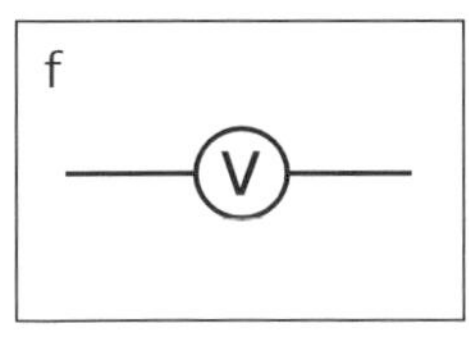

g
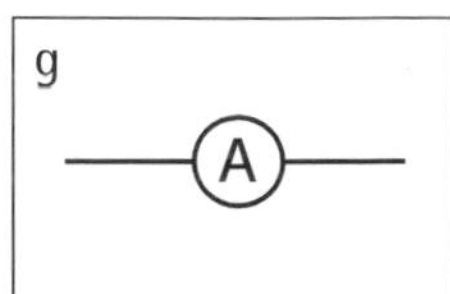

2 Peter is using the circuit below to find the resistance of a lamp.

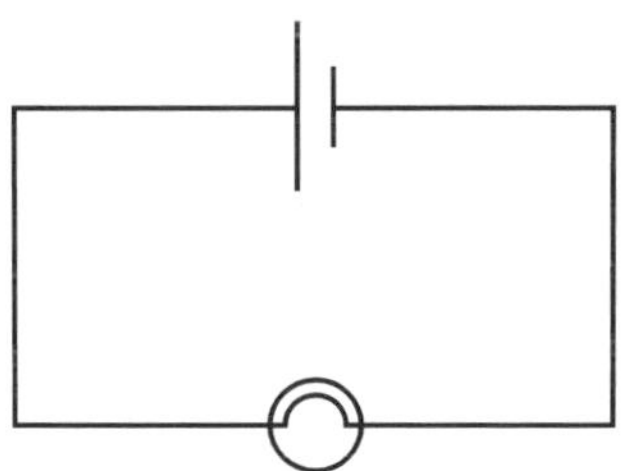

a) Peter uses a voltmeter to measure the voltage across the lamp. Draw a voltmeter on the diagram in the correct position.

b) What meter should Peter use to measure the current? Draw the meter on the diagram in the correct position.

c) When the voltage is 12 V the current is 3 amps. Calculate the resistance of the lamp.

More about electric current

Current–voltage graphs like the ones shown below tell us how the current passing through a component changes as the voltage changes.

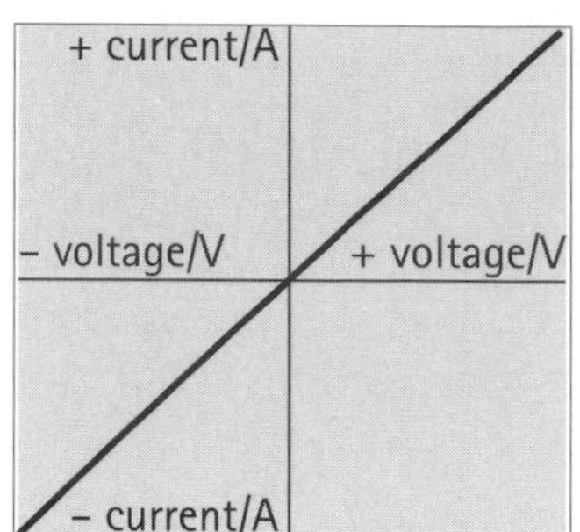

A resistor at a constant temperature has a constant resistance.

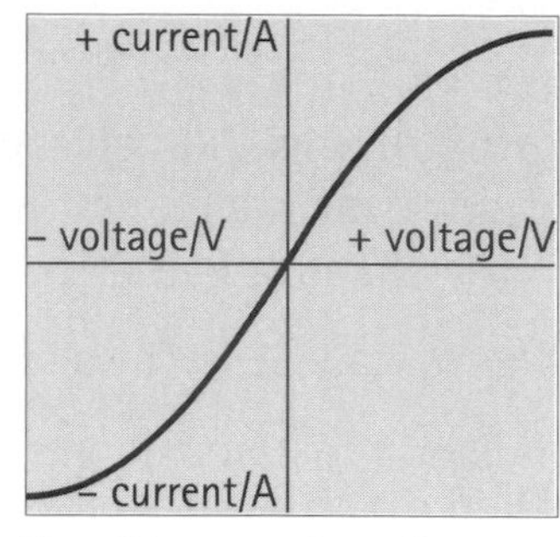

The filament in a lamp gets hotter as the voltage across it increases. As it gets hotter its resistance increases.

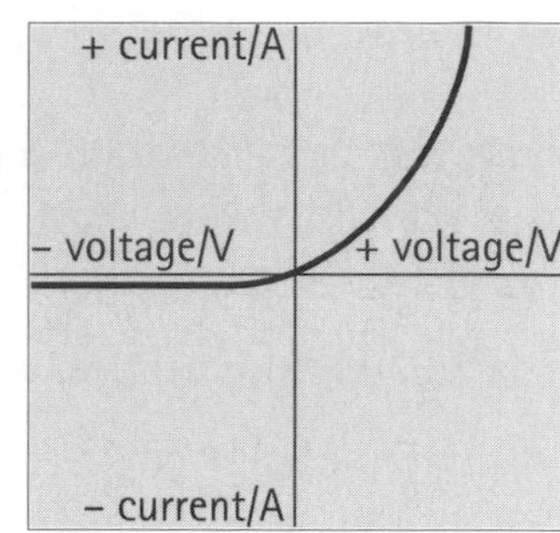

A diode only lets current pass one way. When the voltage is reversed no current passes.

What are the symbols for a resistor, a lamp and a diode?

An LDR is a light-dependent resistor. Its resistance gets less as the light level increases. Its resistance is high in the _________ and low in the _________.

The resistance of a thermistor gets less as its temperature increases. Its resistance is high when the thermistor is _________ and low when the thermistor is _________.

What happens to the current as a thermistor gets warmer?

Electric charge

When some materials are rubbed together they become charged. Electrons are being transferred from one material to the other.

The balloon gains electrons from the jumper and becomes _________ charged. The jumper has lost electrons so it becomes _______________ charged.

If the materials are insulators the charge does not leak away. We sometimes call this static charge:

- two objects with the same charge repel each other
- two objects with opposite charges attract each other

Static charge is used in photocopiers and also to remove ash from smoke in power stations.

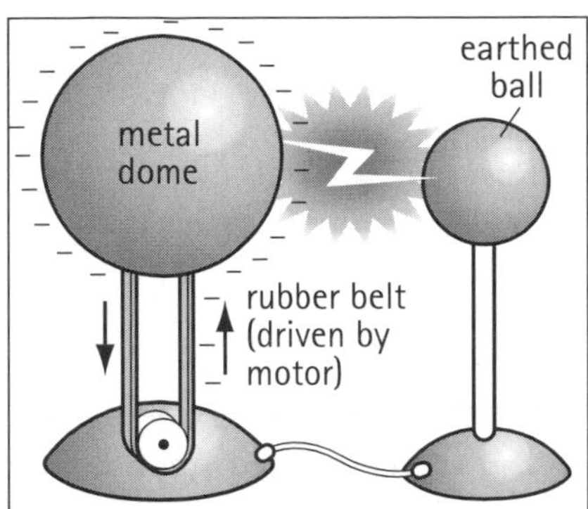

A build up of static charge causes sparking – like in the Van de Graaff generator shown above. This sparking can be dangerous, such as when refuelling aircraft.

Where else does static charge build up and cause problems?

Electric current is a flow of charge. The electric current in a solid conductor, such as metal, is a flow of electrons.

Electrolytes are chemical compounds which conduct electricity when molten or dissolved in water. The current in an electrolyte is a flow of ions. There is more about electrolytes on page 00 of this book.

REMEMBER You need to know this:

charge = current × time
(C) (I) (s)

The unit of electric charge is the coulomb (C). A current of 1 A is a flow of 1 C/s.

Practice Questions – Electricity and magnetism 2

1 Describe and explain what happens to the resistance of a lamp as the voltage in the circuit is increased.

2 When Anna brushes her hair it begins to stick out and stand on end, as shown in the picture on the right. Write an explanation of why this happens.

3 Explain why the hose from a petrol tanker is earthed before petrol is delivered.

Electricity, energy and power

Batteries, solar cells and generators are sources of energy. The electric current transfers the energy to components in the circuit.

Resistors become warm when a current passes through them. Electrical heating is used in many ways in the home.

The rate at which energy is transferred to the circuit is the **power**. Power is measured in watts (W) and kilowatts (kW). One kilowatt is 1000 watts.

> **REMEMBER** You need to know this equation and be able to use it: power = V × I

What is the power rating of a 100 W light bulb in kW?

We calculate electrical power using the equation:

power (watts, W) = voltage (volts , V) × current (amps, A)

Anna uses an immersion heater to heat some water. The voltmeter reads 12 V and the ammeter reads 4 A. What is the power transferred from the power supply to the heater?

> **REMEMBER** (h) The voltage is the energy transferred by each coulomb of charge:
> $$\text{voltage (V)} = \frac{\text{energy (J)}}{\text{charge (C)}}$$

power (W) = voltage (V) × current (A)

power = ____________ V × ____________ A

power = 48 watts

The cost of electricity

The amount of energy transferred to an electrical appliance depends on the time it is switched on and the power of the appliance.

The electricity meter measures the energy supplied by the electricity company. It measures energy in units called kilowatt-hours (kWh). One kilowatt-hour is the energy transferred when 1000 watts is transferred for one hour.

> **REMEMBER** You need to be able to calculate the cost of running an electrical appliance.

We can calculate the energy transferred by an appliance using:

energy (kilowatt-hours, kWh) = power (kilowatts, kW) × time (hours)

The electricity bill tells us how much a 'unit' of electricity costs – that is the cost for one kilowatt-hour. A unit of electricity costs about 7 pence.

What is the cost of running a 2kW electric heater which is switched on for 3 hours?

energy transferred in 3 hours = ____ kW × ____ hours = 6 kWh

cost = ___ units × __ pence per unit = 42 pence

Keeping safe

 Electricity is supplied to houses through the live wire and returns through the neutral wire. Normally the earth wire does not carry a current.

The wires in a mains cable are insulated to make sure no current passes between the live wire and the neutral and earth wires.

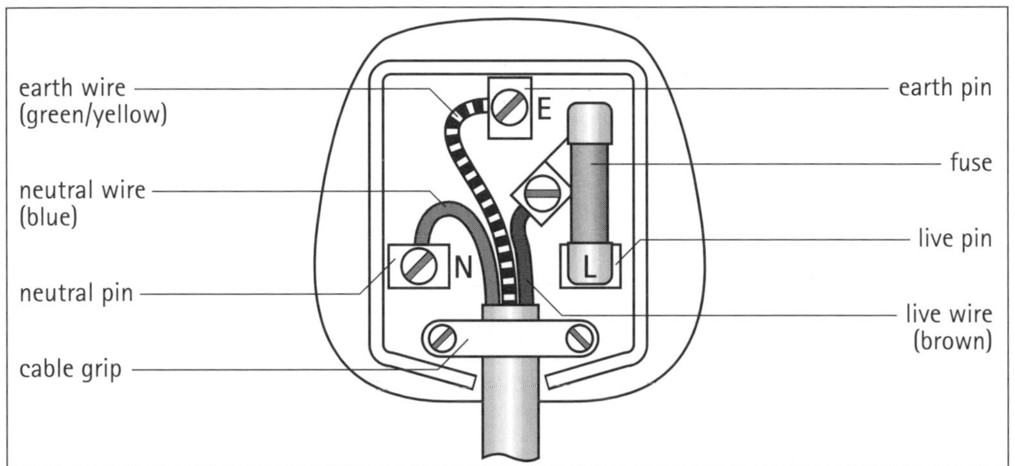

The fuse in the plug shown in the picture above will melt and break the circuit if too much current passes through the live wire.

If a metal part of an appliance, such as the strings on an electric guitar, becomes live due to a fault, the current should flow away through the earth wire. The large current should blow the fuse.

If you touched the live strings the charge would flow through you. It takes a much smaller current to kill you than to blow the fuse. A circuit breaker is much more sensitive to faults in the circuit than a fuse.

REMEMBER You should be able to explain how a fuse and circuit breakers protect a circuit.

Practice Questions – Electricity and magnetism 3

1 A lamp is connected to a 12 V battery. A current of 3 A passes through the lamp. What is the rate of transfer of energy?

2 A 200 W security light is switched on for 10 hours. Electricity costs 7 p per unit.

a) What is the power rating of the light in kilowatts?

b) How much energy is transferred by the light in 10 hours?

c) What is the cost of running the light for 10 hours?

(h) 3 A cooker ring is rated at 920 W. The mains voltage is 230 V.

a) What will be the current passing through the cooker ring?

b) How much charge will pass through the cooker ring in 20 minutes?

Electromagnetism

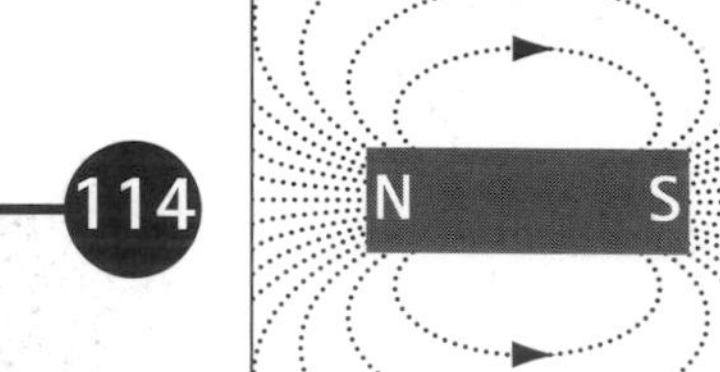

The magnetic field lines around a magnet show the direction of the forces around the magnet, as shown in the picture on the left.

If a magnet is free to turn it will come to rest pointing north-south.

We call the end that points to the north, the north-seeking pole of the magnet, or north pole for short.

The end that points to the south is the ________________ pole.

When two magnets are brought close together their magnetic fields interact. The like (NN or SS) poles repel each other, while opposite poles (N and S) attract each other.

There is a magnetic field near a wire carrying an electric current. The field near a single wire is circular, as shown in the picture below.

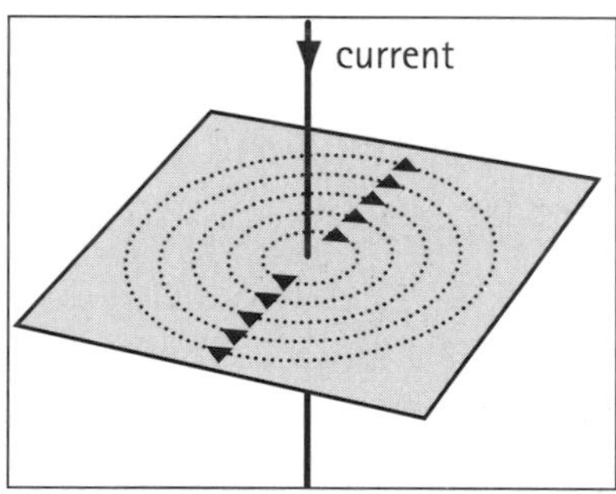

The field near a coil carrying an electric current looks very similar to the field near a bar magnet. It is shown in the picture below.

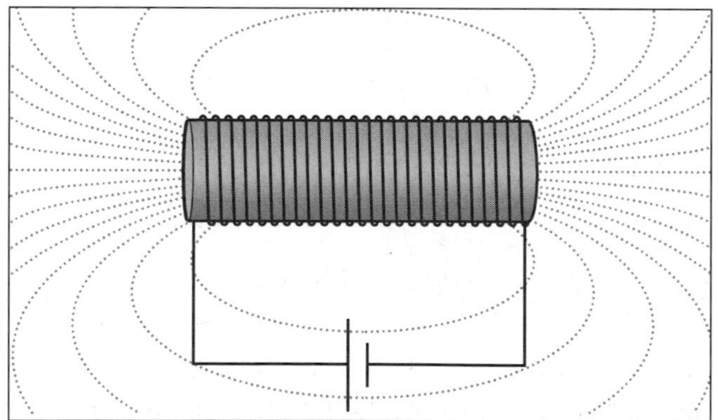

REMEMBER Changing the direction of the current changes the direction of the magnetic field.

We can make the field near a coil stronger by:

- putting an iron bar through the middle of the coil
- increasing the current in the coil
- increasing the number of turns in the coil

Electromagnets are used in bells and relays.

Find out how bells and relays work.

Electric motors

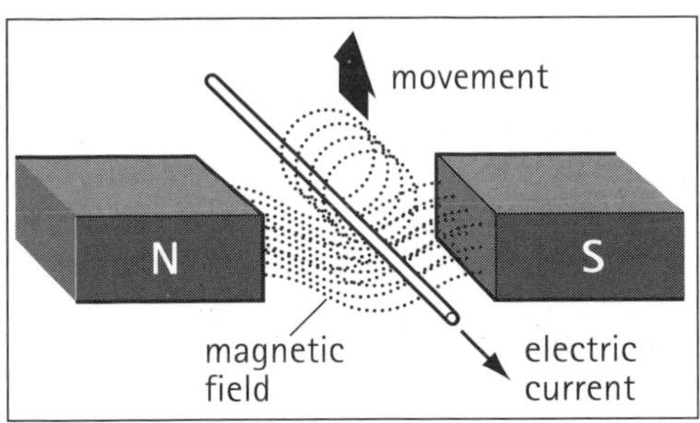

The magnetic field from the current in the wire and the magnetic field from the magnets interact. The wire is forced upwards.
The direction of the force is reversed if the direction of the current or the field is reversed.

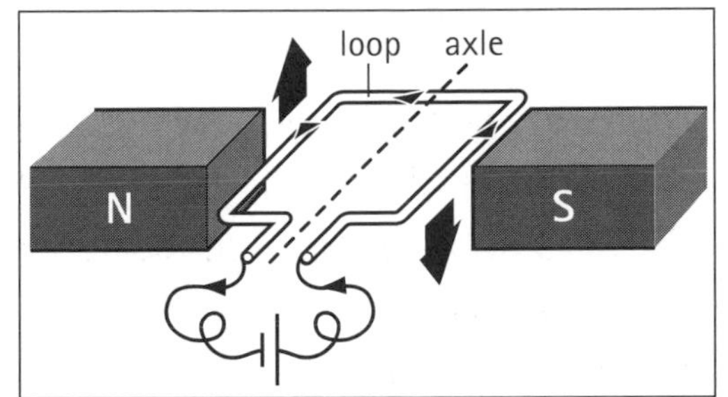

A coil carrying a current is in a magnetic field. The field from the coil interacts with the field from the magnets. All the wires on one side are forced up and all the wires on the other side of the coil are forced down The coil spins. This is a simple electric motor.

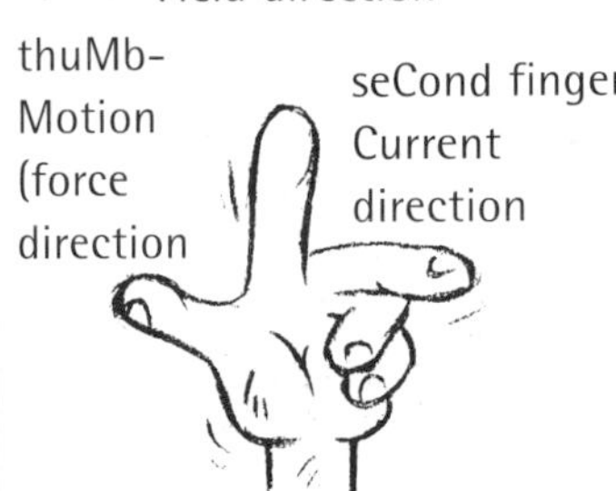

There is a force on a wire carrying an electric current in a magnetic field. The force, the field and the current are all at right angles to each other.

Electromagnetic induction

Moving a magnet into a coil, as shown in the picture on the right, produces a voltage across the ends of the coil. When the magnet is pulled out the voltage is reversed. If the magnet is stationary there is no voltage.

This way of generating a voltage is called **electromagnetic induction**.

Electricity can be generated by rotating a magnet inside a coil or by rotating a coil in a magnetic field.

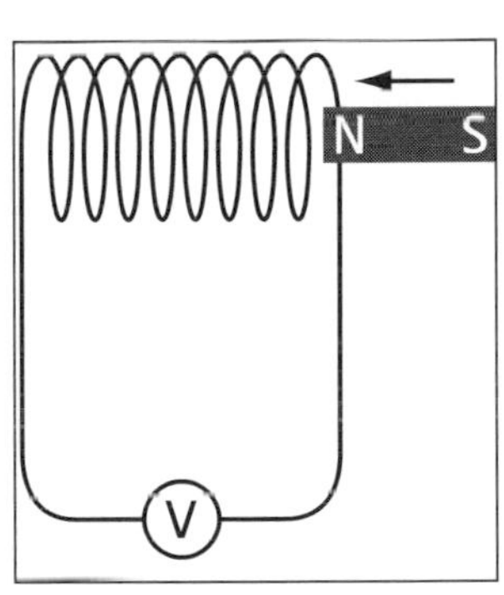

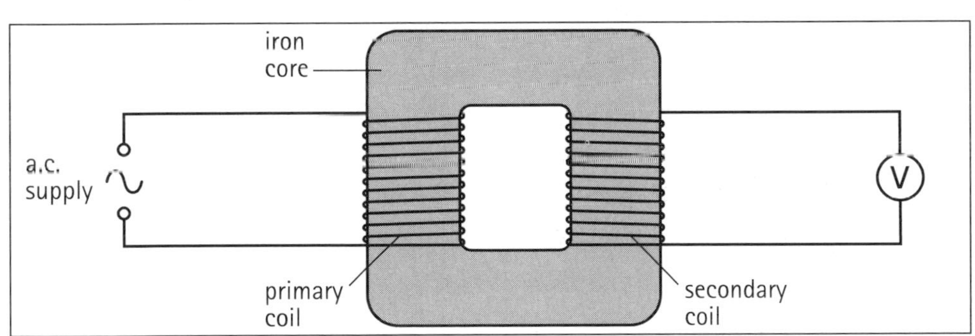

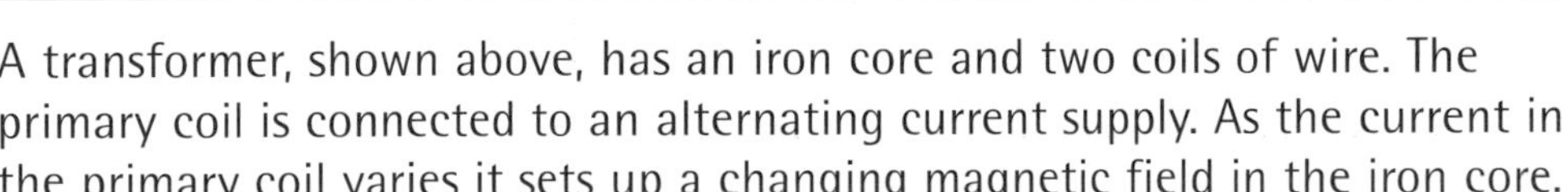

A transformer, shown above, has an iron core and two coils of wire. The primary coil is connected to an alternating current supply. As the current in the primary coil varies it sets up a changing magnetic field in the iron core.

The changing field in the iron core induces a changing voltage in the secondary coil. The voltage in the secondary coil depends on the number of turns on the coil. The bigger the number of turns the bigger the voltage.

REMEMBER You need to know the equation for a transformer. It is given on page 107 of this book

Generation and transmission

Most of our electricity is generated in coal-burning power stations. Coal is burnt in a furnace, and the energy from the coal is used to boil water to produce steam. The steam is used to drive turbines, which turn generators. The generators produce electricity.

Electricity is transmitted around the country on the National Grid – a network of high-voltage cables. Although the cables are good conductors, they are very long and have some resistance. As current passes through the cables, they are warmed and energy is lost.

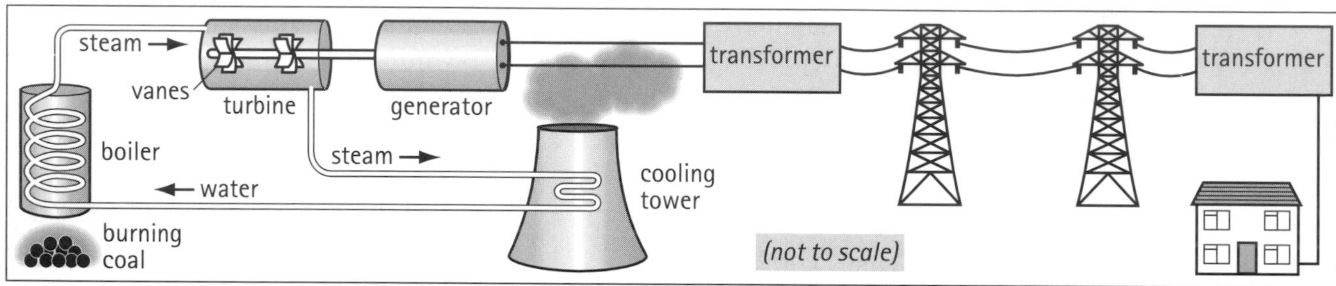

REMEMBER To reduce the energy losses in power lines we use transformers. Transformers only work on a.c.. So we use a.c. for transmission.

Where are the energy losses in generating and transmitting electricity?

Transformers at the power station step up the a.c. electricity to a high voltage for transmission on the National Grid. The higher the voltage, the lower the current, to transmit the same power.

Because the current is low there is less energy lost in heating the power lines. This is more efficient – more energy reaches the customers.

Local step-down transformers reduce the voltage to a safer level for use by customers.

Direct current (d.c.) and alternating current (a.c.)

The current from batteries is direct current. It is always in the same direction and does not change in size.

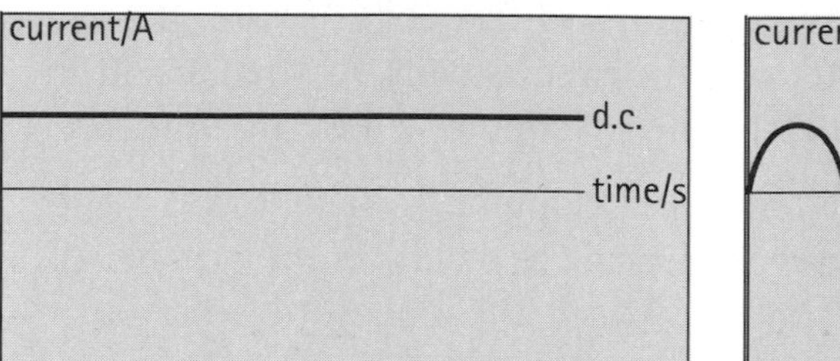

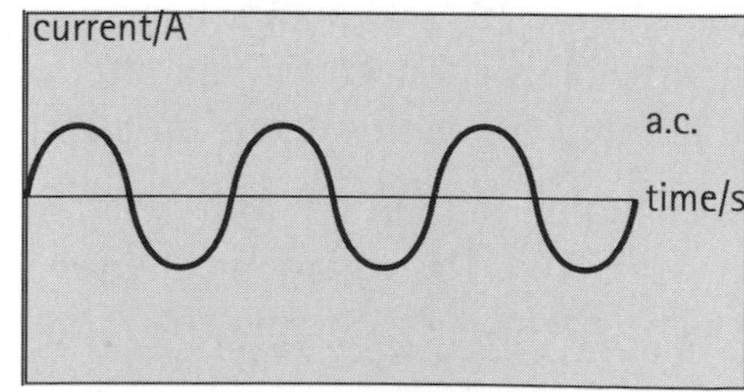

An alternating current is constantly changing direction. Mains electricity is an a.c. supply. The direction of the current changes 50 times per second. The frequency is 50 Hz.

Exam Question – Electricity and magnetism

Joe wanted to find out how the current and voltage changed in a circuit. First he connected three cells, a variable resistor, a lamp and an ammeter as shown in the picture below.

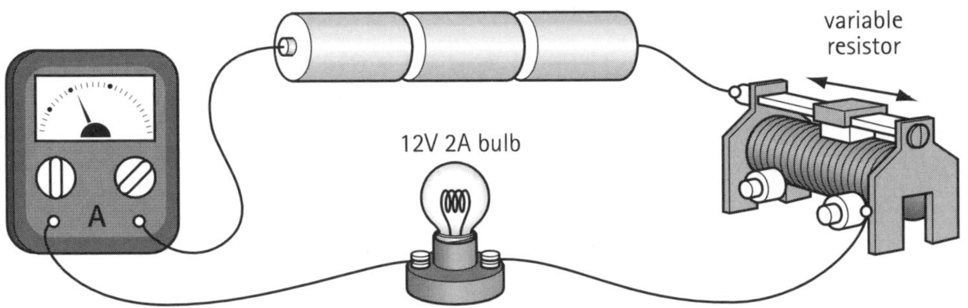

a) Joe did not know where to place the voltmeter to measure the potential difference across the bulb. Add to the diagram by putting the **circuit symbol** for the voltmeter in the correct place.

b) (i) What could Joe do to the variable resistor to increase the brightness of the lamp?

(ii) Explain why this increases the brightness of the lamp.

c) After doing the experiment Joe recorded the results shown in the table.

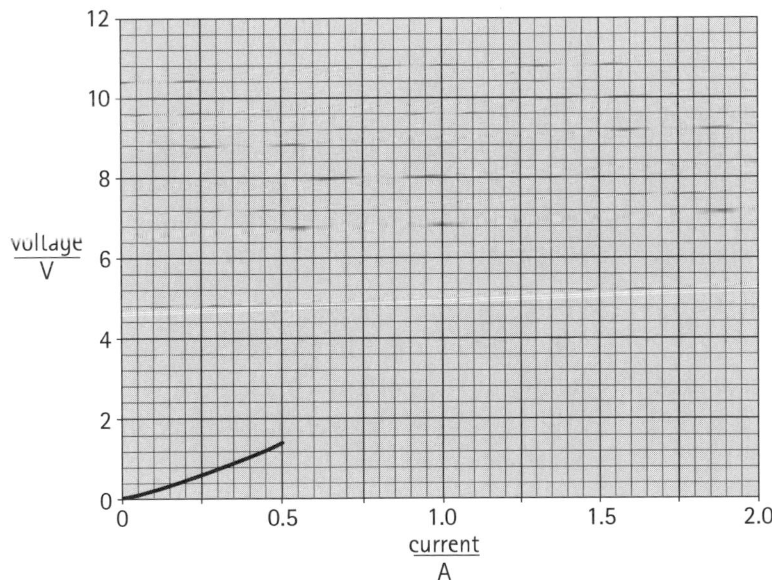

current (A)	voltage (V)
0.00	0.0
0.25	0.6
0.50	1.4
0.75	2.4
1.00	3.6
1.25	5.0
1.50	6.0
1.75	9.0
2.00	12.0

(i) Plot the results on the graph. The first three have been done for you.

(ii) Finish the graph by drawing the best line. It has been started for you.

d) (i) Calculate the resistance of the filament when the potential difference is 6.0 V. Show how you work out your answer.

(ii) Describe how the resistance changes when the potential difference is increased from 0 to 12.0 V. Justify your answer by referring to your graph.

Forces and motion

This section is about

- pressure on solids, liquid and gases
- stretching materials
- distance, speed, velocity and acceleration
- forces affect the motion of objects
- falling objects

There are many forces that may act on an object, for example, gravitational forces, frictional forces and contact forces. These forces might change the shape of an object, change the speed of a moving object or change the direction of a moving object.

Pressure tells us whether a force is concentrated on a small area or spread out over a large area. When a gas is under pressure it takes up less space – the higher the pressure, the smaller the volume (Boyle's Law).

A liquid cannot be compressed. Hydraulic machines rely on the fact that liquids are not compressed. The hydraulic fluid transmits pressure from one place to another.

Some solids change shape when a force is put on them. For example, rubber band or a spring stretches when a force acts on it. Other materials, including metal wires and wood, stretch too.

There are usually several forces acting on an object. If these forces are balanced the object will remain stationary or continue to move at a steady speed in a straight line.

If the forces on an object are out of balance, the object will begin to move, will accelerate (speed up), will decelerate (slow down) or will change direction.

The effect of a force depends on the mass of the object. The bigger the mass, the bigger the force needed to give it an acceleration. The bigger the force applied, the bigger the acceleration.

When an object falls it is being pulled towards the Earth by the force of gravity. An object falling in the Earth's atmosphere will also be affected by air resistance. The size of the air resistance is related to the speed of the moving object – the bigger the speed, the bigger the air resistance.

FactZONE

Some words to know

pressure: the effect of a force on an area

elastic: an elastic material is one that returns to its original shape when the force on it is removed, e.g. rubber

elastic limit: the maximum force that can be put on a material and it still returns to its original shape. Beyond its elastic limit the material is permanently deformed, e.g. an overstretched spring

plastic: a material that keeps the new shape when the force is removed, e.g. clay

gravity: the attractive force between two masses. The force is only noticeable if at least one of the masses is very large (like the Earth or Moon)

friction: the force that resists motion

speed: the rate at which something moves

velocity: tells us the speed of a moving object and its direction

acceleration: the rate at which something changes its speed. A negative acceleration is when something is slowing down. This is also called a deceleration

Some equations to know

$$\text{pressure (N/m}^2\text{)} = \frac{\text{force (N)}}{\text{area (m}^2\text{)}}$$

$$\text{speed (m/s)} = \frac{\text{distance travelled (m)}}{\text{time taken (s)}}$$

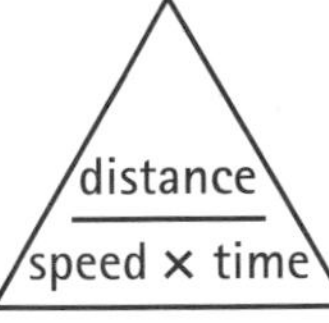

force (N) = mass (kg) × acceleration (m/s^2)

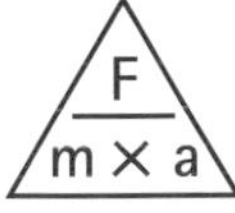

$$\text{acceleration (m/s}^2\text{)} = \frac{\text{change in velocity (m/s)}}{\text{time taken}}$$

Forces on materials

Contact forces

When two objects are in contact they exert equal and opposite forces on each other. These forces are called contact forces or reaction forces. The force from the springs in a chair pushes up on you as your weight pushes down to compress the springs.

Pressure

Why is it easier to cut an apple with a sharp knife than with a blunt one? The effect of a force depends on the area over which it acts. This effect is the **pressure**.

The smaller the area, the more concentrated the force, the __________ the pressure.

A camel has big feet so that it does not sink into the sand.

The bigger the area, the more spread out the force, the __________ the pressure.

We can calculate pressure using the equation:

$$\text{pressure (N/m}^2\text{)} = \frac{\text{force (N)}}{\text{area (m}^2\text{)}}$$

The standard unit for measuring pressure is N/m^2 or pascals (Pa). If the area is measured in cm^2, the pressure will be in N/cm^2.

REMEMBER You need to know and be able to use the equation to calculate pressure.

A person weighing 600 N stands on heels with an area of 3 cm^2. What is the pressure on the floor?

$$\text{pressure (N/m}^2\text{)} = \frac{\text{force (N)}}{\text{area (m}^2\text{)}}$$

$$\textit{pressure (N/cm}^2\textit{)} = \frac{\_\_\_\_\ N}{\_\_\_\_\ cm^2}$$

$$\text{pressure} = 200\ \text{N/cm}^2$$

Pressure in liquids

The force of gravity pulls down on liquids. The weight of the liquid exerts a pressure on the container and anything in it. The pressure is greater the deeper you go.

When an inflatable shark is taken under water, the pressure of the water on the shark compresses the air inside. As the shark rises to the surface the pressure on the outside gets less and the gas expands to fill a bigger space. We see the same effect with bubbles in a bottle of fizzy drink in the picture on the right – they get bigger as they rise to the surface.

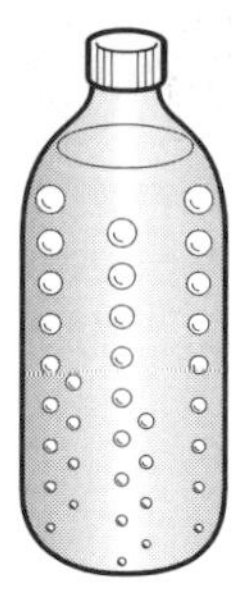

The pressure of liquids acts in all directions. Engineers need to remember this when designing a dam. Other engineers use liquids to transmit forces through the braking system of a car.

Pressure in gases

The molecules in a gas are free to move throughout the gas. They collide with the sides of the container creating pressure. If the pressure outside is greater than the pressure inside, the gas will be compressed until the pressures are equal.

When the inflatable shark in the picture on the right rises through the water the pressure on it gets less and the shark expands.

When the pressure doubles, the volume halves.

When the pressure is three times as big, the volume goes to _________.

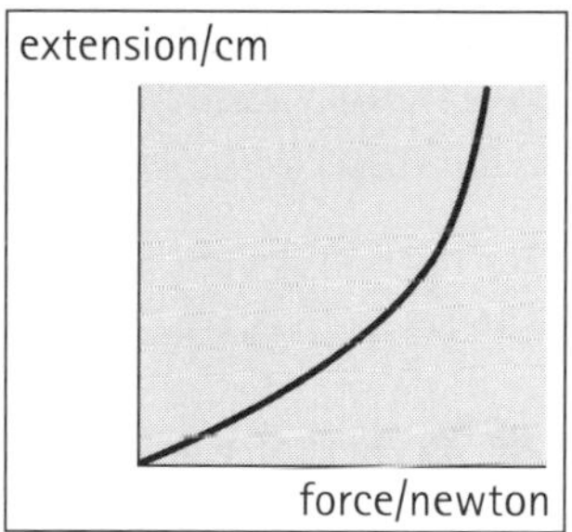

Describe what happened as this spring was stretched.

Name two elastic materials and two plastic materials.

Stretching forces

When a force is applied to a material it changes shape. Some materials keep their new shape when the force is removed. These materials are called plastic or inelastic.

Some materials return to their original shape when the force is removed. We call these materials elastic. When you pull an elastic material it stretches, and the harder you pull the more it stretches.

If you stretch a wire or spring too far it does not go back to its old shape. The material has reached its elastic limit.

Practice Questions - Forces and motion 1

1 A skier weighs 600 N, including his skis. The skis have an area of 3000 cm^2.

a) What is the pressure on the snow when the skier stands on the skis?

b) What happens to the pressure on the ground if he only stands on one ski?

2 The picture shows the springs from a chest expander arranged in three different ways.

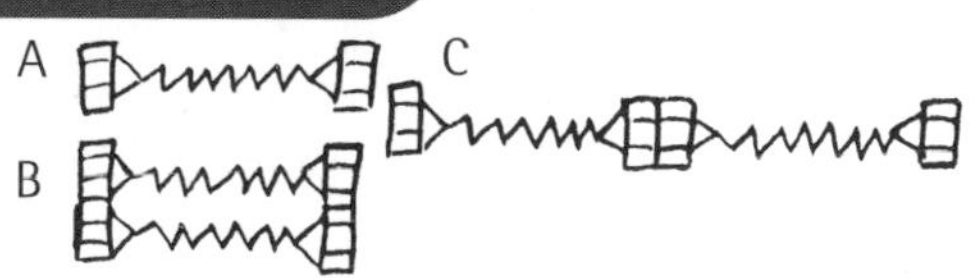

a) Which arrangement is easiest to stretch?

b) Which is hardest to stretch?

c) Explain why the hardest arrangement needs four times the force of the easiest arrangement for the same stretch.

Distance, speed and acceleration

Distance and speed

If an object moves in a straight line, the average speed of the object can be worked out from the distance travelled and the time taken:

$$\text{speed (m/s)} = \frac{\text{distance travelled (m)}}{\text{time taken (s)}}$$

REMEMBER You need to know the equation for speed and how to calculate it. The standard unit for measuring speed in science is metres per second (m/s).

A boy on a bicycle travels 300 m in one minute (60 s). What is his average speed?

$$\text{speed (m/s)} = \frac{\text{distance travelled (m)}}{\text{time taken (s)}}$$

speed (m/s) = $\frac{\_\_\_\_\_\_ m}{\_\_\_\_\_\_ s}$

speed = 5 m/s

A distance-time graph like the one pictured below shows how far something goes in a certain time.

REMEMBER You should be able to describe the journey represented by this distance-time graph.

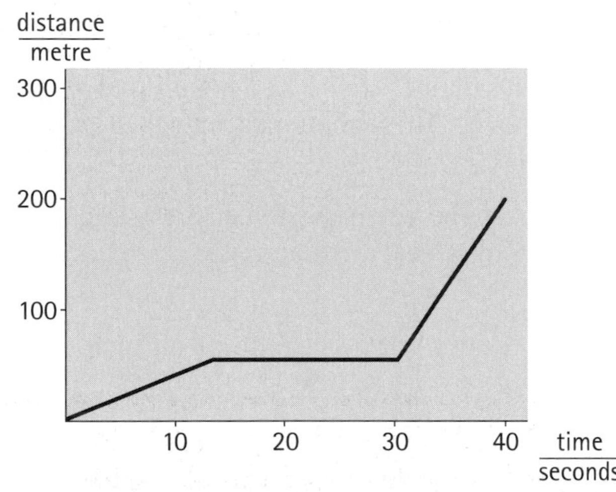

Velocity

The velocity of a moving object tells us the speed *and* the direction. When the space shuttle is being put into orbit, it is crucial that the scientists at NASA know how fast it is going and in which direction.

When the shuttle is in orbit around the Earth it is travelling at a constant speed, but it is changing direction all the time because it is being pulled by the Earth's gravity. Its velocity is constantly changing.

Acceleration

Acceleration tells us how much the velocity changes each second.

$$\text{acceleration (m/s}^2\text{)} = \frac{\text{change in velocity (m/s)}}{\text{time taken (s)}}$$

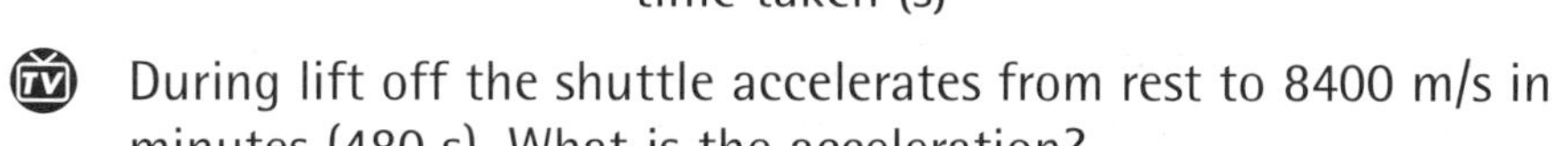

During lift off the shuttle accelerates from rest to 8400 m/s in 8 minutes (480 s). What is the acceleration?

$$\text{acceleration (m/s}^2\text{)} = \frac{\text{change in velocity (m/s)}}{\text{time taken (s)}}$$

acceleration $(m/s^2) = \frac{\_\_\_\_\_\_\_\_\_\_ \ (m/s)}{\_\_\_\_\_\_ \ (s)}$

acceleration = 17.5 m/s^2

What would it feel like to be accelerating at 17.5 m/s^2 *for 8 minutes?*

We can work out acceleration from a velocity-time graph like the one shown on the left:

change in velocity = 25 m/s

time taken = 10 s

$$\text{acceleration (m/s}^2\text{)} = \frac{\text{change in velocity (m/s)}}{\text{time taken (s)}}$$

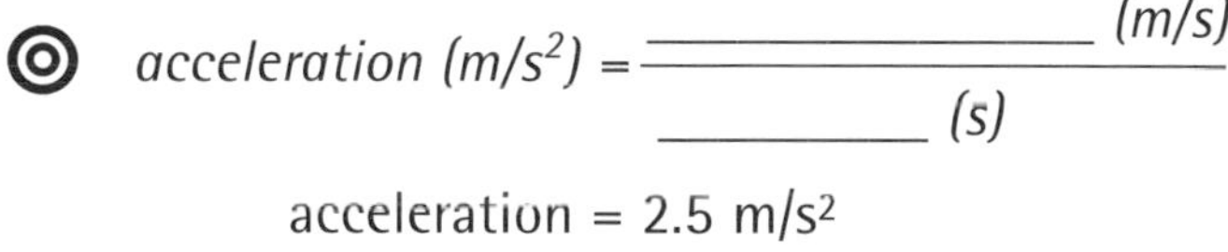

acceleration $(m/s^2) = \frac{\_\_\_\_\_\_\_\_\_\_ \ (m/s)}{\_\_\_\_\_\_ \ (s)}$

acceleration = 2.5 m/s^2

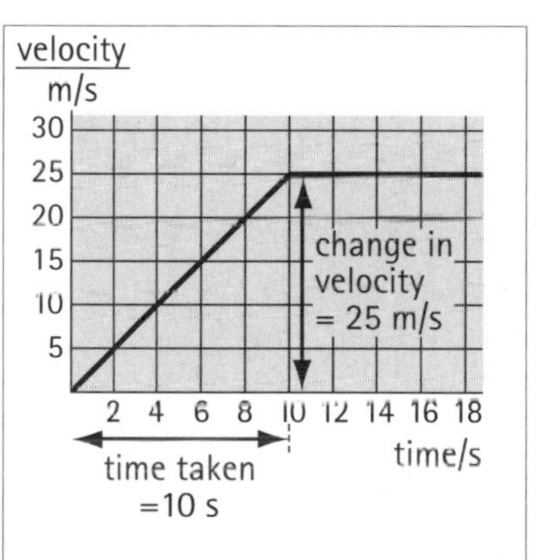

REMEMBER
You need to know the equation for acceleration and you must be able to use it. The standard unit for measuring acceleration is metres per second every second (m/s^2).

Practice Questions – Forces and motion 2

1 A boy runs 400 m in 80 s. What is his average speed?

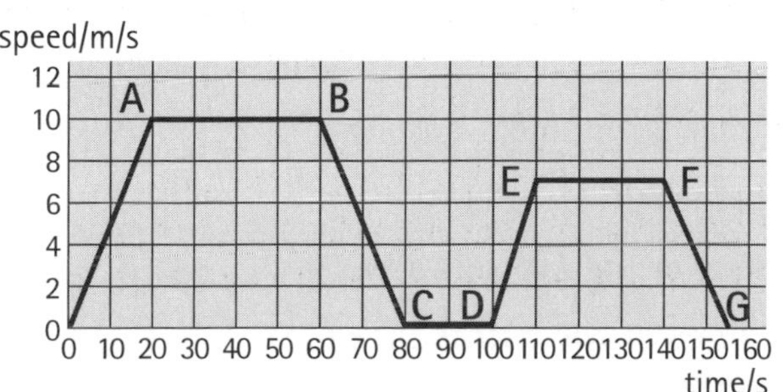

2 Look at the velocity-time graph for a bus shown on the left. Describe what is happening in each part of the journey, O–A, A–B, B–C, C–D, D–E, E–F and F–G.

3 A mini car starts a race by accelerating from 0 to 30 m/s in 10 s. What is the acceleration of the car?

Forces and motion

Forces affect the motion of objects

Different kinds of forces

Gravitational forces are felt near any large, massive object, such as the Sun, Moon, Earth or other planets (see page 00).

Gravity is the force that pulls falling objects to the ground. The force of gravity on an object, its weight, depends on two things:

- the mass of the object
- the strength of the gravitational field, g

weight (N) = mass (kg) × gravitational field strength (N/kg)

$W = mg$

At the surface of the Earth the gravitational field strength (g) is approximately 10 N/kg. This means that the weight of 1 kilogram of matter is 10 newtons.

REMEMBER You need to appreciate the difference between the mass of an object, measured in kilograms and the weight of an object, a force measured in newtons.

What is your mass in kilograms?

What is your weight in newtons on the Earth?

Frictional forces are the forces that resist the movement of an object over a surface or through a liquid or a gas. They are also called resistive forces.

Frictional forces often result in objects warming up as they are slowed down. The space shuttle has insulation to prevent the inside of the orbiter becoming overheated as the spacecraft returns through the atmosphere to Earth.

Forces change the velocity of an object

When there is more than one force on an object:

- If all the forces are in balance, the object will remain as it is – stationary or moving at a steady speed in a straight line.
- If the forces are unbalanced, it might:
  - start to move in the direction of the force
  - speed up (**accelerate**) or slow down (**decelerate**)
  - change direction.
- When an unbalanced force makes an object accelerate:
  - the bigger the force the bigger the acceleration
  - the bigger the mass the smaller the acceleration.

In each of the pictures of the astronaut on the left, say whether he is accelerating, decelerating or moving at a steady speed.

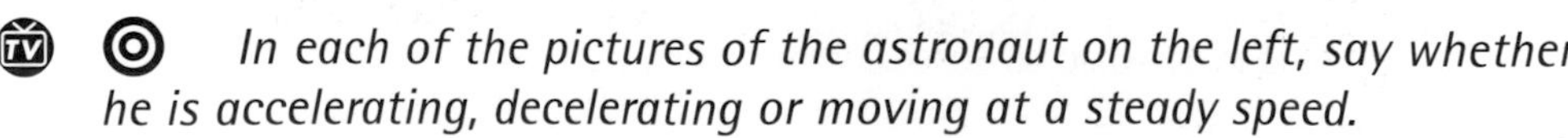

Stopping a car

The force needed to stop a car depends on the mass of the car and its occupants, and its speed.

Braking distance is the distance a car travels before it stops, once the brakes are on.

Thinking distance is the distance the car travels between the driver realising he has to put the brakes on and the brakes actually going on. The thinking distance depends on the **reaction time** of the driver.

stopping distance = thinking distance + braking distance

Measuring forces

We measure force in newtons (N).

(h) Newton's Second law of motion states that: **The acceleration of an object is inversely proportional to the mass and proportional to the force.**

We write this as:

force (N) = mass (kg) × acceleration (m/s^2)

or F = ma

REMEMBER (h) You need to know and be able to use the equation relating force, mass and acceleration. The force of 1 newton will give a mass of 1 kg an acceleration of 1 m/s^2.

Practice Questions – Forces and motion 3

1 Each of the pictures below has two arrows to show the forces on the object. Write down whether you think the object is speeding up, slowing down or stationary, and why.

2 Write down what effect each of the following situations has on the stopping distance of a car and explain why.

a) The car is heavily loaded.

b) The car is moving quickly.

c) The road is wet.

d) The driver is tired.

(h) 3 A car with a mass of 1200 kg accelerates from 0–15 m/s in 10 seconds.

a) Work out the acceleration of the car.

b) Work out the force needed to give this acceleration.

Falling objects

Objects fall because gravity pulls them. Astronauts visiting the Moon showed that objects dropped there fell towards the Moon. The Moon is much smaller than the Earth and so has a much weaker pull. The pull of gravity is not enough to hold on to an atmosphere. When the astronauts dropped a hammer and a feather on the Moon, they fell together – landing at exactly the same moment.

When we do the same experiment on Earth the result is different. Which lands first – the hammer or the feather? Why?

The effect of air on falling objects

REMEMBER You should be able to explain why a falling object reaches terminal velocity.

When an object falls through the air, air resistance acts to reduce the acceleration of the object. Air resistance depends on the shape of an object and its speed.

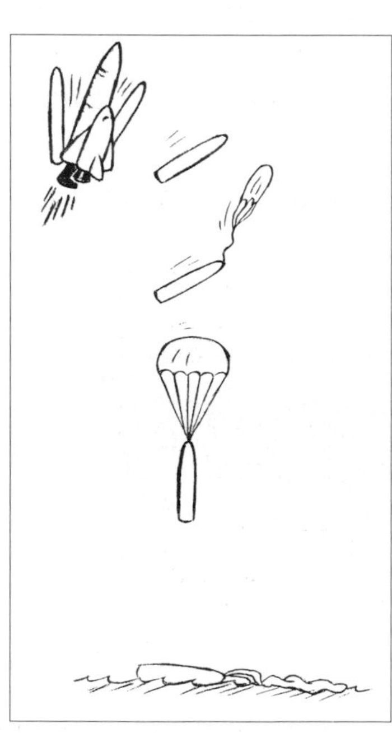

How does the speed of the booster rocket in the picture above change after its release?

As an object speeds up, the air resistance increases. Eventually the pull of gravity – the weight of the object – is balanced by the air resistance. When this happens the object will fall at a steady speed. This steady speed is called the **terminal velocity**.

A parachute acts to increase the surface area of an object. What happens to the air resistance? What happens to the terminal velocity?

Exam Question – Forces and motion

A cyclist is riding along a flat road as shown in the pictures below.

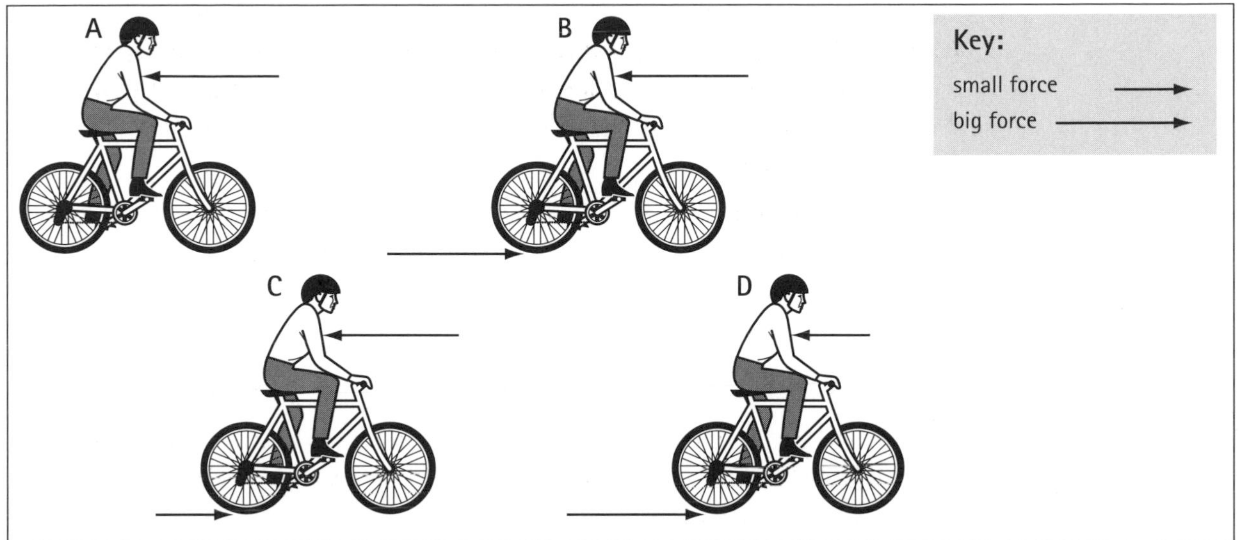

a) The arrows in the pictures show the driving force and the resistive forces acting on her at various stages in her journey. For each picture write down whether she is speeding up, slowing down or moving at a steady speed.

b) The graph below shows the changes in the cyclist's speed during the journey.

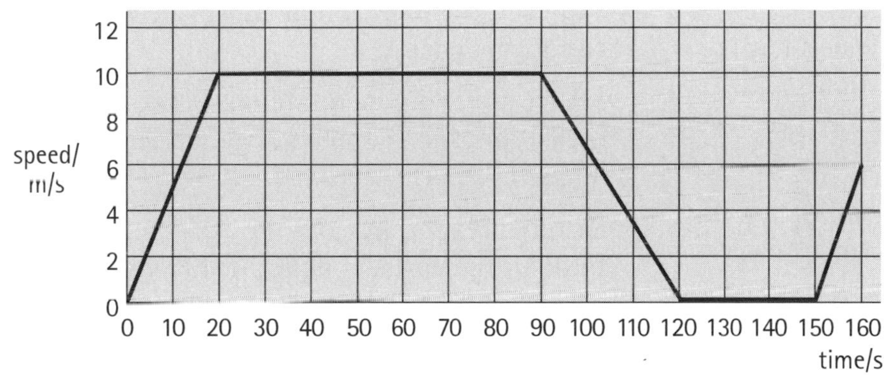

(i) The cyclist **accelerated** between 0 and 20 seconds. What does accelerate mean?

(ii) Describe the motion of the cyclist between 20 and 90 seconds.

(iii) What do you think happened between 120 and 150 seconds?

c) Calculate the acceleration of the cyclist during the first 20 seconds. Show how you work out your answer.

d) The cyclist has a mass of 60 kg. Use your answer to c) to calculate the unbalanced force on the cyclist in the first 20 seconds.

Waves

This section is about

- the behaviour of waves, including light, sound and water waves
- the electromagnetic spectrum
- total internal reflection of light
- sound and ultrasound waves
- the seismic waves that are transmitted through the Earth

There are waves all around us. Most of these waves are invisible, although we use them and see their effects. Waves have many properties in common and it helps to understand what is happening if we look at the behaviour of water waves.

Waves can be reflected: water waves are reflected from a barrier, light waves from a shiny surface such as a mirror, and sound waves are reflected from solid surfaces – we hear this as an echo.

When water waves pass into shallower water they slow down. When they change speed they change direction. This effect is called refraction. Light is refracted when it passes from air into water, perspex or glass.

Many of the waves that are part of everyday life belong to the electromagnetic spectrum.

All these waves travel at the same speed, but they have different wavelengths. The wavelengths range from one millionth of a millionth of a metre to several kilometres.

Electromagnetic waves, like water waves, are transverse, that is the oscillation is at right angles to the direction in which the wave carries the energy.

Sound waves are longitudinal waves. The oscillation is in the same direction as the direction the energy is carried.

Earthquakes set up vibrations that send waves through the Earth. Longitudinal P waves can pass through the liquid core, while the transverse S waves are reflected by the core. We can find out more about the structure of the Earth from the way earthquake waves are transmitted around the globe.

FactZONE

Some words to know

wavelength: the distance from the crest of one wave to the crest of the next wave

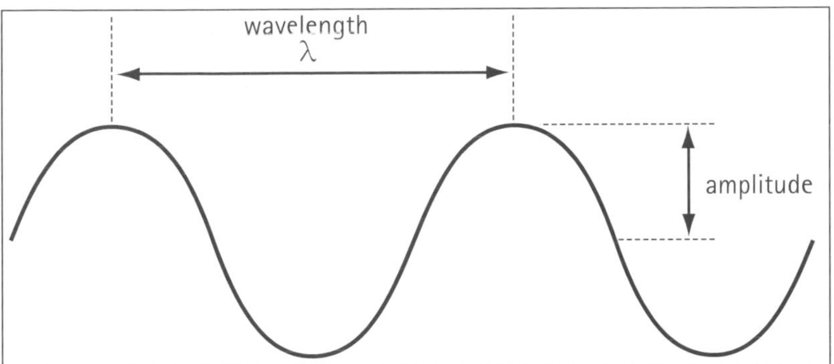

frequency: the number of waves produced each second. The unit of frequency is hertz (Hz)

amplitude: the distance from the crest of a wave to the place where there is no displacement

refraction: the change in direction of a wave when its speed changes because it has passed into a different material (medium)

(h) diffraction: a wave spreads out when it passes through a gap that is about the same width as the wavelength of the wave

electromagnetic spectrum: the family of waves which all travel at 300 000 000 m/s in air

longitudinal waves : waves whose oscillation is in the same direction as the direction in which the energy travels

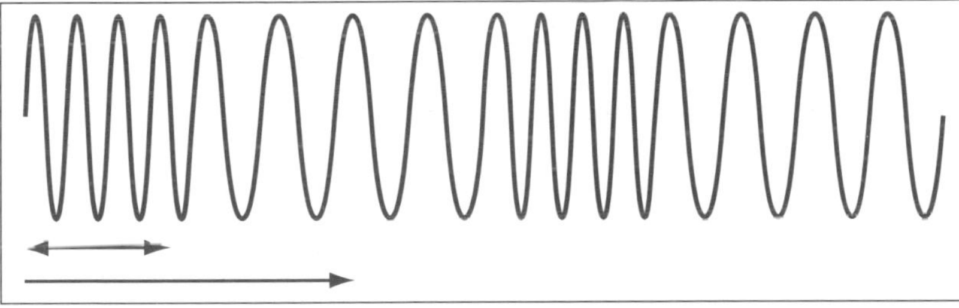

transverse waves: waves whose oscillation is at right angles to the direction in which the energy travels

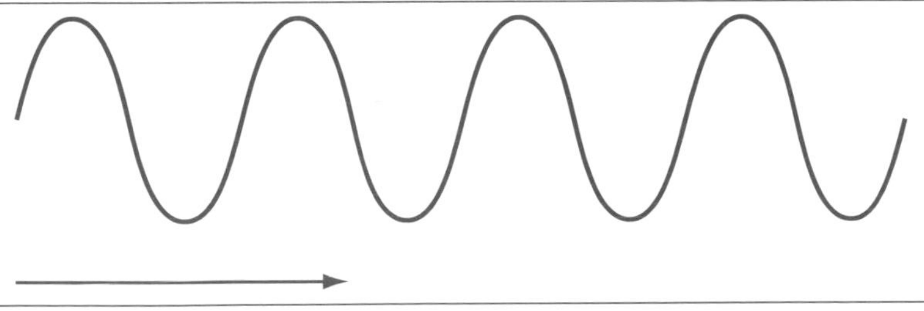

(h) speed of a wave (m/s) = wavelength (m) × frequency (Hz)

$v = \lambda f$

Properties of waves

There are many kinds of waves – light, sound, waves on water and waves on a rope or long slinky spring. All these waves carry energy.

Waves along a rope, light waves and waves on water are all examples of **transverse waves**. This type of wave is illustrated in the picture below.

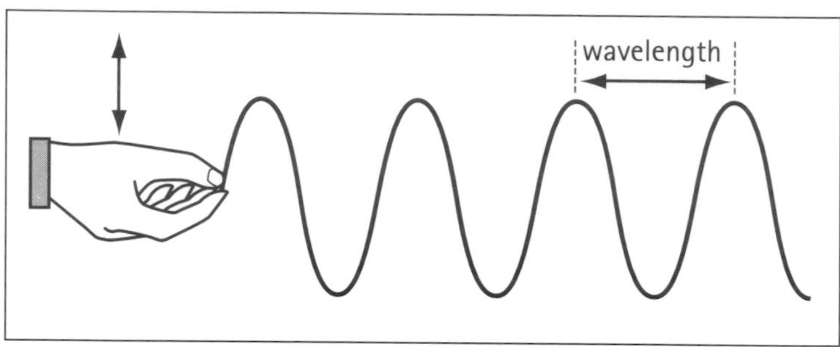

When one end of a rope is moved up and down the rest of the rope begins to move up and down and energy is carried along the rope by a wave. The wavelength is the distance from one crest to the next.

What happens to a cork floating on water when a wave passes?

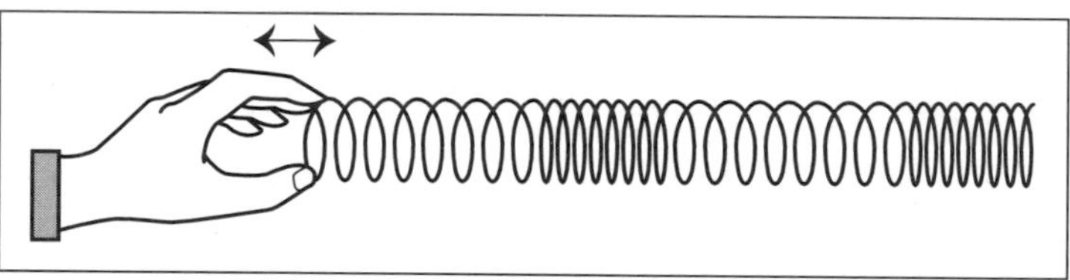

When a slinky spring is pushed backwards and forwards, as shown above, the rest of the spring moves in the same way. Energy is carried along the spring. This is an example of a **longitudinal wave**. Sound is also a longitudinal wave.

How is a sound made?

All these waves can be reflected and refracted.

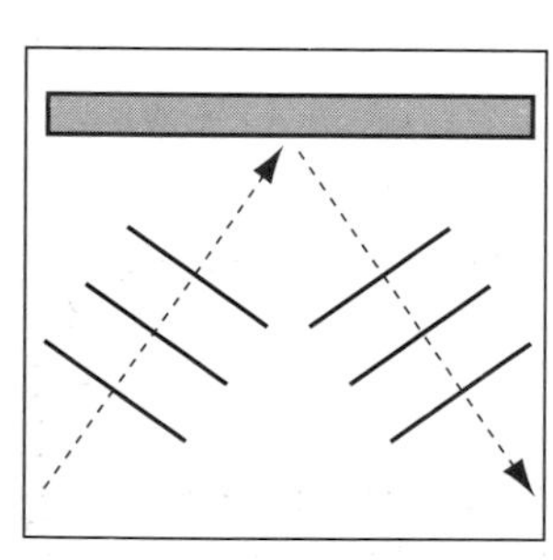

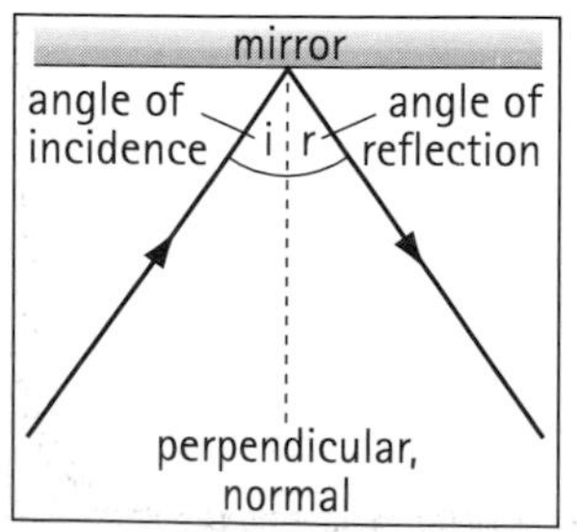

Reflection

When a wave hits a barrier it 'bounces' back, it is reflected, as shown in the picture on the left. The waves reflected from the barrier make the same angle with the barrier as the incoming waves. The wavelength and speed of the wave remain the same.

We see exactly the same effect when light is reflected from a mirror. We measure the angles the ray makes with a line perpendicular to the mirror. (This perpendicular line is called the **normal**.) The **angle of reflection** is equal to the **angle of incidence**. They are shown in the picture on the left.

What evidence is there that sound waves are reflected?

Refraction

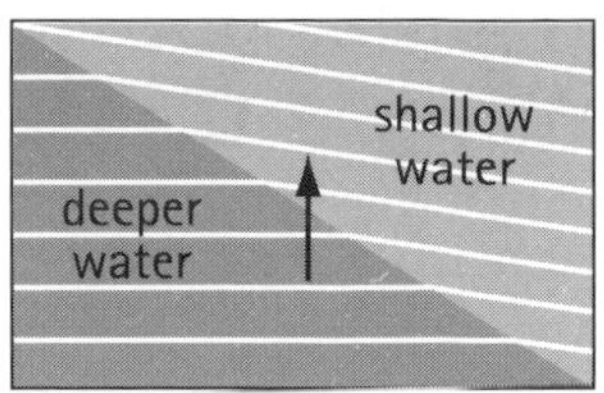

When water waves pass into shallower water they are slowed down. This change in speed makes the wave change direction. The change in direction is called **refraction**. This is illustrated in the picture top right.

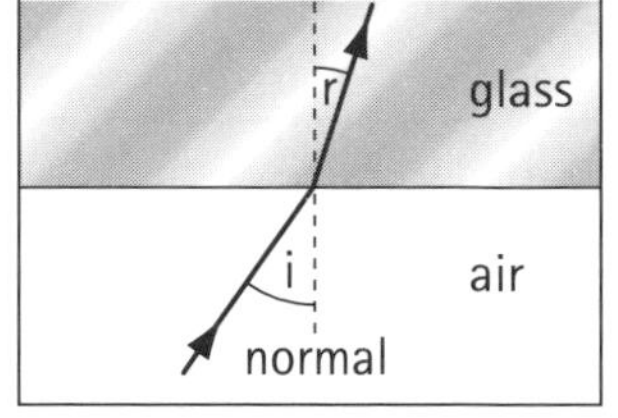

We see the same effect when light passes from air into glass or water. The speed of light in glass is less than in air. As the light slows down it changes direction, as illustrated in the picture middle right. Light is refracted *towards* the normal as it is slowed down.

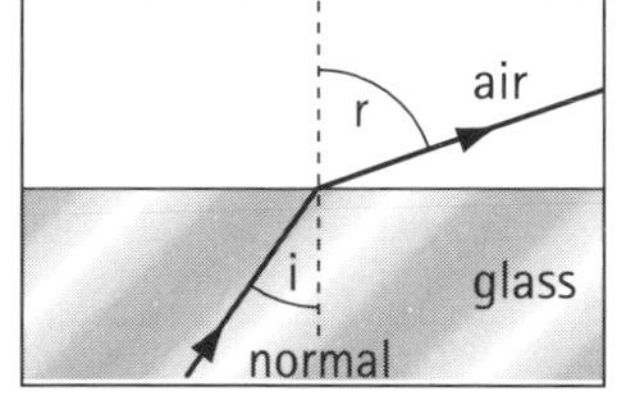

When light emerges into air it speeds up and changes direction again. This time it is refracted *away* from the normal, as shown bottom right.

What evidence is there that light is refracted when it passes into and out of water?

Total internal reflection

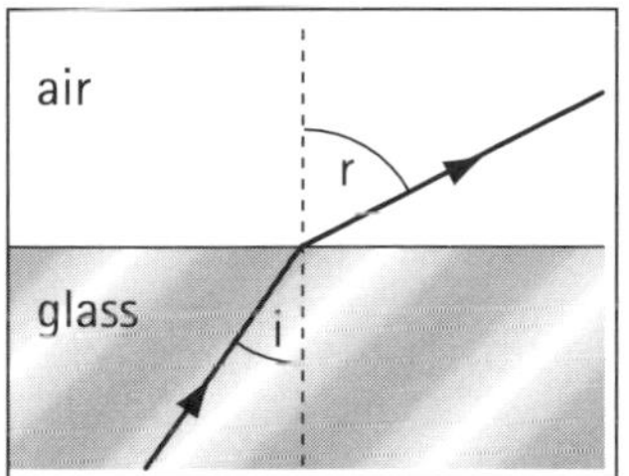

When light reaches the boundary between glass and air, some is reflected back into the glass, but most emerges into the air. The light emerging into the air is refracted away from the normal.

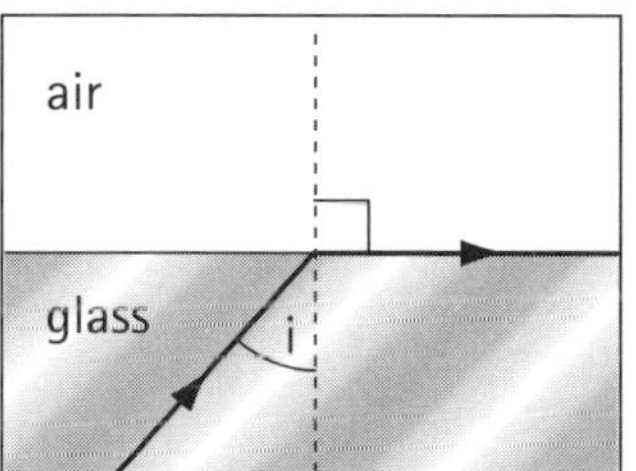

As the angle of incidence inside the glass increases, the angle of refraction outside increases until the emerging ray is passing parallel to the edge of the block. The angle of incidence when this happens is called the **critical angle**.

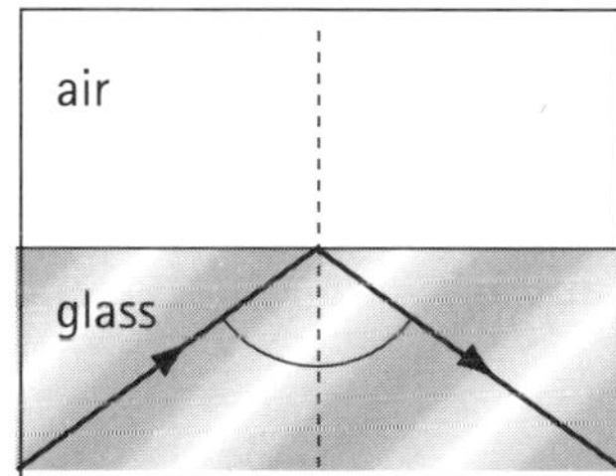

If the angle of incidence inside the block increases any further, the light cannot emerge and is all reflected back inside the block. **Total internal reflection** has occurred.

REMEMBER Total internal reflection occurs when the angle of incidence inside a glass block is greater than the critical angle. The critical angle for glass is 42° and for water it is about 48°.

Practice Questions - Waves 1

1 Complete the ray diagram below to show how total internal reflection occurs when light passes into a right-angled prism.

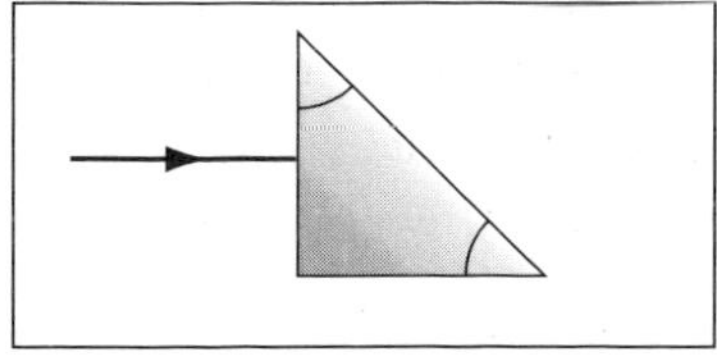

2 Group the following waves into transverse and longitudinal: water waves, light waves, sound waves, waves on a rope.

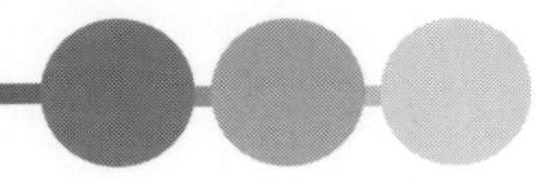

Electromagnetic spectrum

The electromagnetic spectrum is a family of waves that all travel at the same speed in a vacuum. These waves are called electromagnetic waves. White light contains electromagnetic waves of different wavelengths.

short wavelength 0.00000000001 m	high frequency	gamma rays	emitted by some radioactive materials (see page 151) used in medicine to kill cancer cells and to trace blood flow used to kill harmful bacteria on food and to sterilise surgical instruments large doses may damage human cells
		X-rays	pass through soft tissue but not bones or metals used to kill cancer cells and to produce shadow images of bones large doses may damage human cells
		ultraviolet	causes tanning of the skin large doses may cause skin cancer
		visible light violet red	detected by the eye used for vision and through optical fibres in endoscopes to view inside patient's bodies
		infrared	is radiated from warm and hot bodies and causes heating used in grills, toasters and radiant heaters used in remote-control devices, security cameras and communication may cause burning of skin if too much is absorbed
		microwaves	some wavelengths absorbed by water; this is used in cooking but can also damage living cells longer wavelengths used in radar, satellite communications and mobile phones
10 000 m long wavelength	low frequency	radio waves	a broad range of wavelengths used in communication

Using total internal reflection

Many binoculars, periscopes and cameras use total internal reflection to change the direction of light rays, as shown in the diagram below.

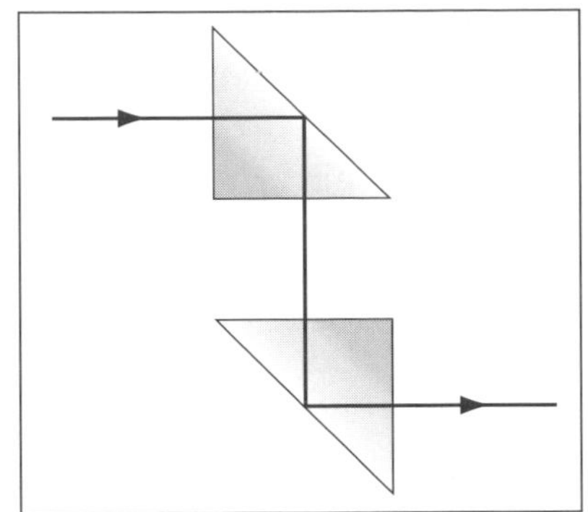

 Total internal reflection is also used to pass a ray of light down an optical fibre, as illustrated in the diagram below. An optical fibre is a thin strand of glass coated in a protective material. The light is reflected off the inner surfaces of the fibre and remains within the fibre even when the fibre bends.

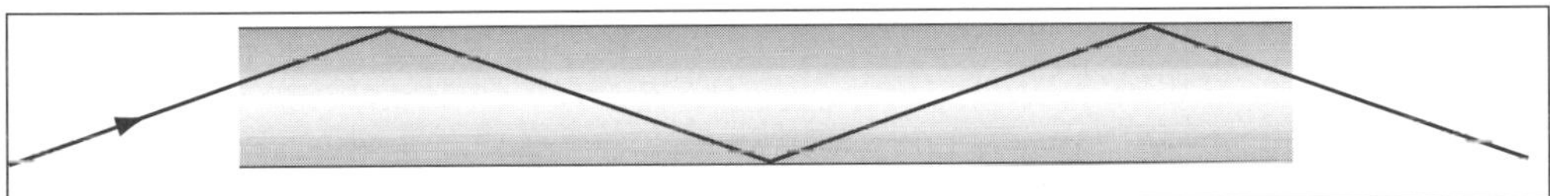

An endoscope is a device used by doctors to see inside patients without the need for an operation. One strand of fibres carries light down into the body and the surgeon looks through a second strand of fibres.

Telephone companies are replacing copper cables with optical fibres. The cables carry light signals, which are converted back into electrical signals at the other end. Many more signals can be carried in a thin optical cable than in a much thicker copper cable.

REMEMBER You need to know the relative position of the different kinds of radiation in the electromagnetic spectrum and about some of their uses and dangers.

Practice Questions - Waves 2

1 Fill in the missing gaps in this electromagnetic spectrum

gamma rays ________ *ultraviolet* *visible* ________ *microwaves* ________

2 Suggest one use and one hazard of each of the following electromagnetic waves:

a) X-rays.

b) microwaves.

c) ultraviolet waves.

Sound

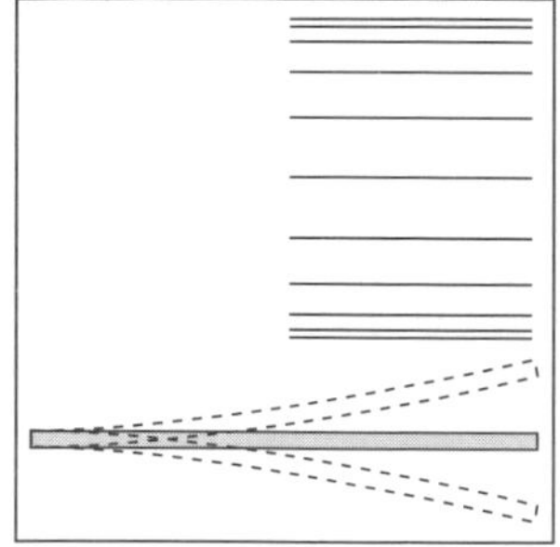

When a ruler vibrates, as shown in the picture on the left, the air ahead of the ruler is made to vibrate. The particles in the air alternately come closer together, creating a compression, and then spread further apart, creating a rarefaction. The sound spreads through the air.

The particles vibrate with the same frequency as the sound and in the same direction as the sound travels.

The sound wave is a ___________ wave.

The energy of the sound causes other objects to vibrate. The sound makes our eardrum vibrate; this is how we detect sounds.

The bigger the amplitude of the vibration, the louder the sound. If the sound is too loud, the large vibrations may damage our ears.

The higher the frequency of the sound, the higher the pitch of the note.

REMEMBER Frequency is the number of vibrations or waves per second. It is measured in hertz, Hz.

1 hertz = 1 vibration per second

The lower the frequency, the ______ the pitch of the note.

Sound is carried by the particles in the medium vibrating. This means that sound cannot travel through empty space.

Echoes and ultrasound

Sound waves are reflected just as other waves. We hear sound waves being reflected every time we hear an echo. The echo is the sound being reflected from a hard surface.

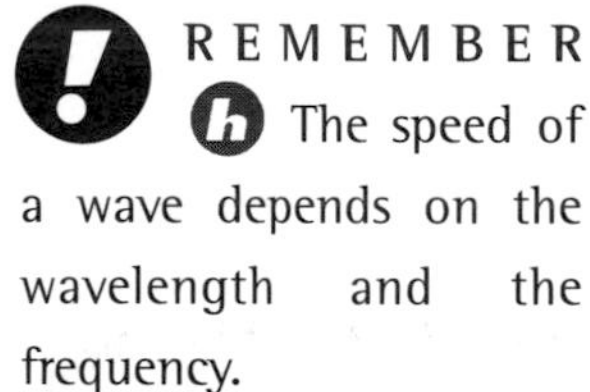

REMEMBER The speed of a wave depends on the wavelength and the frequency.

$v = \lambda f$

Bats use echoes to detect objects around them. They produce a sound with a very high frequency, above 20 000 Hertz. This is too high for us to hear. We call sounds with a frequency too high for us to detect **ultrasound**.

Ultrasound is used to 'look' inside the body. Ultrasound is partly reflected when it meets the boundary between two different organs. The reflected wave is used to build up a picture of the inside of the body. Ultrasound scans are used to look at babies before birth and also to look at other organs.

Why do you think ultrasound is used to look at babies in the womb, rather than X-rays?

Ultrasound can also be used in industry, for example, for detecting flaws inside metal casting.

Diffraction of waves

When water waves pass through a gap in a barrier, they spread out as they pass through to the other side, as shown in the diagram on the right. This spreading out of waves as they pass through a gap is called **diffraction.** The diffraction happens best if the wavelength of the waves is about the same as the width of the gap.

Diffraction gives us more evidence that light, water waves and sound all behave in the same way.

We can hear what is being said in another room, even if the people talking are out of sight. Sound is diffracted as it passes through the doorway. This happens because the wavelength of the sound is about the same as the width of the doorway.

We do not notice the diffraction of light very often because the wavelength of light is very small. This means that light only diffracts noticeably when the gap is very small too.

We use the fact the radio waves diffract every day. The radio waves that carry signals for our televisions have much longer wavelengths than light. The waves diffract past buildings, so that there is less 'shadow' where the signal does not reach. This is illustrated in the diagram below.

Practice Questions – Waves 3

1 a) A ruler makes 100 vibrations in 2 seconds. What is the frequency of the vibration?

b) How could you use the ruler to make a higher-pitched note?

2 A bat sends a signal out. It is reflected from the wall of the cave 0.2 seconds later. The cave wall is 30 m away. What is the speed of sound?

3 What evidence is there that sound waves are diffracted?

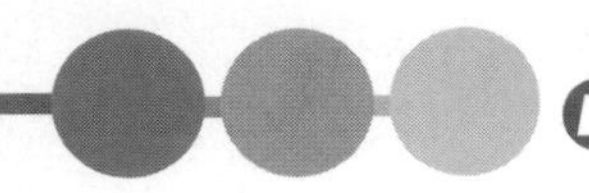

Waves through the Earth

The Earth is shaped like an orange. There are three parts to the structure of the Earth. The surface crust, the mantle and the core. Earthquakes can give us evidence about this structure.

When an earthquake occurs the energy travels from the site of the earthquake, which we call the epicentre. The energy is carried by different kinds of waves.

What happens to the energy of the wave when it reaches the Earth's surface?

The primary 'P' waves are longitudinal waves, which travel at 8 to 13 km/s. They can pass through both the mantle and the core. P waves are refracted as they pass through the core, as shown in the diagram below.

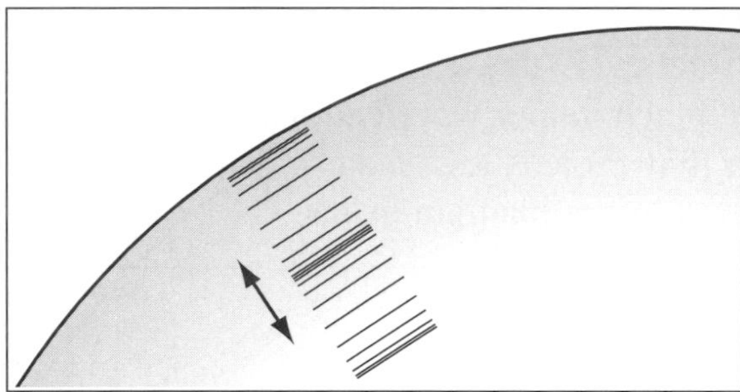

The secondary 'S' waves are transverse waves. These travel through the mantle at 4 to 7 km/s and are reflected by the core, as shown below.

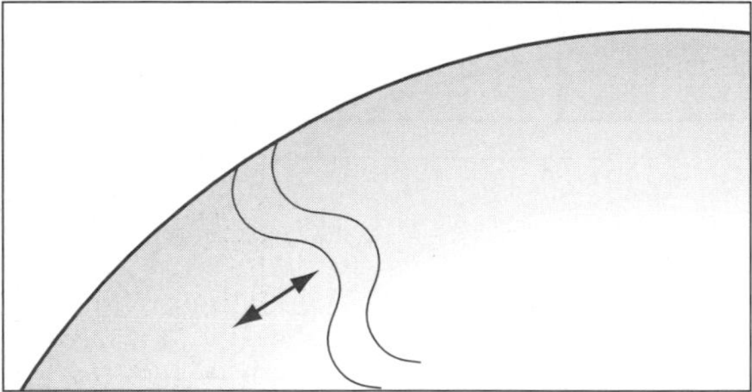

Seismometers are used to detect the waves. The P and S waves have different speeds and arrive at the surface at different times. Seismologists can use the information from earthquake stations around the world to tell them more about the structure of the Earth, as illustrated below.

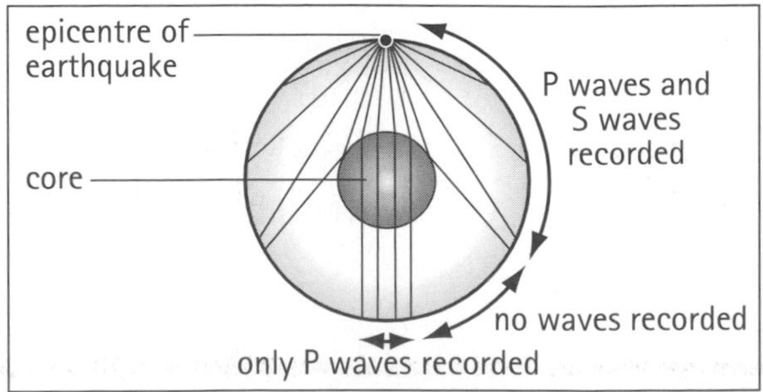

Exam Question – Waves

The diagram below shows a ray of light about to enter a short section of an optical fibre.

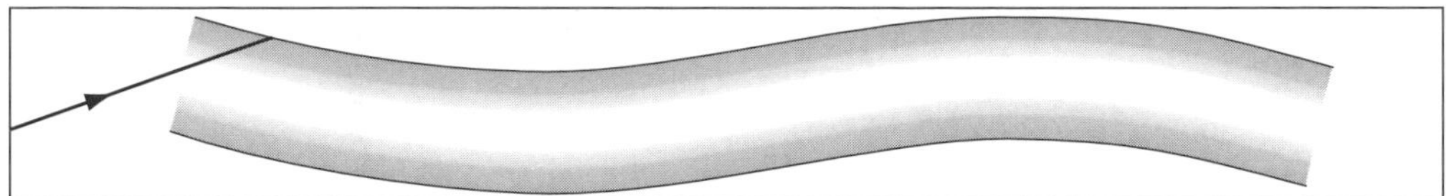

a) (i) On the diagram continue the path of the light through the section of fibre as accurately as you can. [3]

(ii) What is the advantage of using optical fibres to transmit light from one place to another? [1]

b) Endoscopes are used to look deep inside the human body. They consist of two bundles of fibres arranged as in the diagram below right.

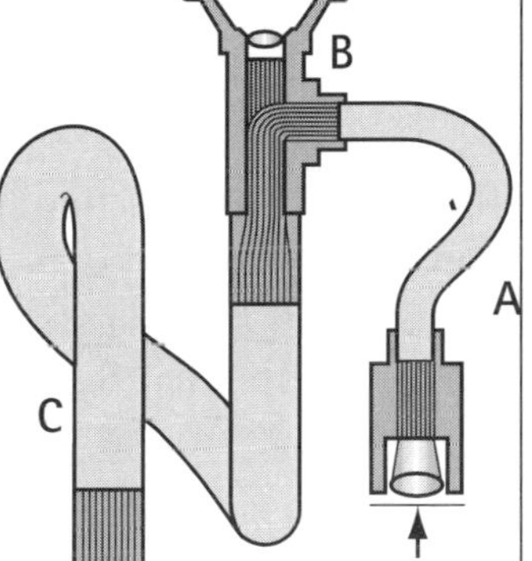

Tube C contains two bundles of optical fibres. The fibres in tube A are wrapped around the fibres from B.

(i)Why are the fibres in A needed to carry light? [1]

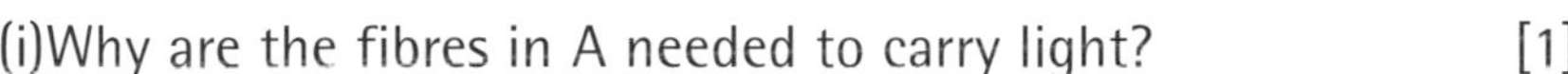

(ii) Why must the inner bundle of fibres be arranged in exactly the same pattern at C as they were at B? [1]

(iii) Write down **two** advantages of using endoscopes rather than X-rays for examining the inside of the body. [2]

c) Doctors use ultrasound to scan babies in the womb, as shown below. The ultrasound probe gives out a pulse of ultrasound and also detects ultrasound.

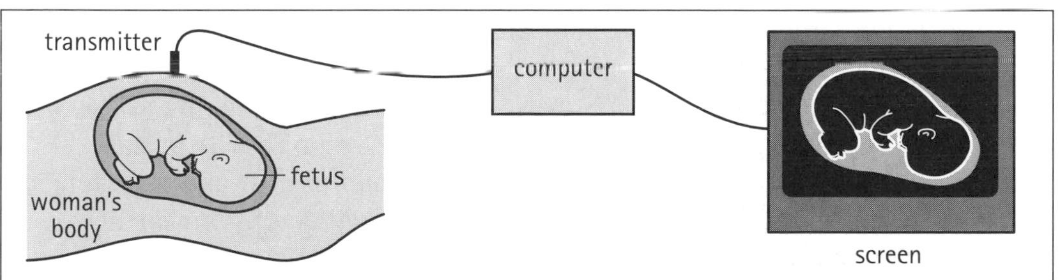

(i) What is ultrasound? [1]

(ii) What property of ultrasound allows the detector to receive information about the baby? [1]

d) In many parts of the country optical fibres are replacing the copper cables used for telephone cables. Write down **two** advantages of using optical fibres. [2]

The Earth and beyond

This section is about

- the Earth, Moon, Sun, planets and other bodies in the Solar System and their place in the Universe
- the gravitational forces that determine the movements of planets, moons, comets and satellites
- how stars evolve over a long time-scale
- some ideas used to explain the evolution of the Universe into its present state

The Earth is one of nine planets that orbit the Sun. Together with comets and other space debris, such as the asteroid belt, these bodies make up the Solar System. All these bodies are held in orbit around the Sun by gravity.

The Earth and some of the other planets have one or more moons. These moons are natural satellites, they too are held in orbit by gravity. Our Moon makes one orbit of the Earth every month.

There are also many man-made satellites in orbit around the Earth. They may be placed in orbit to transmit radio signals around the planet or to study what is happening on the Earth. Other satellites, such as the Hubble telescope, are designed to make observations of the rest of the Solar System and beyond.

The Solar System is centred around our Sun, which is just one of many stars that make up the galaxy called the Milky Way. We can see the stars that are fairly close to us as individual points of light in the night sky. The Milky Way appears as faint band of light in the night sky.

Our galaxy is just one of many millions of galaxies in the Universe. Some of the galaxies appear as points of light in the night sky.

Stars are formed when clouds of dust and gas are pulled together by the force of gravity. Gravity also holds stars in their galaxies. When a star reaches the end of its life it may explode into a cloud of dust and gas. Some of this dust and gas will go on to make new stars.

FactZONE

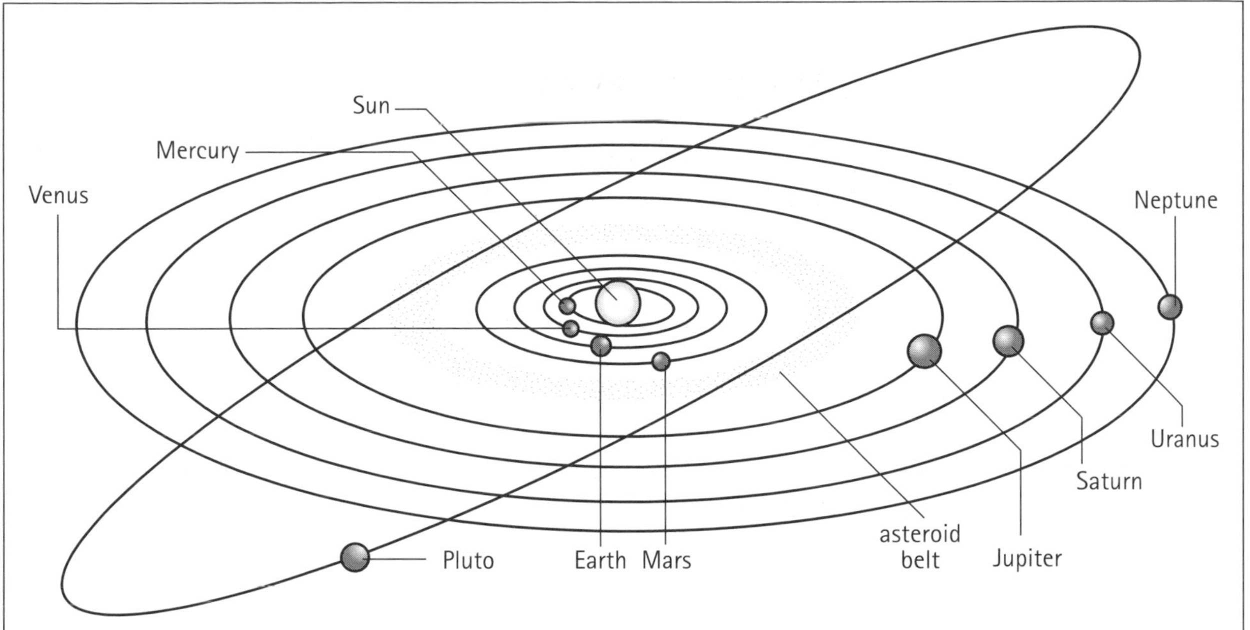

- The Solar System consists of the Sun, nine planets, the asteroid belt and a number of comets.
- All the planets except Pluto have elliptical orbits in the same plane.
- The orbit of Pluto is more elliptical and at an angle to the plane of the other planets.
- Between the four inner planets and the outer planets lies the asteroid belt, made up of dust and rocks.
- All the bodies orbiting the Sun are held in orbit by the force of gravity.
- The gravitational force between two bodies depends on the mass of the bodies and how close together they are.
- The time taken for a planet to orbit the Sun is its year. The further a planet is from the Sun, the weaker the pull of gravity on it and the greater its orbit. The further from the Sun a planet is, the longer its year.
- The Moon is a natural satellite of the Earth. Some other planets have natural satellites too. The time taken for the Moon to make one orbit of the Earth is one month.
- Artificial satellites are put into orbit around the Earth. Those close to the Earth orbit much more quickly than those in higher orbits.
- Comets make very eccentric orbits of the Sun. They pass close to the Sun, when they can be seen, and then travel far beyond Pluto. When comets are close to the Sun they move faster, when they are far away they move more slowly.

Our place in the Universe

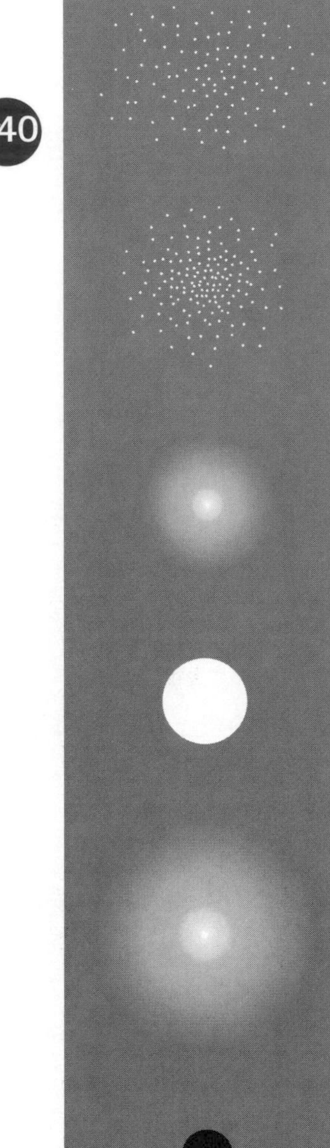

The life history of a star

Stars are formed from massive clouds of dust and gas in space. Gravity pulls the dust and gas together. As the mass falls together it gets hot. A star is formed when it is hot enough for the hydrogen nuclei to fuse together to make helium. The fusion process releases energy, which keeps the core of the star hot.

During this stable phase in the life of the star, the force of gravity holding the star together is balanced by the high pressures caused by the high temperatures. Our Sun is at this stable phase in its life.

When all the hydrogen has been used up in the fusion process, larger nuclei begin to form and the star may expand to become a red giant.

When all the nuclear reactions are over, a small star, like our Sun, may begin to contract under the pull of gravity. It becomes a white dwarf, which fades and changes colour as it cools down.

A larger star with more mass will go on making nuclear reactions, getting hotter and expanding until it explodes as a supernova. An exploding supernova throws hot gas and dust into space leaving a neutron star, which eventually shrinks to a black hole.

The life history of the Universe

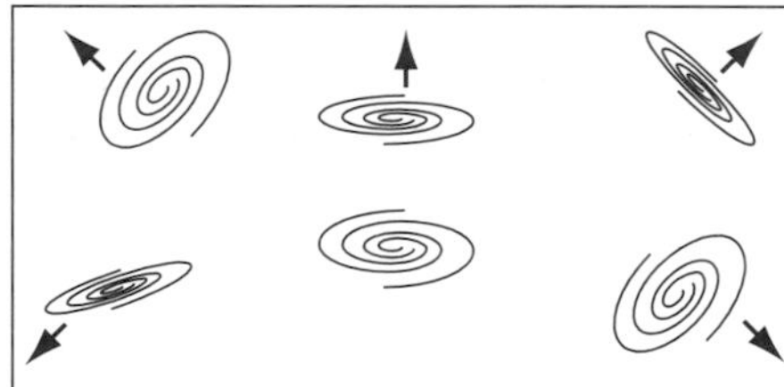

Observations of light from other galaxies show that it appears to be shifted towards the red end of the spectrum. The further a galaxy is away, the greater the red shift.

An explanation for these observations is that all the galaxies in the Universe are moving apart very fast. The distant galaxies, with the bigger red shift, are moving away faster than those nearer to us. This suggests that the Universe was formed by a big bang, which threw all the matter out in different directions.

The future of the Universe depends on exactly how much matter there is and how fast it is moving. The Universe is held together by gravitational forces. If there is enough matter, the force of gravitation may slow down the expansion and eventually make it contract. If there is less matter the expansion may go on for ever.

Exam Question – The Earth and beyond

The table below gives information about the five innermost planets. Use the information in the table to answer the questions.

planet	average distance from the Sun (millions of km)	time for one orbit of the Sun (Earth years)
Earth	150.00	1.0
Jupiter	778.00	11.90
Mars	228.00	1.90
Mercury	58.00	0.24
Venus	108.00	0.60

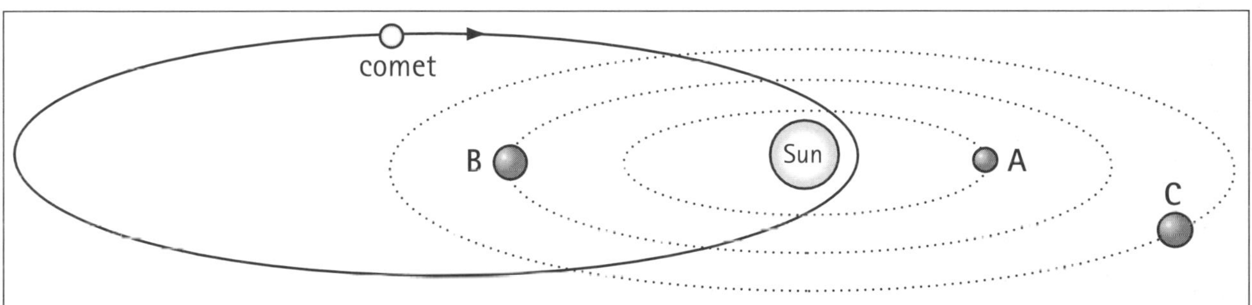

a) The diagram above shows the three planets nearest the Sun and a comet. What are the names of planets **A**, **B** and **C**?

b) Which planet has the shortest year?

c) There are many asteroids in orbit around the Sun. One of these asteroids is called Ceres. It takes Ceres about four Earth years to make one orbit of the Sun. Between which two planets are the asteroids found?

d) Comets go around the Sun in elliptical orbits.

(i) Draw an arrow on the diagram to show the force from the Sun on the comet.

(ii) At which point in its orbit does the comet have its slowest speed?

Energy

This section is about

- work, energy, power and efficiency
- kinetic energy, potential energy and work
- how differences in temperature can lead to transfer of energy
- the need for economical use of energy resources

Energy is all around us. We cannot live without it, yet it is difficult to define. It is easiest to describe what happens when energy is transferred from one place to another.

When we use a force to make something move, we do some work, and we are transferring energy. Our bodies burn food to give us the energy to do work.

When we burn coal in a power station to generate electricity, energy from the coal is used to turn the generators.

Of course not all the energy from the coal is transferred to the electric current. A lot of energy is lost in heating the water, and the area around the boiler house will get warmer. The water flowing through the cooling towers warms up the surroundings too. The energy transfer is not completely efficient.

When something gets hot it loses energy to its surroundings. Energy is conducted through solids by the vibrations of atoms.

Liquids and gases expand when they get hot. This makes them less dense and so the warmer part of a liquid or gas floats above the colder, denser part. The energy is transferred by convection.

All warm bodies emit radiation. The hotter the body, the more energy it radiates. Energy from the Sun reaches us by radiation.

Much of the energy we use comes from fossil fuels, such as coal and natural gas. Reserves of these fuels will not last for ever. We need to find ways to conserve them. We can do this by finding alternative ways of generating electricity and providing energy for transport. We should also find ways of using less energy.

FactZONE

Some words to know

work: we do work when we apply a force to make something move

kinetic energy: the energy of a moving object

gravitational potential energy: the energy an object gains when it is lifted up

power: the rate at which work is done or energy is transferred

conduction: energy is transferred from the warm part of a solid to the cooler part by conduction

convection: energy is transferred by fluids (liquids or gases) by the movement of less dense warm fluid above denser cold fluid

radiation: warm bodies emit infrared radiation

evaporation: molecules near the surface of a liquid leave the liquid

Some equations to know

work done (J) = force (N) × distance (m)

$$\text{power (W)} = \frac{\text{work done or energy transfer (J)}}{\text{time taken (s)}}$$

$$\text{efficiency} = \frac{\text{useful energy output}}{\text{total energy input}}$$

(h) gravitational potential energy = mass × gravitational field strength × height

J kg N/kg m

(h) kinetic energy = ½ × mass × velocity^2

J kg m/s

Work, energy and power

REMEMBER You need to know and be able to use the equation for work done. The standard unit for work is joules.

Work

When we lift a weight we do some work. We transfer energy from our muscles to the weight.

We say that the weight has **gravitational potential energy**. This means it has energy because it is lifted up in the Earth's gravitational field.

How can we get that energy back?

The work done when a force is exerted depends on the size of the force and the distance the force moves:

work done (joules) = force (newtons) × distance (metres)

REMEMBER The pull of gravity is 10 newtons on every kilogram.

REMEMBER (h) You need to be able to use the equation for potential energy on higher tier papers: PE = mgh

If the weightlifter in the picture above lifts 100 kg through 1.5 metres how much work does he do?

He needs to exert a force of 1000 N to lift 100 kg.

work done (J) = force (N) × distance (m)

work done (J) = _______ N × _____ m

work done = 1500 J

Potential energy and kinetic energy

REMEMBER (h) You need to be able to use the equation for kinetic energy on higher tier papers: KE = $\frac{1}{2}mv^2$

When a weightlifter lifts the weight, he is using his muscles to transfer energy from food to the potential energy of the weights.

What happens if the weight lifter drops the weights?

The weights fall to the ground, losing potential energy and gaining kinetic energy. Kinetic energy is the energy an object has because it is moving.

But what happens to the energy when the weights hit the ground?

Power

Power measures how quickly energy is transferred. We can calculate the power from the equation:

$$\text{power (W)} = \frac{\text{work done or energy transfer (J)}}{\text{time taken (s)}}$$

> **REMEMBER** You need to be able to use the equation for power. The standard unit for power is watts (W). 1kW = 1000 watts.

In the picture on the right, a boy with a mass of 50 kg runs up a flight of stairs in 5 seconds. The height he has risen is 20 m. How much power did he develop?

◎ *He used a force of __________ N to lift his mass of 50 kg.*

The work done in going up stairs = force (N) × distance (m)

◎ *work done (J) = 500 N × ________ m = 10 000 J*

$$\text{power (W)} = \frac{\text{work done or energy transfer (J)}}{\text{time taken (s)}}$$

◎ h power (W) = $\dfrac{\text{10 000 J}}{\text{\_\_\_\_\_\_ s}}$ = ______ W

How will the boy feel at the top of the stairs?

Not all the energy from food will have gone to getting him upstairs. The boy will feel pretty hot too!

> **REMEMBER** You need to be able to use the efficiency equation.

Efficiency

Efficiency tells how much of the energy input is transferred to useful energy output.

$$\text{efficiency} = \frac{\text{useful energy output}}{\text{total energy input}}$$

Practice Questions – Energy 1

1 A cyclist exerts a constant force of 50 N while pedalling 100 m.

a) Calculate how much work did she did.

b) She cycled the 100 m in 20 seconds. Calculate the power of the cyclist.

2 A coal-fired power station has an efficiency of 35%. What does this mean?

Energy transfers

Energy is transferred when there is a temperature difference between two bodies, i.e. when one is hotter than the other.

Conduction

Why is it not sensible to have a saucepan handle made of metal?

Energy is transferred from the hotter part of a solid to the colder part by conduction. Metals are good conductors, whereas most non-metals are poor conductors.

Poor conductors are used as insulators. Most liquids and gases are poor conductors.

Energy is transferred by the particles in the material. The particles in the hot part are vibrating more. These vibrations are passed on to the cooler particles next to them, so the energy spreads through the material until all particles have the same energy.

The free electrons in metals have more kinetic energy when the metal is hot. The electrons help to transfer energy from the hot part of a metal to the cooler part.

Convection

Convection is the transfer of energy by the movement of a liquid or gas.

When a liquid or gas becomes warm it expands and becomes less dense. The warmer fluid floats above the cooler fluid, which sinks. This creates a flow which is called a convection current.

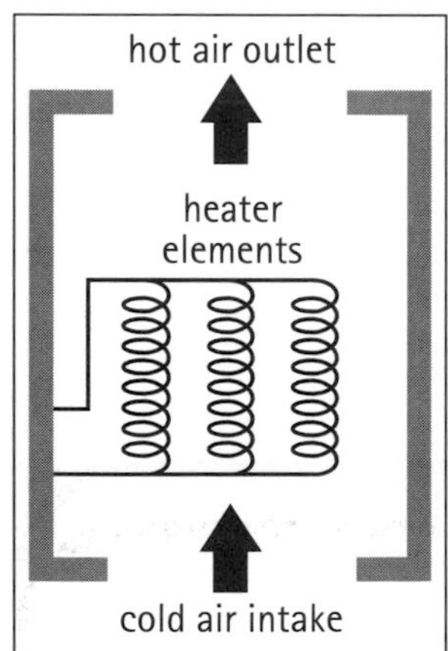

How do convection currents warm up the whole room?

Evaporation

Evaporation is when the particles near the surface of a liquid leave the liquid and become a vapour. The escaping particles take some energy with them, so leaving the liquid cooler.

The particles that escape are those with higher-than-average energy – otherwise they would not have enough energy to escape. Because the liquid loses its higher energy particles, the liquid that is left has less energy so it becomes cooler.

How does sweating help us keep cool?

Radiation

Everything radiates energy. The energy radiated because something is warm is the infrared radiation, and is part of the electromagnetic spectrum.

Dark, dull surfaces emit more radiation than light shiny surfaces. They also absorb radiation well. Light, shiny surfaces do not absorb radiation well – they are good reflectors.

Radiation can pass through space.

Which of the two cars in the picture above will get hotter on a sunny day – the black car or the white car?

Can you suggest methods of cooking that use each of: conduction, convection and radiation?

Practice Questions – Energy 2

1 Suggest materials that could be used to insulate the roof space in a house.

2 Give at least two reasons why the element is put at the bottom of a kettle.

3 Suggest why the central heating radiators in houses should perhaps be called 'convectors'.

Energy resources

Where does electricity come from?

Electricity is a very convenient way of supplying energy. Most of our power stations use fossil fuels – coal, oil and gas – as the diagram below shows. One day these fuels will run out. As well as producing electricity, power stations produce pollution and excess carbon dioxide, and they warm up the surroundings. These are all good reasons for using electricity more wisely.

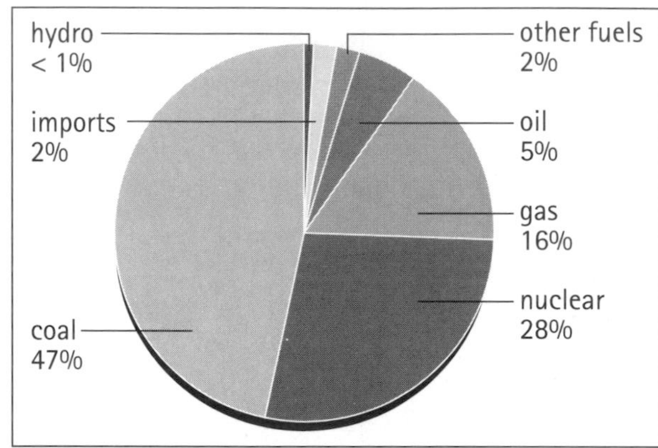

We also use fossil fuels to power our cars. What has happened to the energy from the burning petrol by the end of the journey?

How else do we use fossil fuels, apart from burning as a fuel?

Save it!

We could make more efficient use of energy in our homes. The picture below shows the heat losses from a typical house.

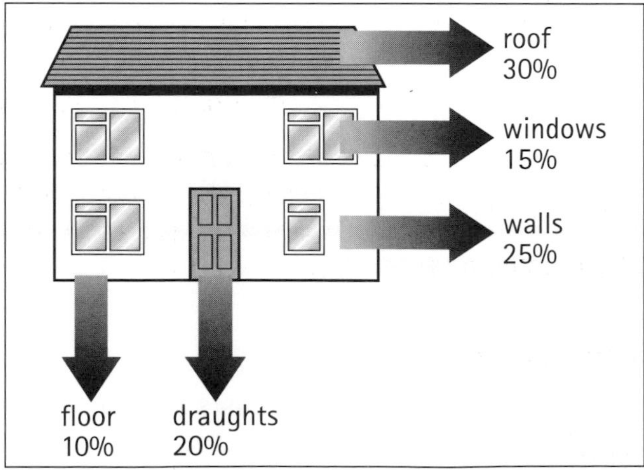

How would better insulation help us use less energy?

We could use more public transport and private cars less.

How would using public transport save energy?

What are the alternatives?

There are other ways of turning a generator than using a steam turbine. Wind and water are both used to turn generators.

What are the advantages and disadvantages of using wind or water to generate power?

Exam Question – Energy

The diagram below shows a car travelling at 30 m/s on a level road. At this speed the car has to overcome a total force opposing motion of 600 N.

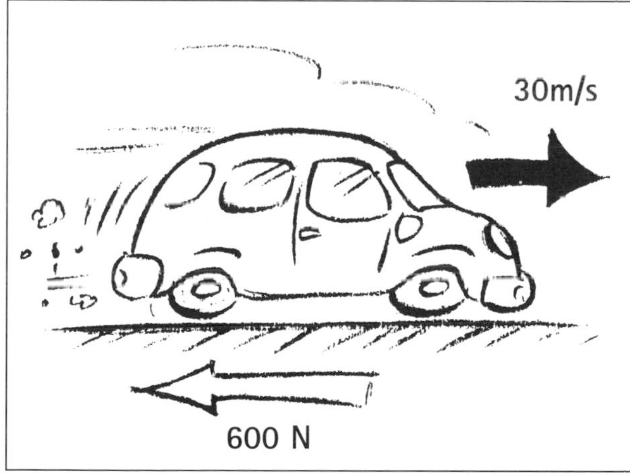

a) How far does the car go in 10 seconds?

b) How much work is done by the engine in this time?

c) What is the power transferred by the engine?

d) What happens to this energy?

e) In a crash, the seat belt locks and the belt stretches, as shown in the picture above. Explain why a material that does not stretch is unsuitable for use in seat belts.

f) Explain why a fully loaded car does not accelerate away from the traffic lights in the same way as an identical car that contains only the driver.

Radioactivity

This section is about

- the three main types of radioactive emission
- the effects of radiation on matter and living organisms
- the meaning of the term 'half-life'

Radioactivity is a random process that takes place in some elements. The nuclei of these materials are unstable and spontaneously emit radiation, which can ionise molecules. The radiation can be detected with a Geiger-Müller tube and a counter.

There are three kinds of radiation – alpha (α) radiation, beta (β) radiation and gamma (γ) radiation. Each type of radiation has different properties, but they can all cause ionisation.

Radiation can cause ionisation of the molecules in living cells. This may damage the cells and can cause cancer. Doctors also use ionising radiation to kill cancer cells.

The nucleus of an atom is made up of protons and neutrons. The protons are positively charged and the neutrons carry no charge. Some nuclei are unstable because they have too many neutrons. When alpha or beta particles are emitted the number of protons in the nucleus changes. This means a new element has been formed.

Radioactive decay is a random process that helps the nucleus to become more stable. We cannot predict when a particular nucleus will decay. However, we can say that after a certain amount of time half the nuclei in a sample of the material will have decayed. We call the time it takes for half the nuclei to decay the half-life.

We are surrounded by radioactive substances, in the air we breathe and in the rocks under the ground and from which some buildings are made. Radioactive particles also reach us from Outer Space. All these sources of radiation are called background radiation.

Our bodies are used to these low doses of background radiation, but if the amount of radioactive material in our surroundings becomes too high, there could be problems for our health.

We have to take the background radiation into account when we are taking radioactivity measurements.

FactZONE

Ionising radiation

radiation	what is it?	how far can it travel in air?	what stops it?	what happens in a magnetic field?
alpha α	particles – positive helium nuclei	few centimetres of air	thin paper	small deflection
beta β	particles – negative electrons	stopped by a few metres of air	thin aluminium	large deflection
gamma γ	electromagnetic radiation	several kilometres	thick lead	no deflection

All ionising radiation can be harmful. The radiation ionises the molecules in the cells of the body. This may damage or even kill the cell.

Care must be taken when handling radioactive materials. People who work with ionising radiations must be particularly careful – the greater the dose, the greater the risk of damage.

Large doses of radiation are used to kill cancer cells in the body. Their use is carefully controlled. There is sometimes some short-term damage to other healthy cells.

Radiation is absorbed by the material through which it passes. The thicker the material, the greater the absorption. This effect is used to monitor thickness of materials in production.

Some radioactive materials are used as tracers in industry and medicine. The material can be put into a fluid system, such as piped water. The radiation emitted shows where the fluid has flowed to. This can be used to identify blockages or leakages.

Background radiation is the radiation that is all around us. It comes from out of space, the rocks in the ground and the food we eat, as well as from artificial sources, such as nuclear power stations and hospitals.

h **Half-life** is the time it takes for half a quantity of radioactive material to decay. Half-lives range from fractions of seconds to thousands of years.

Half-life

The amount of radiation emitted from a sample depends on how many radioactive nuclei are in the sample. As the nuclei decay, there will be fewer left to decay, so the decay rate will decrease. A graph showing how much radioactive material is present will show the rate at which the material decays.

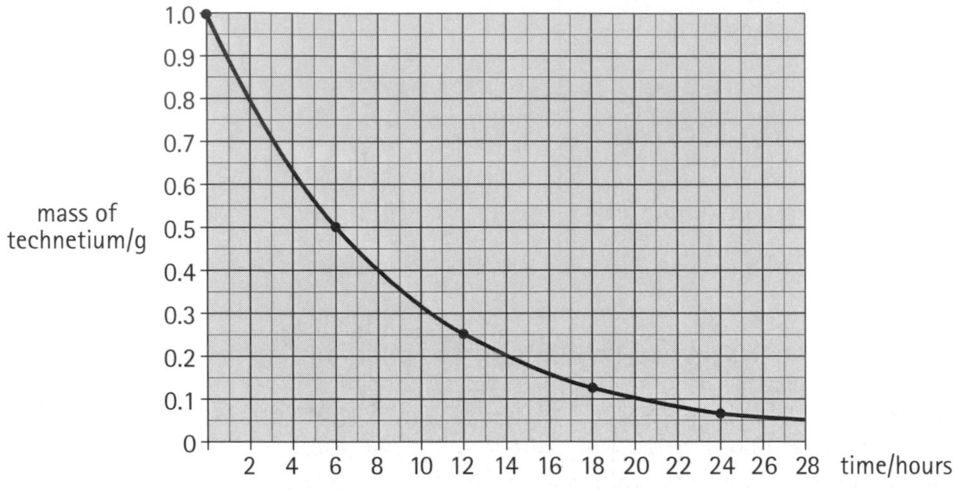

The diagram above shows how a sample of technetium decays. Technetium is commonly used as a tracer in medical investigations. Technetium-99 has a half-life of 6 hours. This means that if there is one gram at the start, then after 6 hours this will have decayed to half a gram and another 6 hours later there will only be one quarter of a gram left.

How much will be left after another 6 hours?

How much 24 hours from the start?

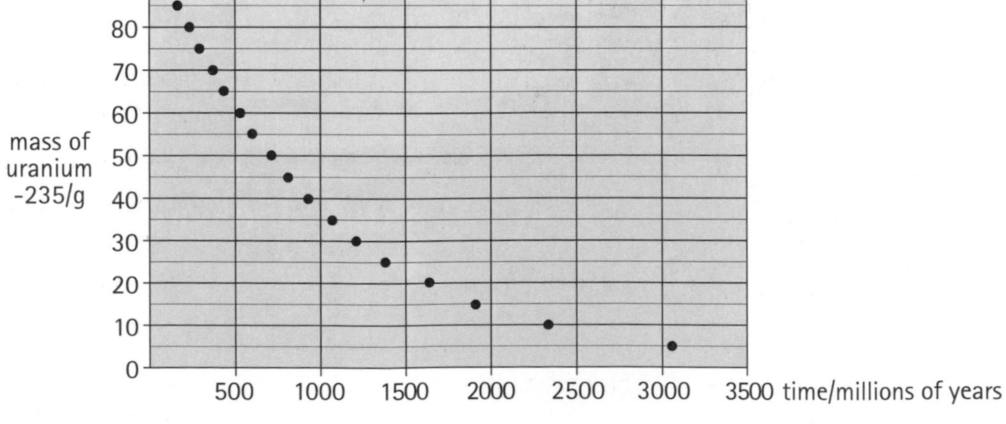

Uranium-235 occurs in some igneous rocks. It gradually decays to lead-207. The graph at the bottom of the previous page shows how much uranium-235 would be left from a sample of 100 g. Scientists compare the amount of uranium to the amount of lead in a rock to estimate the age of the rock.

How old would the rock be if there were 60 g of uranium to 40 g of lead?

Exam Question – Radioactivity

1 The diagram below shows how radiation is used to destroy a brain tumour. The three sources give out the same type of radiation.

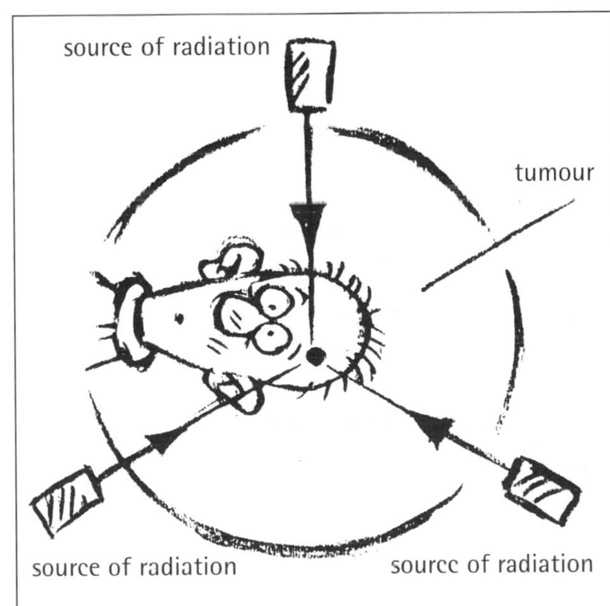

a) What type of radiation would be most suitable? [1]

Give a reason for your choice [1]

b) Why are there **three** sources of radiation arranged as shown? [2]

2 Radioactive isotopes are sometimes used as tracers. They can be used to find out if an organ in the human body is working properly. A radioactive material is injected into the bloodstream. The radiation that it emits can then be detected later to find its position in the body.

a) Write down **two** properties that the radioactive material must have. For each property explain why it makes it suitable. [4]

b) (h) A particular radioactive isotope has a half-life of 2 days. Twelve milligrammes of the isotope are injected into the patient. After 6 days:

(i) how many half-lives have passed? [1]

(ii) how much of the isotope will remain in the patient? [1]

Answers to Questions

Life processes 1 (page 13)

1 a) Photosynthesis.

b) **Nerve cell** has an elongated fibre to carry impulses more rapidly around the body. **Red blood cell** has a large surface area to allow rapid diffusion of gases. **Sperm cell** has a tail which allows the cell to swim and move towards the egg cell. **Root hair cell** has a large surface area to allow rapid absorption of water. **Egg cell** has a large amount of cytoplasm which contains the parts of the cell (organelles) needed for rapid growth and development to begin. **Leaf cell** has chloroplast to transfer Sun's energy and carry out photosynthesis.

2 a) Growth is an **increase** in size, which happens because the number of **cells** increases.

b) Mature organisms can create new lives by a process called **reproduction**.

c) During **respiration**, energy is transferred from food. Humans need **oxygen** to carry out this process.

d) Getting rid of waste is called **excretion**. Two examples of human waste are **carbon dioxide** and **urine**.

Humans as organisms 1 (page 17)

1 Lightly cooked vegetables and raw foods contain the maximum amount of minerals and vitamins because none have been lost in cooking.

2 Too much fat in the diet, eating too much generally, not enough exercise.

3 High protein foods such as meat, fish and cheese.

4 a) Children are more active than elederly people and need more energy for their daily activities. Children are growing rapidly and need energy and raw materials for this process.

b) Aidee might reduce the amount of high energy foods she eats.

5 a) Carbohydrate foods.

b) Glucose molecules are smaller than starch molecules and can pass through the semi-permeable membrane.

c) To show that the water does not contain any starch or sugar at the start, so any present at the end must have come through the membrane.

Humans as organism 2 (page 19)

1 a) Observe on each side top and bottom: 2 incisors, 1 canine, 2 premolars, 3 molars = 32 total, depending on extractions and whether all teeth have developed. Incisors are flat and sharp for cutting/biting, canines are pointed for stabbing food and ripping it up, premolars and molars are broad on the top surface with cusps for grinding.

b) The nervous system.

2 Softening of food by saliva, some digestion of starch and chopping up of food in the mouth; protein digestion in the stomach; digestion of all remaining carbohydrates, proteins and fats in the first part of the small intestine; absorption in the latter part of the small intestine; water absorption from waste remains in the large intestine.

3 a) The rate of enzyme action increases with temperature between 10 and 50°C; above 50°C the enzyme is destroyed and does not work.

b) pH in the mouth is alkaline, but in the stomach it is very acidic. Stomach acid stops the enzyme working because enzymes work best at a specific pH.

4 Barium meal is swallowed before an X-ray so the intestines are seen more clearly.

5 a) A ring muscle.

b) Sphincters close the stomach and so make it into a temporary 'bag' to hold food while digestion occurs.

6 It helps to prevent food poisoning and illness caused by contaminated food.

Humans as organisms 3 (page 21)

1 a)

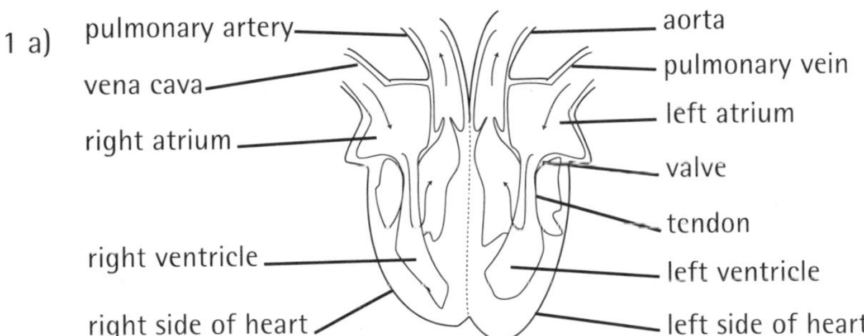

b) There are valves between the atria and ventricles; they are open as the atria and ventricles are filling and are closed when the ventricles contract, to prevent backflow of blood. There are valves at the base of the large arteries; they are open when the ventricles contract and are closed when the ventricles are filling, to prevent backflow of blood.

2 a) (i) Pulmonary artery.

(ii) Aorta.

b) The pulmonary artery has a lower oxygen content than the aorta because it is passing to the lungs carrying blood which has already circulated around the body. The aorta carries blood which has been oxygenated in the lungs. The pressure of blood in the pulmonary artery is lower than in the aorta, preventing damage to the delicate tissues of the lungs; also the blood does not need to circulate as far so less pressure is required.

Humans as organisms 4 (page 23)

1 a) Usually an infection.

b) An injury.

c) A lifestyle habit.

d) Mental illness.

e) An inherited condition.

2 It stops loss of blood and seals wounds, preventing germs from entering.

3 a) Substances made by some white blood cells, which lock on to antigens so they are more easily destroyed by other white blood cells.

b) They increase protection against infection by making it easier for the body to kill invading organisms.

Humans as organisms 5 (page 25)

1 a) They have a large surface area, very thin walls and a rich blood supply.

b) Carbon dioxide and oxygen.

3 a) 16 breaths per minute.

b) 0.4 litres.

c) (i) 16 x 0.4 = 6.4 litres per minute.

(ii) 24 x 0.5 = 12 litres per minute.

(iii) Rate of respiration and demand for oxygen is greater during and immediately after exercise, so ventilation rate increases to cope with this.

(iv) Increased carbon dioxide levels cause breathing to speed up.

Humans as organisms 6 (page 27)

1 a) To get energy needed for chemical reactions that take place in the cells.

b) Aerobic respiration is the breakdown of food in the presence of oxygen; anaerobic respiration happens in the absence of oxygen.

2 b) (i) Running.

(ii) Energy is needed for all the life processes which continue while someone is sleeping, e.g. breathing movements, brain activity.

(iii) 42 kJ/min x 30 min = 1260 kJ

3 a) Monterey shrew.

b) (i) 0.5 cm^3/g/h.

(ii) Sonoma shrew is respiring faster.

c) Short-tailed shrew.

d) When body mass is smaller, the ratio of surface area of the body compared to volume is higher, so more energy is transferred to the surroundings and the shrew must respire faster to keep warm.

4 a) It contains a lot of energy which is readily available for use by the body.

b) oxygen + glucose → carbon dioxide + water

Humans as organisms 7 (page 29)

1a) The students' reaction times were longer, because ethanol (alcohol in beer) is a sedative.

b) Jo's reaction time returned to normal within an hour.

2 a) Light rays do not come to focus on the retina.

b) In short sight the light rays are brought together in front of the retina, but in long sight they come to focus behind the eyeball.

Humans as organisms 8 (page 31)

1 The pituitary gland is activated by the hypothalamus via nerve connections.

2 Ovaries in females; testes in males.

3 By diffusion.

Humans as organisms 9 (page 33)

1 a) A period, days 1–4; lining of the womb thickens, days 5–15; ovulation, day 14; fertilisation may occur, days 14–17.

b) October 8th–12th.

2 a) To supply milk for a newborn baby.

b) To allow the growth and development of a fetus.

c) Sperm are the male sex cells needed for fertilisation.

Humans as organisms 10 (page 35)

1 Ovary – produces eggs; oviduct – eggs may be fertilised as they pass along here; uterus – a secure place for a fetus to develop; vagina – sperms enter through here.

2 a) They produce sex cells (sperm)

b) It delivers sperm into the vagina.

3 High survival rate of offspring.

Humans as organisms 11 (page 37)

1 Keratin in surface layers of skin makes the skin waterproof; sweat glands produce sweat which cools the body, also contains urea (excretory product); receptors (pain, temperature, etc.) detect changes in the environment; sebaceous gland makes sebum, an oily secretion which conditions the hair and skin; hair can be raised to trap extra air layers and help insulate the body; capillary network supplies skin cells with nutrients and oxygen, and control of blood flow throught them helps in controlling body temperature.

2 Endotherms can control their body temperature to a great extent; the body temperature of ectotherms is mostly determined by the temperature of their surroundings.

3 Humans can live in a wide variety of climates and exploit many different environments.

4 Evaporation of sweat uses energy from the body, and this has a cooling effect. The more someone sweats the greater the cooling effect. When blood flows near the surface of the skin, heat radiates from the skin to the surroundings, which has a

cooling effect. Blood flow near the surface of the skin can be controlled by widening or narrowing the size of the blood vessels. The more blood flow there is near the surface of the skin the more cooling effect, and vice versa.

5 Sun's radiation causes the pigment melanin to develop in surface skin layers of pale skin, giving suntanned appearance; can cause skin burns and inflammation; damages cell layers causing the effects of ageing; can damage DNA within cells, leading to skin cancer.

Humans as organisms 12 (page 39)

1 a) In food and drink.

b) How active someone is; how hot the day is; the clothing they are wearing.

c) The more water lost as sweat, the less urine is produced, unless someone drinks a lot.

2 a) Glomerulus in the capsule.

b) The part of the tubule called the loop of Henle.

c) The second part of the tubule.

3 a) Blood pressure.

b) Most of the water is reabsorbed into the blood.

4 Dialysis takes a lot of time and has to be repeated regularly; a transplant acts as if the person has their own working kidney.

Green plants as organisms 1 (page 43)

1 a) (i) Carbon dioxide and water.

(ii) Glucose and oxygen.

b) (i) Stomata.

(ii) Roots.

(iii) Vascular tissue.

c) Growing areas such as new buds and root tips.

2 c) 37 bubbles per minute with lamp at 10 cm.

d) (i) It increases because the plant receives more light, which is an energy source for photosynthesis.

(ii) It decreases because a cooler temperature reduces the rate at which enzymes work, and enzymes catalyse the reactions of photosynthesis.

e) carbon dioxide + water → glucose + oxygen.

Green plants as organisms 2 (page 45)

1 a) The leaf surface is not totally impermeable. Water is lost by evaporation from cell surfaces as the water diffuses out of stomata.

b) By absorption from the soil through the roots.

2 Advantages: cheap; easy to apply; know what is being applied and how much; type

can be selected according to specific pests (any two). Disadvantages: can spread to other areas outside the application region; may enter food chain; may affect organisms other than target pest (any two).

3 a) By using manure or an inorganic fertiliser.

b) By using compost.

4 Improved growth of plants; larger healthier plants; more blooms; more fruit.

Variation and inheritance 1 (page 49)

1 a) The difference in characteristics between individuals within a population of the same species.

b) Because individuals grow up in different environments and because of genetic/inherited differences between individuals.

c) An inherited characteristic may be an advantage to an individual and help it to survive longer than other individuals and therefore to reproduce more. If this is the case, the next generation of offspring which inherit the characteristic will also be more successful and over a long period of time the population will evolve as this new characteristic becomes a feature of this species. However, the new characteristic may be a disadvantage to an individual, or even lethal. Such a characteristic can lead to a population becoming extinct if it is passed on to all the offspring.

2 a) 6% recaptured in unpolluted area; 52% recaptured in the polluted area.

b) More dark moths were recaptured in the polluted area because they survived better where buildings and vegetation were darkened by soot. The dark moths would be more conspicuous in the unpolluted area.

c) A decrease in the population of dark moths.

Variation and inheritance 2 (page 51)

1 50% or 1 in 2 chance. 50% of children would be dd and 50% Dd.

2 a) Freckles are dominant, so two ff alleles must be present.

b) Both of his children have freckles, so they probably inherited f from their mother and F from their father, and F is dominant and hides f.

c) Tariq could have Ff, but this is less likely since then only 50% of his children would be expected to have freeckles.

d) Sadiq does not have freckles so must have inherited the alleles ff.

e) Bindi and Raj both have freckles yet they had a child without, so they must both have had the alleles Ff, giving a 25% chance of a child with no freckles.

Living things in their environment 1 (page 55)

1 a) The crop plants are growing well in the field but are shorter next to the hedge.

b) Light; space; minerals from the soil; water; carbon dioxide (any three).

c) The hedge could be taking the water and minerals away from the crop plants growing nearby; the hedge could be shading light from the crop plants nearby.

2 a) The fox.

b) It will begin to reduce as its food supply is less.

3 a) Sulphur dioxide and oxides of nitrogen from the burning of fossil fuels.

b) (i) Fish and other aquatic life cannot survive in acid conditions so acid rain in waterways reduces wildlife.

(ii) Acid rain on soil causes damage to plants, killing them and leading to deforestation.

c) To protect the soil and trees growing in it from acid rain which is brought to Sweden on the winds from countries further west.

Living things in their environment 2 (page 57)

1 a) Leaves → rabbit → fox

b) (i) A producer can make its own food from simple raw materials. Consumers need ready-made organic food sources.

(ii) Oak tree is a producer; all the animals are consumers.

c) Owl.

d) More insects could survive because their natural predators would be absent. Less toads would survive or they would need to find a new food source.

2 a) 25 – 10 – 12 = 3 kJ per square metre per day.

b) 0.2% of 8500 kJ = 17 kJ.

Chemical reactions and rates 1 (page 63)

1 Two.

2 a) It is balanced already.

b) $2H_2 + O_2 \rightarrow 2H_2O$

c) $2Na + 2H_2O \rightarrow' 2NaOH + H_2$

3 a) $CuO(s) + Mg(s) \rightarrow MgO(s) + Cu(s)$

b) $2Fe(s) + 3Cl_2(g) \rightarrow 2FeCl_3(s)$

Chemical reactions and rates 2 (page 65)

1 a) Hydrogen peroxide → oxygen + water.

b) Catalyst.

d) The reaction slowed down because there are less particles to react.

Chemical reactions and rates 3 (page 67)

1 Hydrogen.

2 a) The reaction between an acid and a base, producing a salt and water.

b) Cleaning your teeth. The toothpaste (which is a base) neutralises the acid on your teeth.

3 a) A weak acid has few hydrogen ions in solution and a strong acid has many hydrogen ions in solution.

b) Dilute hydrochloric acid has more water than concentrated hydrochloric acid.

Materials and their properties 1 (page 73)

1 a)

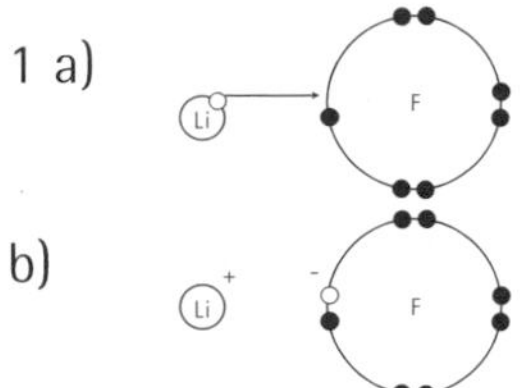

b)

c) Ionic.

The periodic table 1 (page 77)

1 Because they have the same number of electrons in their outermost shell.

2 a) Potassium hydroxide and hydrogen.

b) Fizzing; potassium sets alight; potassium floats on the water (any two).

c) pH changes because potassium hydroxide is formed, and this is alkaline.

The periodic table 2 (page 79)

1 a) +110°C to +125°C (+114°C is the correct value).

b) They get larger because there are more shells of electrons.

c) They get less reactive as you go down the group. Fluorine is the most reactive because it gains electrons most easily.

d) Potassium chloride and bromine.

e) Solid at room temperature.

The periodic table 3 (page 80)

1 Because they have full shells of electrons, so are stable.

2

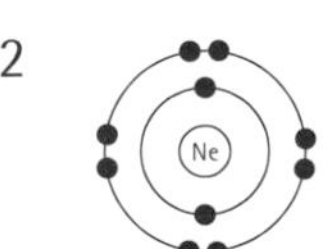

The periodic table 4 (page 81)

1 Iron; manganese; copper; zinc.

2 They form coloured compounds; they have high melting points; they have high densities; they are often used as catalysts (any three).

The periodic table 5 (page 83)

1 Fizzing.

2 Potassium set alight; fizzing.

The periodic table 6 (page 85)

1 Step 1: Work out number of moles of calcium carbonate:

1 mole = 40 + 12 + (16 x 3) = 100 tonnes

50 tonnes = 50/100 = 0.5 moles

Step 2: Look at equation – 0.5 moles of $CaCO_3$ produces 0.5 moles CaO

Step 3: Work out mass of 0.5 moles of CaO:

1 mole = 40 + 16 = 56 tonnes

0.5 moles = 56 x 0.5 = 28 tonnes

Industrial processes 1 (page 89)

1 a) (i) Nitric acid.

(ii) Neutralisation.

b) (i) It dissolves and is washed into rivers.

(ii) It is soluble in water.

(iii) It causes them to grow and multiply.

(iv) There are too many algae, which then die. Bacteria grow on the algae and take oxygen from the water. Fish die because they do not get enough oxygen.

Industrial processes 2 (page 91)

1 From dead sea creatures which were trapped in sediments for millions of years.

2 By fractional distillation.

Industrial processes 3 (page 93)

1 a) (i) A compound containing hydrogen and carbon only.

(ii) CH_4.

b) (i) Gas.

(ii) Exothermic.

(iii) Carbon dioxide (CO_2) and water (H_2O).

Industrial processes 4 (page 95)

1 a) Coke and limestone.

b) Hot air.

c) Molten iron.

d) Nitrogen from the air and sulphur dioxide from impurities in the coke and limestone.

e) Heat produced in the reaction between carbon (coke) and oxygen.

Industrial processes 5 (page 97)

1 Anhydrous copper sulphate and water to form hydrated copper sulphate. It can be reversed by heating to remove water from hydrated copper sulphate.

$CuSO_4 + 5H_2O \rightleftharpoons CuSO_4.5H_2O$

anhydrous hydrated

2 The forward reaction and the backward reaction both have the same rate.

3 The position of the equilibrium would move to the left (the back reaction) because an increase in temperature increases the endothermic reaction.

Earth and air 1 (page 101)

1 a) (i) Magma rising and cooling to form new ocean floor.

(ii) Sea/ocean floor spreading – plates moving away; volcanoes/earthquakes – plates moving together.

b) New crust is formed where rising convection current reaches the crust. Old crust disappears where convection current starts to fall causing land masses to move slowly. This will continue to happen at the rate of about 2 cm per year.

Earth and air 2 (page 103)

1 a) A – metamorphic; B – igneous.

b) By compression.

c) By plates colliding.

Earth and air 3 (page 105)

1 a) Burning; respiration; decay by bacteria.

b) (i) Photosynthesis.

(ii) Decreases it.

c) (i) Increase it.

(ii) Greenhouse effect, causing temperature to rise.

Electricity and magnetism 1 (page 109)

1 a resistor; b lamp; c switch; d diode; e battery or cell; f voltmeter; g ammeter.

2 a)

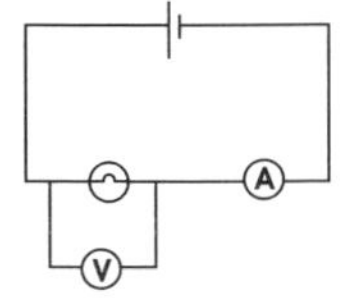

b) ammeter

c) $R = \frac{V}{I}$

$$R = \frac{12\ V}{3\ A} = 4\ W$$

Electricity and magnetism 2 (page 111)

1 As the voltage increases, the current increases and the wire gets hotter. The hotter wire has a higher resistance.

2 Electrons are transferred from the hair to the brush. Hairs all have positive charge so they repel each other.

3 When the hose is unravelled it may become charged. The charge may cause sparking. The sparks may explode any petrol fumes.

Electricity and magnetism 3 (page 113)

1 rate of energy transfer = power

power = VI

power = 12 V x 3 A = 36 watts.

2 a) 200 W = 0.2 kW.

b) energy = power x time

energy = 0.2 kW x 10 h = 2 kWh.

c) 7p/unit x 2 units = 14 pence.

3 a) P = V x I

$$\frac{I}{V} = P$$

$$I = \frac{920\ W}{230\ V} = 4\ A.$$

b) Q = It

Q = 4 A x (20 x 60)s = 4800 coulombs.

Exam Question – Electricity and magnetism (page 117)

a) Voltmeter in parallel with bulb.

b) (i) Reduce resistance by moving control knob.

(ii) Less resistance increases current which increases brightness.

c) You should show each point with a cross and draw a smooth curve through the points.

d) (i) $R = \frac{V}{I}$

$$R = \frac{6\ V}{1.5\ A} = 4\ W$$

(ii) The current does not increase as quickly as the voltage because the resistance increases.

Forces and motion 1 (page 121)

1 a) $$\text{pressure (N/cm}^2\text{)} = \frac{\text{force (N)}}{\text{area (cm}^2\text{)}}$$

$$\text{pressure (N/cm}^2\text{)} = \frac{600 \text{ N}}{3000 \text{ cm}^2} = 0.2 \text{ N/cm}^2$$

b) Pressure doubles because area is half.

2 a) Two springs in series (C).

b) Two springs in parallel (B).

c) Springs in series each need only half the force of a single spring; springs in parallel need twice the force of a single spring; so parallel is four times as hard as series.

Forces and motion 2 (page 123)

1 $$\text{speed (m/s)} = \frac{\text{distance (m)}}{\text{time (s)}}$$

$$\text{speed (m/s)} = \frac{400 \text{ m}}{80 \text{ s}} = 5 \text{ m/s.}$$

2 OA accelerates (speeds up) from 0 to 10 m/s; AB steady speed of 10 m/s for 40 s; BC decelerates (slows down) from 10 m/s to 0 in 20 s; CD stationary for 20 s; DE accelerates from 0 to 7 m/s in 10 s; EF steady speed of 7 m/s for 30 s; FG decelerates from 7 m/s to 0 in 15 s.

3 $$\text{acceleration (m/s}^2\text{)} = \frac{\text{change in speed (m/s)}}{\text{time taken (s)}}$$

$$\text{acceleration (m/s}^2\text{)} = \frac{30 \text{ m/s}}{10 \text{ s}} = 3 \text{ m/s}^2$$

Forces and motion 3 (page 125)

1 Car – driving force is greater than frictional force, so car accelerates; parachutist – air resistance equals weight, so parachutist falls at a steady speed (terminal velocity); weightlifter – pull of gravity on weights equals weightlifter's push upwards, so weights remain stationary; cyclist – driving force is less than frictional force, so cyclist slows down.

2 a) Increases stopping distance – bigger mass means a smaller deceleration by the brakes, so it takes longer to stop.

b) Increases stopping distance – higher initial speed means it takes longer to stop for the same deceleration.

c) Increases stopping distance – less frictional force, so smaller deceleration means it takes longer to stop.

d) Increases stopping distance – driver has increased reaction time, so a longer thinking distance and so it takes longer to stop.

3 a) $$\text{acceleration (m/s}^2\text{)} = \frac{\text{change in speed (m/s)}}{\text{time taken (s)}}$$

$$\text{acceleration (m/s}^2\text{)} = \frac{15 \text{ m/s}}{10 \text{ s}} = 1.5 \text{ m/s}^2.$$

b) F = ma

force (newtons) = 1200 kg x 1.5 m/s^2 = 1800 N.

Exam Question – Forces and motion (page 127)

a) A slowing down – only frictional forces acting; B moving at a steady speed – forces balanced; C slowing down – frictional forces greater than driving force; D accelerating – driving force greater than frictional forces.

b) (i) Increase speed.

(ii) Moving at a steady speed of 10 m/s.

(iii) Stopped.

c) $$\text{acceleration (m/s}^2\text{)} = \frac{\text{change in speed (m/s)}}{\text{time taken (s)}}$$

$$\text{acceleration (m/s2)} = \frac{10 \text{ m/s}}{20 \text{ s}} = 0.5 \text{ m/s}$$

d) F = ma

force (newtons) = 60 kg x 0.5 m/s = 30 N.

Waves 1 (page 131)

1

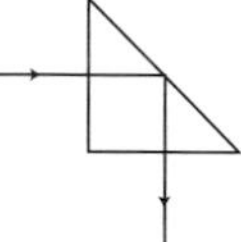

2 Transverse: water, light, waves on a rope. Longitudinal: sound.

Waves 2 (page 133)

1 gamma rays **X-rays** ultraviolet visible **infrared** microwaves **radio waves**

2 a) X-rays used for 'seeing' inside bodies; can damage cells in the body. Microwaves used in communication and for cooking; can damage living cells. Ultraviolet waves used for killing germs; can cause skin cancer.

Waves 3 (page 135)

1 a) 50 vibrations per second or 50 Hz.

b) A shorter length of ruler vibrating will make a higher-pitch note.

2 Sound travels 60 m in 0.2 seconds (there and back)

$$\text{speed (m/s)} = \frac{\text{distance (m)}}{\text{time (s)}}$$

$$\text{speed (m/s)} = \frac{60\text{ m}}{0.2\text{ s}} = 300\text{ m/s.}$$

3 Sounds can be heard through an open window even when the source of the sound is not directly in front of the window.

Exam Question – Waves (page 137)

a (i) The wave bounces backwards and forwards through the fibre; the angle of reflection equals the angle of reflection each time.

(ii) Light does not spread out so there is no loss of energy.

b (i) To illuminate the object inside the body.

(ii) So that the image is not distorted.

(iii) Less harmful than X-rays; can see a moving image; X-rays only show bone structure (any two).

c) (i) High pitch/frequency waves.

(ii) Reflection from the baby.

d) Lighter cables; less interference; less signal loss so less amplification needed; better quality signal (any two).

Exam Question – The Earth and beyond (page 141)

a) Mercury, Venus, Earth.

b) Mercury.

c) Between Mars and Jupiter.

d) (i) Force from Sun shown by arrow pointing from comet to Sun.

(ii) When it is farthest from the Sun.

Energy 1 (page 145)

1 a) work done (J) = force (N) x distance (m)

work done (J) = 50 N x 100 m = 5000 J.

b)

$$\text{power (W)} = \frac{\text{work done (J)}}{\text{time taken (s)}}$$

$$\text{power (W)} = \frac{5000\text{ J}}{20\text{ s}} = 250\text{ W.}$$

2 Only 35% of the energy input to the power station is put out as useful energy; 65% is wasted, mostly in heating up the surroundings.

Energy 2 (page 147)

1 A loft is insulated with fibre glass blanket which has many air pockets which act as insulator, or it can be insulated with loose-fill polystyrene which is a poor conductor.

2 It only needs a small amount of water to cover the element; warm water rises above cold water by convection, so an element at the top would not heat the cold water at the bottom.

3 They warm the air near the radiator and this air then rises up in the room and cooler air moves in to replace it. In this way the warm air circulates around the room by convection.

Exam Question – Energy (page 149)

a) 300 m.

b) work done (J) = force (N) x distance (m)

work done (J) = 600 N x 300 m = 18000 J.

c) $$\text{power (W)} = \frac{\text{work done (J)}}{\text{time taken (s)}}$$

$$\text{power (W)} = \frac{18000\ \text{J}}{10\ \text{s}} = 1800\ \text{W}.$$

d) Energy warms up tyres, brakes, atmosphere through exhaust gases, car and air through frictional forces.

e) When a seat belt stretches it absorbs some of the energy of the moving person and allows the person to stop over a longer time so there is a smaller acceleration and a smaller stopping force.

f) A fully loaded car has a greater mass and so a smaller acceleration for the same driving force.

Exam Question – Radioactivity (page 153)

1 a) Gamma, the most penetrating.

b) All sides of the tumour receive radiation; there is less effect on healthy cells through which the radiation passes.

2 a) Radiation must be able to penetrate the body so that it can be detected; radioactive material must have a short half-life so it does not stay in the body too long.

b) (i) Three half-lives.

(ii) One eighth remains.